ON WINGS
OF HEALING

ON WINGS OF HEALING

The Story of The Airborne Medical Services
1940-1960

by

Lieut.-Colonel HOWARD N. COLE
OBE, TD, FRHistS

With a Foreword by

Lieut.-General Sir FREDERICK BROWNING
GCVO, KBE, CB, DSO, DL

The Naval & Military Press Ltd

Published by
The Naval & Military Press Ltd
Unit 10 Ridgewood Industrial Park,
Uckfield, East Sussex,
TN22 5QE England
Tel: +44 (0) 1825 749494
Fax: +44 (0) 1825 765701
www.naval-military-press.com
www.military-genealogy.com
www.militarymaproom.com

Published on behalf of
The Airborne Medical Society

In reprinting in facsimile from the original, any imperfections are inevitably reproduced and the quality may fall short of modern type and cartographic standards.

The World would lose
If such a man as you
Should vanish unrecorded.

      Tennyson.

FOREWORD

by

LIEUT.-GENERAL SIR FREDERICK BROWNING,
GCVO, KBE, CB, DSO, DL.

IT is both an honour and a pleasure to write a Foreword to the history of the Airborne Medical Services.

I am proud to have been connected, even in a remote way, with their raising and formation in 1941. In view of the fact that their organisation needed little adjustment in the years ahead, great credit is due to the Senior Medical Officer, Brigadier A. Austin Eagger. He raised the Airborne Units in the 1st Airborne Division with a thoroughness and foresight that were an inspiration to all ranks, who proved themselves in battle to be second to none and well ahead of most. The problems were not simple or straightforward. Fresh ground was being broken in designing Medical Services which could be carried by air, both parachute and glider. The technical achievement was outstanding, but equally so was the training of all ranks who were called upon to learn the many things connected with air transport, the loading and landing phases and the vital efficiency of operating immediately and effectively when on the ground.

That all this was achieved in the short space of time available reflects, as I have said, credit to the organiser, but the results achieved were due to the devotion to duty, efficiency and self-sacrifice of all ranks.

This book is one which those who took part will read with pride, interest and satisfaction.

I also feel the story will be of interest to a wider public, especially the medical profession as a whole, and I trust and believe that the history of the Airborne Medical Services will be read by many people in all walks of life.

I sincerely wish it the success it deserves.

MENABILLY,
  PAR,
    CORNWALL.
      January 1963.

DEDICATION

IN spite of all that has been written on the exploits of Airborne Forces, members of the Airborne Medical Society, which was founded in 1942, were of the opinion that there was still a story to tell and that the history of the Airborne Medical Services should not be allowed to sink into oblivion. Lieut.-Colonel Howard N. Cole is to be congratulated on the way in which he has undertaken the by no means easy task of presenting a record of this Medical Service from the initiation in 1941 to the present day. He has gained this information from a study of the War Diaries, various Reports by Senior Officers and personal interviews. Probably this has allowed the whole picture to be seen in a better perspective than if the story had been written by any of those who served with Airborne Forces.

Of necessity, much detail has had to be omitted, and there well may be some feeling of disappointment by individuals that certain events are not given the prominence which they may feel they deserve. All who served, however, were members of a team to whom had been entrusted a great responsibility under conditions for which there was no precedent. Every man was inspired by the desire to prove worthy of this unique responsibility. They succeeded in gaining the confidence and respect of the combatant units and worthily upheld the traditions of the Royal Army Medical Corps, in which they were proud to serve.

The casual reader might gain the impression from the frequent references to commissioned officers that they played the major part in achieving the objective. Nothing could be further from the truth, and all officers would readily confirm that the success of Airborne Medical Services was due to the efficiency, self-sacrifice and loyalty of the 'Other Ranks' who, in the hour of trial, were never found to be wanting. They came from many walks of life and all were volunteers. Some were conscientious objectors who were not prepared to take life but were prepared to sacrifice their own lives to save others.

It would be the wish of all officers that this book should be dedicated to these Warrant Officers, Non-Commissioned Officers and Men who served in the Royal Army Medical Corps, the Royal Army Dental Corps, the Royal Army Service Corps, and the Army Catering Corps with Airborne Medical Units. As individuals they could well say "Without me you could never have done it", and how right they would be.

Many did not return, and this book may serve to remind us of what we owe to them, and of the increased responsibility for the future which, by their sacrifice, they placed on us.

A. AUSTIN EAGGER.

PREFACE

IN the autumn of 1942, whilst attending a course at the Staff College, Camberley, I was present at a demonstration of an airborne landing on Salisbury Plain. At that time the methods of employment of airborne forces were not widely known or generally appreciated, and the lectures, the précis handed out, and the demonstration itself, left a considerable impression on those of us who had not hitherto encountered the work of parachute troops.

As time went by news and reports of airborne operations all went towards the general pattern of the war, but, as one who was never in personal contact with airborne forces, the indelible impression of that airborne demonstration on Salisbury Plain was always foremost in my thoughts when one read 'Airborne forces landed on the night of the. . . .' I could always visualise the individual parachutist coming down, alone in a strange and hostile land, very much the individual, very much alone, although the next man in his 'stick' might be but a hundred yards away; it was always, in my view, a triumph of training and an operation calling for considerable courage and daring on the part of every man—of which I was even more convinced after I had been over the dropping zone on the west bank of the Rhine shortly after the landing of the 6th Airborne Division in 1945, with the signs of battle still much in evidence, particularly the battered gliders with their bullet-shattered perspex windscreens and torn bodies.

With this feeling of high regard for the services of the airborne forces, it was with considerable pleasure that I accepted the privilege of compiling this history of the Airborne Medical Services, for my respect for the men who wore the red beret was matched with that for the Royal Army Medical Corps as a whole, and their airborne units in particular.

It is my hope that this record will be considered worthy of all ranks of the RAMC whose story it is, together with those of the other arms which make up the Airborne Medical Services.

In writing the story the aims and objects have been threefold. Firstly to record factually the history of the Airborne Medical Services from 1940 until the end of the British Mandate in Palestine (and, with some reference to the activities since then of the one remaining Regular Parachute Field Ambulance (The 23rd) and their Territorial Army counterparts). Secondly to paint the background picture to their history and to link this with the operations in which they participated. Lastly, to add, where possible, certain medical and technical information of historic professional interest in reference to types and numbers of casualties, operations performed and stores and equipment carried, in order that, in some small way, this may be accepted as a work of reference on the Airborne Medical Services in the Second World War.

My work has been considerably facilitated by having access to the personal records of members of the Airborne Medical Society, who have given me their full co-operation at all times in making available notes they made when the details of their work in the various theatres of operations were still fresh in the minds of those who participated, and, in recording, for this book, their personal reminiscences of the actions in which they served.

It is from this valuable collection of contemporary records that this work has been compiled, and fitted into the broad picture of the airborne operations of the 1st and 6th Airborne Divisions, the full story of which is available in the official HMSO publication ' By Air to Battle ', and ' The Red Beret —The Story of the Parachute Regiment at War, 1940-45 ', both by Hilary St George Saunders. It was essential to draw upon the history of the Parachute Regiment as a whole, in order to give the framework for the story of the Airborne Medical Services which formed an integral part of each airborne operation from Bruneval to the end of the war.

The accent on this story is, of course, on the actual airborne operations, for not only are they the best recorded in the material available, but because this was work of a totally different character to that in normal operations, and because, after the airborne landing, when the airborne forces operated in an infantry rôle, the work of the Parachute and Airlanding Field Ambulances was, in fact, similar to that of the Field Ambulance in an armoured or infantry division.

The accepted principle governing the evacuation of casualties in war had always been for the wounded to be withdrawn from the scene of action as soon as possible and dispatched to the Casualty Clearing Stations—where urgent surgical treatment could be given—and on to the General Hospitals on the Lines of Communication or the Base, where proper care and attention could be given in far more favourable conditions than was possible in the forward areas. However, in airborne operations the medical services were faced with a situation never before envisaged. The rapid evacuation of casualties as in normal operations was impossible and the Parachute and Air Landing Field Ambulances, with their surgical teams, had to be prepared to hold all casualties until evacuation was possible, a situation which, although undesirable, had on occasions to be accepted.

Greater space has been devoted to the work of the RAMC at Arnhem, and after, than to other operations in which the Airborne Medical Services participated; for this was unique in medical military history as vouched at the time, for, as the glider pilot author of 'Arnhem Lift' has recorded in describing his visit to a Regimental Aid Post outside the perimeter and meeting the Medical Officer in charge: 'He was a big, cheerful man, and said to me: "You're watching medical history being made"'—indeed it was, but so it had been ever since RAMC units had become an integral part of the airborne forces—back in 1942, in the Temera Valley in North Africa, a surgical team of the 16th (Parachute) Field Ambulance had carried out major operations in slit trenches and dugouts but a hundred yards to the rear of the 2nd Parachute Battalion whilst it was in action.

In the preface to his great work 'The Red Beret—The Story of the Parachute Regiment at War, 1940-45', Hilary St George Saunders wrote: 'This is the story of the Parachute Regiment ... they were not, however, the only members of the British Army to wear the distinguished headgear. Those who dropped with them belonging to the Royal Engineers, the Royal Artillery, the Royal Corps of Signals, The Royal Army Service Corps and the Royal Army Medical Corps, and those who went to battle in gliders also wore it and added lustre to its fame. Their story will, I hope, one day be told, when the facts have been collected and are available '.

This work, in part, fulfils his wish, for the facts concerning the great work of the Airborne Medical Services have now been collected to enable this record to be made.

I would particularly express my thanks and appreciation to the following who made their records and/or private papers available to me and upon which I have drawn upon extensively in the compilation of the story : Brigadier A. Austin Eagger, CBE ; Brigadier Graeme Warrack, DSO, OBE, TD ; Colonel M. McEwan, DSO, OBE, DFC, TD ; Colonel Guy Rigby-Jones, MC, TD ; Lieut.-Colonel J. S. Binning, RAMC (TA) ; Lieut.-Colonel A. D. Young, DSO ; Colonel T. F. Redman ; Colonel P. R. Wheatley, DSO ; Lieut.-Colonel D. C. G. Whyte, DSO ; Major C. J. Longland ; Major A. S. Baker ; Major J. L. Kilgour ; and also to Major-General R. E. Barnsley, CB, MC, the Curator of the RAMC Historical Museum.

My appreciation must not exclude reference to the great assistance afforded to me by the first five named who, as the members of the History Committee of the Airborne Medical Society, so carefully and helpfully went through the typescript of the book checking, from their personal experiences, details and accuracy. In this I must refer particularly to Lieut.-Colonel John Binning, the Secretary of the Society, and to Brigadier Graeme Warrack, Chairman of the History Committee of the Society.

I also record my thanks to Colonel J. C. Watts, OBE, MC, for his permission to quote from his own book ' Surgeon at War ' ; to Colonel Harry Pozner, MC, for his help in preparing the chapter dealing with the Airborne Formations of the Indian Army and to quote from his articles on the Burma Campaign ; to Mr Spencer Curtis Brown for permission to quote from Hilary St George Saunders' book 'The Red Beret'; to Messrs Sampson Low, Marston & Co. Ltd. for permission to quote from General Sir Richard Gale's book 'With the 6th Airborne Division in Normandy'; to the Director of Publications, Her Majesty's Stationery Office, for permission to quote from 'By Air to Battle'; and to the honorary editors of 'The Journal of the RAMC' and 'The Army Medical Services Magazine' to quote material published in those journals.

'Not least were they in the Crusade' the men of the Airborne Medical Services . . . to-day some are still serving in the Royal Army Medical Corps, others are surgeons and physicians of repute working in Harley Street or in the great hospitals up and down the country, others are general practitioners. The locally well-known Dr Brown, that grey-haired, kindly doctor who now turns out after midnight on a cold misty night to tend the old lady in Laburnum Grove; the arrival of Mrs Smith's second baby on the council estate, or hurries to the local cottage hospital to attend young Bob after his motor-cycle crash at the roundabout—few know that but seventeen years ago that same doctor leapt from a Dakota one dark night to land, by parachute, in the middle of a battle, to give attention to the leg of a shell-shattered corporal of the Parachute Regiment or to go out, amid the crash of mortar bombs, to give morphia to a dying gunner as he lay, under enemy fire, by a belt of French woodland . . . a far cry from the battle-ground of Normandy to St Mary's Hospital at the top of the well-lit High Street.

The Other Ranks are scattered far and wide. Few know that Mr Jones, of the Packing Department of Namrons Furniture Company, who is entrusted with the key of the first-aid box on the ground floor, was once Sergeant Jones, RAMC, who was mentioned in despatches for his work one night in bringing in the wounded to a stable in a remote Sicilian village, or that Mr Robinson, the Chief Clerk in the Costing Department in Ruggmores Ltd—The Carpet Cleaners, was once Corporal Robinson who won his MM near Hammelkeln on the Rhine when he saved three men from a blazing glider, or, that the milkman who calls before we are up each morning and limps a little as he carries the bottles to the door, limps because of a wound he received whilst crossing a bullet-swept side street on the outskirts of Arnhem, carrying a load of medical supplies to an isolated Regimental Aid Post. . . . Such to-day are the men who have made this story, those who wore the Red Beret *and* the Red Cross brassard.

HOWARD N. COLE.

TONGHAM,
    January 1963.

CONTENTS

CHAPTER		PAGE
	Parachute Drop	*Frontispiece*
	Foreword	vii
	Dedication	ix
	Preface	xi
I	Red Berets for the RAMC	1
	Formation and Training of the Airborne Medical Services	
II	The First Action	12
	A Sea-borne Section at Bruneval	
III	Into Action in Africa	14
	The 16th (Parachute) Field Ambulance in Algeria and Tunisia	
IV	Operations 'Husky', 'Ladbroke', and 'Fustian'.	34
	The Invasion of Sicily	
V	Into Italy	51
	With the 1st Airborne Division and the 2nd Independent Parachute Brigade Group	
VI	Operation 'Anvil'	59
	With the 2nd Parachute Brigade in the South of France	
VII	War and Civil War	65
	The 127th (Parachute) Field Ambulance in Greece	
VIII	The Normandy Beachhead	78
	With the 6th Airborne Division from 'D' Day onwards	
IX	'Not Least in the Crusade' . . .	108
	The Airborne Medical Services at Arnhem	
X	After Arnhem—	136
	The 1st Airborne Division's Military Hospitals in Occupied Holland	
XI	Into the Breach	154
	With the 6th Airborne Division in the Ardennes	

XII	OVER THE RHINE	158
	The 6th Airborne Division's Airborne Landing	
XIII	FROM THE RHINE TO THE BALTIC . . .	170
	The Advance through Germany	
XIV	THE LIBERATION OF NORWAY	179
XV	IN INDIA AND BURMA	183
	With the Airborne Formations of the Indian Army	
XVI	MALAYA AND JAVA	195
	The 225th (Parachute) Field Ambulance in the Far East	
XVII	INTERNAL SECURITY	201
	Palestine, 1945-48	
XVIII	SINCE THEN	211
	The Airborne Medical Services, 1947-61	
	THE COMPOSITION OF A PARACHUTE FIELD AMBULANCE ROYAL ARMY MEDICAL CORPS . .	222
	BIBLIOGRAPHY	224
	ABBREVIATIONS	226

MAPS

By the Author

1.	THE NORTH AFRICAN CAMPAIGN . .	*Facing page*	32
2.	THE SICILY LANDINGS	,, ,,	48
3.	SICILY AND ITALY	,, ,,	64
4.	GREECE	,, ,,	76
5.	THE NORMANDY LANDING . . .	,, ,,	80
6.	THE ARNHEM BATTLE AREA . . .	,, ,,	116
7.	THE RAMC AT OOSTERBEEK . . .	,, ,,	134
8.	THE RHINE CROSSING	,, ,,	168
9.	FROM THE RHINE TO THE BALTIC .	,, ,,	178
10.	BURMA AND SOUTH-EAST ASIA . .	,, ,,	192

CHAPTER I

RED BERETS FOR THE RAMC

THE FORMATION AND TRAINING OF THE AIRBORNE MEDICAL SERVICES

'WE ought', wrote Mr Winston Churchill on 22nd June 1940, when, as Prime Minister, he sent an instruction to General Ismay, then the Chief of the Military Wing of the War Cabinet Secretariat, ' to have a corps of at least five thousand parachute troops. . . . I hear that something is being done already to form such a corps. . . . Advantage must be taken of the summer to train these forces, who can none the less play their part meanwhile as shock troops in home defence. Pray let me have a note from the War Office on the subject.'[1]

Earlier that month the Air Ministry had decided to establish a parachute training centre, called The Central Landing School, at Ringway, Manchester's civil airport, where a combined Army and RAF staff set to work in planning and organising the airborne forces. At this same time Commando units were being raised, and, as the method by which it was intended that these units should go into action was to be varied, their training for transport by air and parachuting was essential. No 2 Commando was selected for this training. By the beginning of August every member of the unit had completed three jumps from Whitley aircraft and in the first six months of the life of the School between four and five hundred men underwent initial training in parachuting. In November a demonstration was given on Salisbury Plain by the 11th Special Air Service Battalion (as No 2 Commando had been redesignated), during which fifty officers and men landed by parachute and moved into a ' mock ' action. In the following month the Battalion was divided into a para-

[1] ' By Air to Battle ' (HMSO) (1945).

A

chute wing and a glider wing, the former becoming, in September 1941, the 1st Parachute Battalion.[1] In that month the Battalion was moved to Hardwick Hall, near Chesterfield, where the 1st Parachute Brigade was forming, the Brigade being destined to become part of an airborne division, to be composed of parachute and glider-borne troops, which was raised in October.

The Headquarters of the Airborne Division was formed in November 1941 under the command of Major-General F. A. M. Browning, DSO,[2] who took a very keen interest in the organisation and development of the Airborne Medical Services. He demanded the highest standards of efficiency and frequently stressed to all unit commanders the importance of the medical services.

On 29th November 1941 Colonel A. Austin Eagger, OBE, was posted to the Division as the Assistant Director of Medical Services (ADMS) and, of the officers then serving with the 1st Parachute Brigade, Captains T. R. B. Courteney and W. A. Owen, and Lieutenants M. H. Haggie and J. Rutherford were retained within the formation, and were in effect thereby the first volunteers for the Airborne Medical Services, and served in numerous operations with great distinction throughout the war.

On 1st December Captain T. R. B. Courteney was appointed Deputy Assistant Director of Medical Services (DADMS) of the Division and took an active part in devising and making practical trials of the special equipment required for this new rôle for the Royal Army Medical Corps. He was one of the first, and certainly the first medical officer, to make a parachute descent with a kit-bag tied to his leg when this method was under consideration.[3]

In the training of the men for the airborne forces, all

[1] The Regimental Medical Officer was Captain W. A. Owen, RAMC.
[2] Now Lieut.-General Sir Frederick Browning, GCVO, KBE, DSO.
[3] In October 1942 Captain Courteney was sent under orders from the War Office to Australia to assist in the formation of the Airborne Medical Services with the Australian Forces and subsequently saw active service with the 7th Australian Division in its airborne rôle in the operations in New Guinea. Captain Courteney returned to England to rejoin the 1st Airborne Division in January 1944, and was posted as second in command of the 133rd (Parachute) Field Ambulance, with which he served at Arnhem.

aspects of medical considerations were explored. For example, in December 1941, a conference was held at Ringway, under the chairmanship of Colonel A. Austin Eagger, the ADMS of the airborne forces, to decide on recommendations, as a result of experience and trials, to be made to combat air-sickness by different forms of training, modifications to equipment, and procedures. At this conference the need for a large transport aircraft which could be adapted for medical purposes was felt to be urgent, and the need for a light stretcher which could be 'thrown down' was explained; a design for a trailer which would be capable of taking two stretchers was asked for by the ADMS; and definite information as to the size of containers which could be used for packing medical stores for the Parachute Brigade was called for.

It was from this type of discussion, following experiments and trials, that gradually the scales and types of special equipment for use by the airborne forces was evolved.

Colonel Eagger attended numerous conferences attended by representatives from the War Office, Air Ministry, the Medical Research Council, the commanders of the combatant units of the Division and Royal Air Force officers, at which every aspect of airborne equipment and training and planning for operations were considered.

Reports and recommendations were submitted by the ADMS on a wide variety of subjects. These included methods of selection of personnel; physical standards; special clothing—in particular the airborne smock and the 'Brinje' vest; rations; attainment and maintenance of physical fitness; and new, or modifications to, equipment to enable the numerous items required by the medical services to be either carried on the man or dropped in suitable containers.

Controlled trials were held under the supervision of the Medical Research Council to ascertain a method of overcoming air-sickness, which, in exercises, was found to seriously incapacitate some 80 per cent of glider-borne troops.[1] Experience in operations however proved that this

[1] A tablet containing hyoscine was found to be effective for some 50 per cent.

problem was but of minor importance. Men were still airsick but made an immediate recovery on landing through the psychological stimulus of going into action.

In March 1942 the Parachute Brigade moved to Bulford. It was whilst on Salisbury Plain that the distinctive headdress, the red beret, was adopted by all ranks of the airborne forces and, in May, the famous airborne forces badge was introduced.[1]

Training and organisation continued throughout 1942, the 2nd Parachute Brigade was raised, and on 1st August all parachute infantry became one Regiment, to be known henceforth as the Parachute Regiment.

In step with the formation of parachute battalions units of supporting arms were raised, so that the 1st Parachute Brigade became a complete brigade group with its own services, including the RAMC.

On 14th November 1941 the 181st Field Ambulance joined the Airborne Division and moved to Hungerford, and in January 1942 was reorganised as an 'Airborne Field Ambulance' and commenced specialist training. In March the unit moved to Chilton Foliat, Wilts., and on 1st April was re-designated 181st (Air Landing) Field Ambulance.

During March it had been decided to raise another airborne field ambulance, and on 3rd April Major P. R. Wheatley, with a cadre drawn from the 181st (Air Landing) Field Ambulance composed of fifteen RAMC Other Ranks (ORs) (including one Quartermaster-Sergeant (QMS) and a staff-sergeant) and five ORs Royal Army Service Corps (RASC), moved by road to report to the Commanding Officer (CO) of the 2nd Parachute Battalion at Hardwick Hall, near Chesterfield, to act as a 'depot unit' to a new field ambulance whilst it was forming. That same day authority was given by the War Office for the raising of the 16th Airborne Field Ambulance, which was destined to be the first parachute-trained medical unit, and parachute training soon commenced at Ringway, near Manchester.

[1] The badge, depicting Bellerophon, astride the winged horse, Pegasus, his spear held high, his cloak flowing out behind him, in light blue, set on a maroon square, was designed by Edward Seago, the Staff Officer (Camouflage) at Headquarters, Southern Command.

By 6th April 151 ORs had been posted to the unit,[1] and Lieut.-Colonel M. MacEwan, DFC, TD,[2] was posted to command from the 128th Field Ambulance, together with Major P. R. Wheatley as Second-in-Command and Captain A. D. Young, from 199th Field Ambulance, and Lieutenant J. H. Keesey (RMO 2nd Gloucesters).

After initial parachute training the unit was re-designated 16th (P) Field Ambulance, and some months elapsed before the ' (P) ' was substituted by the word ' Parachute '.

At this time all units of the 1st Parachute Brigade wore distinguishing lanyards, so the Field Ambulance also chose one, it was dull cherry—the RAMC colour—and sky blue.[3]

The second parachute field ambulance to be formed was the 127th. This pre-war Territorial Army (TA) field ambulance, from Manchester,[4] became, in 1941, a light field ambu-

[1] This was the first Parachute Field Ambulance to be raised—not being formed by the conversion of an existing unit, and all the officers and ORs were volunteers from throughout the RAMC. The Unit was allotted the number ' 16 ' which had not been used since the disbandment of the 16th Field Ambulance RAMC after the 1914-18 War during which that Regular Army unit had served in France and Flanders with the 6th Division.

[2] During the 1914-18 War Colonel McEwan had served with mountain batteries, RA and the Royal Flying Corps. In the years between the wars he had served in the Territorial Army, with the Royal Artillery, being appointed to command the 58th (Suffolk) Medium Brigade RA(TA) at Ipswich in 1935. He commanded the 16th (Parachute) Field Ambulance from its formation until the end of the operations in North Africa in 1943, and later became the first ADMS of the 6th (Airborne) Division.

[3] This distinguishing lanyard is worn today by the remaining parachute field ambulance of the Regular Army—the 23rd.

[4] The 127th (East Lancashire) Field Ambulance RAMC(TA) had mobilised at Manchester on 2nd September 1939. The unit formed part of the 42nd (East Lancs.) Division, and, with that formation joined the BEF in April 1940. On 2nd May 1940 the 42nd Division relieved the 5th Division, taking over a sector on the Franco-Belgian frontier and, from here, on 14th May had moved into Belgium. The Field Ambulance first went into action at Beuvrey Nord on 19th May, where it opened an Advance Dressing Station (ADS) and set up three Casualty Clearing Points (CCPs) to evacuate casualties from that sector of the River Scarpe between St Amond and Raches, held by the 127th Infantry Brigade. The Field Ambulance took part in the operations leading to the withdrawal from Dunkirk, and on 1st June operated an ADS established on the promenade at Bray Dunes, where it dealt with a large number of casualties. The unit was evacuated off the beaches the following day.

lance with the 42nd Armoured Division and was converted to a parachute field ambulance on 17th July 1942.

Three more parachute field ambulances and another air landing field ambulance were raised in 1943.[1]

Not only did the newly raised Airborne Medical Services have the normal RAMC responsibilities within the Division—namely the advice and technical assistance to the Commander to enable him to maintain the health of the troops ; the care and evacuation of wounded and sick ; the administration of the medical units and the provision of medical stores, equipment and supplies—but, in addition, were responsible for the physical and psychological aspects of parachuting ; the normal responsibilities when training (*i.e.*, medical care in cases of sickness or accidents) ; and when employed in support of infantry, but also the unique aspect of airborne operations when no evacuation of casualties would be possible until contact was made with ground forces on linking up after an airborne landing. This necessitated the provision of full medical and surgical facilities to treat all types of wounds, to hold and nurse the patients up to ten to fourteen days.[2] At this stage this period was not directly associated with the actual time before the link-up with the ground forces, but was in fact the time during which abdominal cases could be moved after operations.

---

[1] The 133rd (Parachute) Field Ambulance came into existence in Palestine in January 1943 by the conversion of the 133rd Field Ambulance of the 44th (Home Counties) Division. (See page 31.)

The 224th (Parachute) Field Ambulance was formed in December 1942 by conversion of the 224th Field Ambulance.

The 225th (Parachute) Field Ambulance was formed at Castle Cary on 7th June 1943, taking its number from the 225th Light Field Ambulance of the Guards Armoured Division which had been disbanded in January 1943. 225th Field Ambulance had been raised on 2nd September 1940 from a cadre from the 128th Field Ambulance, at Bulmershe Court, Earley, Reading. In October 1941 it had joined the Guards Armoured Division in Somerset, became a light field ambulance and redesignated 225th Guards Light Field Ambulance.

The 195th (Air Landing) Field Ambulance was formed on 1st October 1943 by conversion of the 195th Field Ambulance.

[2] The period of ten to fourteen days was chosen for clinical rather than tactical reasons. No surgeon would wish to move a serious abdominal case sooner than ten days.

The other major problem in the organising and training of airborne medical units was the complication, special to airborne forces, that all personnel and stores required to carry out their task had to go by air, and the allocation of space in the aircraft allotted to a force was strictly limited in light of the main object of the use of airborne troops—to get the maximum number of fighting men on to the objective at the outset of the operation.

The airborne field ambulances were so organised and equipped that they could evacuate casualties from the Regimental Aid Posts (RAPs) to the Main Dressing Station (MDS); sort out the cases according to the urgency and treatment necessary; resuscitate cases of shock and haemorrhage by transfusion of plasma; and carry out nursing after operations. All operations were to be carried out by field surgical teams, six to the Division, two per field ambulance.

Medical planning for airborne operations depended on the estimate of casualties; likely sites for the Dressing Station(s) (DS); forecast of the period of the isolation phase and facilities for evacuation of casualties on the link-up with the ground forces.[1]

During training the RAMC organisation for dealing with casualties was fully tested. In all exercises an assessment was made of the anticipated numbers and types of casualties, and men were detailed as such; they were issued with labels on which was written the nature of their 'wound' or 'injury' and instructed to behave in such manner. So much did these men enter into the spirit of the exercises that, on occasions, their behaviour and attitudes on the ground was so realistic as to cause genuine consternation among observers.

The Field Ambulance personnel collected their 'casualties' on the Dropping Zones (DZ) and carried them off to the ADS, and, records Lieut.-General Sir Richard Gale,[2] 'then went through all the make-believe of being operated

---

[1] In the Normandy landing the link-up was forty-eight hours after the 'drop'; in the Rhine crossing the isolation period was only twenty-four hours, but at Arnhem there was no medical link-up at all until capture by the enemy.

[2] 'With the 6th Airborne Division in Normandy' by Lieut.-General R. N. Gale, CB, DSO, OBE, MC (Sampson Low, Marston & Co., Ltd.). (1948.)

upon—the surgical teams doing everything but actually cutting the soldiers to bits '—in this manner the Airborne Medical Services learned how to deal with casualties and how to hold them in the ADS until evacuation was possible.

By the end of the war experience in airborne operations had shown that 10 per cent of casualties needed urgent surgery; surgical teams could average 1.8 operations per hour, but had to be relieved after twelve hours if they were to work again the next day. In all a field ambulance could cope with some 330 cases in twenty-four hours. Later experience also showed that the overall mortality of cases reaching the Field Ambulance was but 1 per cent, and of these the mortality from abdominal wounds was between 30 and 40 per cent.

As time went by special medical airborne equipment, stores and their method of packing was devised and introduced. These included the folding airborne stretcher; the folding trestle (both of which were adopted by many other units); the folding suspension bar; the airborne operating table; the airborne inhaler, devised by Professor Sir Robert Mackintosh; and special containers for whole blood and plasma produced under the direction of Sir Lionel Whitby.

Packs called 'Don' and 'Sugar'[1] were standardised throughout the Airborne Medical Services. The former contained sufficient dressings, drugs and medical comforts for twenty patients, the latter providing dressings for ten surgical cases. Both packs were used extensively for second-line supply.

Within forty-eight hours of his appointment the ADMS had been asked by General Browning to submit his recommendations for the establishment of a parachute and an air landing field ambulance. The basis of the organisation of these units was taken from that of the old cavalry field ambulance, and, apart from minor details, remained un-

---

[1] The 'Don' pack was composed of anaesthetics; drugs; serum; dressings; tins of tea, milk and sugar powder; cubes of meat extract; cigarettes; soap and candles. The 'Sugar' pack also included anaesthetics and drugs and bandages, gauze, swabs and plaster of Paris.

changed throughout the war. It proved to be flexible and easily adapted for a variety of circumstances.

The War Establishment of a parachute field ambulance consisted of a HQ with two surgical teams and four sections. It comprised a total of 9 RAMC officers and 108 ORs, and with attached personnel [1] making the total strength of the unit 11 officers and 166 ORs. The War Establishment of an air landing field ambulance was similar except that, having five instead of four sections, the total RAMC officers was 10 and ORs 129, whilst an increased number of attached personnel brought the total strength to 12 officers and 192 ORs.

To enable skilled first-aid to be immediately available in action RAMC nursing orderlies were permanently attached to each infantry battalion and were distributed among the companies. Approval for this innovation, subsequently generally adopted, was not obtained without some difficulty, but, in practice it proved invaluable.

The respect and confidence which these nursing orderlies gained in the early airborne operations ensured that room was found for them on all subsequent occasions despite the limited number of aircraft made available for combatant units.

The first air landing field ambulance to be formed was the 181st. The unit had been raised as a field ambulance in 1939 at Beaminster in Dorset.[2]

In November 1941 it was selected for conversion into an airborne unit. At that time the Field Ambulance was at Llandysull, in Cardiganshire, commanded by Lieut.-Colonel Norman Gray Hill, MC.[3] In December the unit moved to Standen Manor at Hungerford, and it was here that thirty-eight ORs were posted away as being unfit for

[1] Royal Engineers ; Royal Army Service Corps ; Army Dental Corps (became Royal Army Dental Corps in 1946) ; Army Physical Training Corps and Army Catering Corps.
[2] Raised from a cadre of two officers and nine ORs from the 132nd Field Ambulance.
[3] Lieut.-Colonel Norman Gray Hill, MC, TD, was succeeded in command in August 1942 by Lieut.-Colonel G. M. Warrack. Colonel Gray Hill was killed in an air crash in Italy in the autumn of 1943 when ADMS HQ L of C.

airborne duties. By January 1942 the strength of the Field Ambulance was twelve officers and 202 ORs and they moved to Chilton Foliat. Three weeks later one section commanded by Captain A. S. Baker was in action on the French coast, taking part in the Bruneval raid.[1]

In March 1942 a new War Establishment was introduced, on 1st April the unit received its new designation, that of 181st (Air Landing) Field Ambulance, RAMC, and in May it moved to Carter Barracks at Bulford Camp on Salisbury Plain. A new phase of training then commenced. Men were given experience of being transported in gliders; airsickness and night-vision tests were carried out, and, as it had been decided that the unit would be armed, weapon training was added to the programme. Exercises were held to test the stamina, efficiency and organisation of the unit. In October they marched thirty-one miles in eight and a half hours; early in November an experimental carry with airborne stretchers was conducted.

Finally the Airborne Medical Services of the British Army comprised five parachute field ambulances, the 16th, 127th, 133rd, 224th, and 225th, and two air landing field ambulances, the 181st and 195th.

The 16th and 133rd (Parachute) and 181st (Air Landing) Field Ambulances formed the medical services of the 1st Airborne Division; the 224th and 225th (Parachute) and 195th (Air Landing) Field Ambulance served with the 6th Airborne Division, whilst the 127th (Parachute) Field Ambulance, after serving with the 1st Airborne Division in Italy, became the medical unit of the 2nd Independent Parachute Brigade Group in Italy and Greece. Parachute field ambulances were also raised in India for service with the 50th Indian Parachute Brigade in 1943 and later with the 44th Indian Airborne Division,[2] which was raised in May 1944, from elements of the 44th Indian Armoured Division.[3]

In addition to the airborne medical units there were also

---

[1] See Chapter II.
[2] 7th (British) Parachute Field Ambulance and 60th (Indian) and 80th (Indian) Parachute Field Ambulances.
[3] See Chapter XV.

all the RAMC officers and ORs who served as RMOs and medical orderlies with the battalions of the Parachute Regiment; the Airborne Light Regiments, Royal Artillery; the Parachute Field Squadrons, Royal Engineers; the battalions of the Air Landing Brigades, and as medical staff officers of the 1st (British) Airborne Corps, 1st and 6th Airborne Divisions, and the 2nd Independent Parachute Brigade Group. Individual officers and men of the Airborne Medical Services also saw service in many different parts of the world, in the Middle East and in Burma; with the 7th Australian Division (in its airborne rôle) in New Guinea; with Wingate's 'Chindits' in their glider-borne landings astride the Irrawaddy in March 1944; with the 11th Battalion The Parachute Regiment in the airborne landing on Cos in the autumn of 1943, in Jugo-Slavia, where medical officers dropped by parachute to give aid to the Partisan forces; and last, but not least, with The Special Air Service units.[1]

---

[1] The very nature of the independent rôle of the SAS units presented difficult problems to the RAMC personnel accompanying them. The treatment and disposal of casualties among SAS troops was, of necessity, opportunist. When sufficiently large parties were engaged they were accompanied by a doctor who carried a full scale of equipment including anaesthetics, plasma and surgical instruments. The doctor had either to deal with wounded or sick himself and hold them in the SAS base, or to make contact with local doctors through the resistance movement where such existed. Smaller parties were accompanied by RAMC medical orderlies and all medical personnel dropped by parachute on SAS operations carried skeleton medical equipment in their rucksacks, so that they could still function if their containers and panniers (which were filled with medical stores; blankets, groundsheets, stretchers and stretchers and splints) went astray in the drop.

CHAPTER II

THE FIRST ACTION

A Sea-Borne Section at Bruneval

THROUGHOUT 1941 the Germans established a chain of radio-location stations along the coastline of occupied Europe in order to establish early warning posts to detect the approach of both ships and aircraft. The existence of these posts, and the location of many, were known to the Intelligence service, and photographic reconnaissance units of the RAF brought back many photographs of these stations. It was considered that the capture of the apparatus from one of the posts would be invaluable so that it could be examined by scientists and technicians to find out what progress had been made by the enemy and how accurate their equipment had become.

The planning staff at Combined Operations HQ in London considered how such could be achieved. The RAF and representatives from the 1st Airborne Division were called in for consultation, and, early in 1942, decisions were taken which led to the launching of the operation against the radio-location station located in an isolated chateau near the village of Bruneval, about twelve miles to the north-east of Le Havre.

The position was studied from maps and air photographs. About 400 yards from the chateau was a farmhouse, called Le Presbytere, encircled by a wood. This farm was the HQ of a small garrison which manned fifteen defensive posts in the area. Not far inland was an infantry regiment and a panzer battalion, both of which could provide immediate reinforcements.

Not far from the chateau the cliffs ran down to a small cove.

It was decided that the operation should be entrusted to a small force of trained parachutists, and that if they could seize the chateau, hold it as long as necessary to remove the radiolocation apparatus, the force could then withdraw down

THE FIRST ACTION

the cliff path to the cove, from whence they would be taken off by the Royal Navy.

The unit selected for the operation was 'C' Company of the 2nd Parachute Battalion, commanded by Major J. D. Frost, and training for their rôle commenced on Salisbury Plain, at Alton Priors.

This airborne force was to be supported by a 'sea tail' which included a section from the 181st (Airborne) Field Ambulance, commanded by Captain A. S. Baker, composed of twenty non-commissioned officers and men, with Sergeant Sanders as the senior NCO.

The Field Ambulance was then at Chilton Foliat, and together with the Company of the 2nd Parachute Battalion the Section moved up to Inveraray for special training, the RAMC learning their rôle in Assault Landing Craft (ALCs) based on a former Belgian ship, the MV *Prins Albert*, of some 3,000 tons, and this seaborne training was subsequently continued off the Dorset coast.

At last all was ready and the parachutists moved to Thruxton Airfield to emplane in Whitley aircraft on the evening of 27th February.

The RAMC Section embarked on the *Prins Albert* at Gosport, except for Captain Baker, who went aboard a Motor Torpedo Boat (MTB) based on HMS *Hornet*. The Section was transhipped halfway across the Channel and divided among three ALCs, and together with the three MTBs continued across the Channel. The seaborne force waited off the French shore for about two hours before moving into the beaches to take off the parachutists, who included several casualties who were dealt with by the RAMC personnel at the small beach DS. Fortunately there were few casualties, but the plan had been that any urgent surgery would have been carried out in the MTBs; Captain Baker being in one, with Royal Naval medical officers in the other two. The force withdrew as soon as all the airborne troops had been embarked, and turned back to England with an escort of Spitfires, and so it was that the first airborne RAMC unit went into action, although not in an airborne rôle, except for the medical orderlies who dropped with Major Frost's company of the 2nd Parachute Battalion.

CHAPTER III

INTO ACTION IN AFRICA

THE 16TH (PARACHUTE) FIELD AMBULANCE IN ALGERIA AND TUNISIA

THE invasion of North Africa in November 1942 was the first major campaign in which British airborne forces participated as an integral part in the plans for the initial operations, although they were subsequently employed in a normal infantry rôle. The 1st Parachute Brigade (composed of the 1st, 2nd, and 3rd Battalions of the Parachute Regiment), the medical unit of which was the 16th (Parachute) Field Ambulance, RAMC, formed part of the First Army for the invasion of Algeria.

Two companies of the 3rd Battalion, together with No 3 Section of the 16th (Parachute) Field Ambulance, commanded by Captain J. H. Keesey, left Bulford towards the end of October for Netheravon, and from there, on 5th November, moved to Hurn Airfield, near Christchurch, whilst the remainder of the Brigade entrained for Greenock to embark and sail 'under sealed orders'.

The 3rd Battalion contingent, with the RAMC Section, emplaned on the evening of 9th November in American-piloted Dakotas; taking off, in a fog, they flew through the night, landing at dawn in Gibraltar.

Whilst the men rested at the airfield, the CO reported to the Fortress HQ, where he learned that the small airborne force was to take off immediately, their objective being the airfield at Bone.

Hurriedly the Dakotas were reloaded to meet the tactical needs, and this task was completed in the beams of searchlights after darkness fell. At half-past four in the morning of 11th November the first of the Dakotas took off for the airfield at Maison Blanche, near Algiers. The other Dakotas followed; one aircraft, in which were Captain Keesey, the Officer Commanding (OC) of the Section of the Field Ambulance, and two RAMC ORs, crashed into the sea.[1] Another was hit by anti-aircraft (AA) fire whilst flying over Algiers Harbour.

By nine o'clock in the morning twenty-nine Dakotas were drawn up at the Maison Blanche ready to take off. This airborne force of 360 officers and men was to seize the Bone airfield without delay, for it was learned from First Army HQ that there was a German parachute battalion in Tunis which would no doubt have the same objective.[2]

As the American pilots [3] were inexperienced in the location of DZs at night and in the dropping of parachutists, it was decided to take off at dawn.

At 8.30 in the morning the string of Dakotas came over the target, and the parachutists jumped out to drift down on the airfield. Due to the atmospheric conditions the landing was described as 'far heavier than any to which they had become accustomed'; thirteen casualties resulted, of which one man was killed.

On landing, the airfield appeared completely deserted, but as the men formed up crowds of Arabs began to converge upon them and quite a lot of stores and parachutes were looted. Later in the day the airfield was attacked by enemy dive-bombers, but it was held by the Parachute Battalion until relieved by No 6 Commando and the arrival of an RAF squadron of Spitfires. The RAMC Section, then commanded by Staff-Sergeant E. O. Stevens, set up a DS and treated casualties from among the parachutists, Commandos and RAF.

The rest of the Parachute Brigade, with the 16th (Parachute) Field Ambulance (less one section), commanded by Lieut.-Colonel M. McEwan, DFC, TD, which had left

[1] All the men were rescued by the crew of an American ship which was bound for New York. The men picked up from the sea travelled to the USA and rejoined the 3rd Battalion two months later.

[2] The actual parachute drop early the next day was, in fact, witnessed by a formation of JU.52s carrying the German parachutists to the same objective, but on seeing the British landing they turned and made back to Tunis.

[3] The majority of the American pilots had come to the US Air Force from civil air lines and this was to be their first operational flight.

England on 1st November, arrived by sea at Algiers on 11th November and had lain in the harbour for two days subjected to intermittent bombing until they disembarked on the evening of 13th November. Marching from the docks straight through the town they reached the village of St Charles, eighteen kilometres outside Algiers. By 15th November the whole Brigade had arrived and assembled in the Maison Blanche area where they were joined, on 19th November, by the two companies of the 3rd Battalion which had seized Bone Airfield, together with No 3 Section of the 16th (Parachute) Field Ambulance.

The task of the First Army, which had landed at Algiers, was to capture Bizerta and Tunis, and, despite adverse weather conditions, the smallness of the force and a lack of transport, the formation immediately prepared to carry out this eastwards move. The advance, by three infantry brigades and a tank brigade, commenced on 15th November.

The next day the parachute troops were employed in an airborne rôle with the object of repeating at Souk el Arba the success achieved at Bone. The task of seizing the key point of the airfield and road junction at Beja, some ninety miles east of Tunis, was allotted to the 1st Battalion The Parachute Regiment, who were accompanied by No 1 Section of the 16th (Parachute) Field Ambulance commanded by Lieutenant D. Wright, with No 1 Surgical Team under command of Lieutenant C. G. Robb.[1] They took off at seven o'clock in the morning of 15th November, but after being airborne for an hour and a half the weather worsened to such an extent that they were forced to turn back to Maison Blanche. The operation was re-mounted the following day.

The RAMC element of the airborne force took off at eleven o'clock in the morning. They flew for two hours along the African coast, then turning inland came over the DZ at a quarter past one. Out went the trolley and containers, followed by the first ' stick ' of men. The trolley became detached from its parachute in the descent and was com-

---

[1] Professor C. G. Robb, MC, MCh, FRCS, who after the war became Professor of Surgery at St Mary's Hospital, London, and New York University.

pletely smashed but all containers were collected intact. The other medical 'sticks' dropped over a thousand yards away and they all came together in the assembly area, and marched with the Battalion into the nearest village, where they were enthusiastically received by the villagers and some French troops. One man was killed in the drop and one other casualty was treated on the DZ. Arrangements were made to take over a part of a small local French hospital where thirty beds were available. Later in the day three men of the Parachute Battalion and a Sapper NCO were admitted, having been wounded in the accidental discharge of a sten gun.

The Battalion moved forward that evening, arriving outside Beja about eight o'clock, spending the night in a bivouac, and marching into the town early the next day. Here the Field Ambulance Section and the Surgical Team moved into a small military hospital of twenty beds set up in the garrison school. The French MO then made arrangements for the use of the town's Civil Hospital, some 250 yards away, and here Lieutenants Robb and Wright and three orderlies were installed, the remainder of the Surgical Team and the Section set themselves up in the Military Hospital.

The Battalion had deployed into defensive positions around the town, Captain Haggie establishing an RAP at the Battalion HQ. Later one company went forward towards the village of Sidi N'Sir, the RMO accompanying them. Five battle casualties were admitted to the MDS at Beja the following day, one NCO of the 1st Battalion and four Germans, all of whom were operated upon.

During that day it was learned that a large French military hospital was situated about fifteen kilometres away at Souk el Khemis. Contact was made with the French Medical Service, who were extremely helpful, offering X-ray facilities and the use of a hospital train based at Souk el Khemis for the westward evacuation of casualties. This liaison was fully developed when on 20th November Beja was dive-bombed by fifteen Stukas, leaving behind a trail of ruins and many casualties. Some sixty French and Arab civilians were killed and over 150 injured were collected from the shattered

B

buildings and the rubble-strewn streets. The French Ambulance Section helped in bringing in the wounded and the British Surgical Team linked up with the French in treating the casualties, at the outset Lieutenant Wright acted as anaesthetist to the French surgeon at the Civil Hospital whilst Lieutenant Robb set up his own theatre to deal with the flow of other air-raid victims. Lieutenant Robb performed 162 operations, many of which were carried out during the bombing of the town, with Lieutenant Wright acting as anaesthetist. During this time a bomb fell just outside the building and Lieutenant Robb was injured, his left tibia being fractured, the fracture running onto the knee joint; in spite of this he carried on operating, and the next day after performing another twenty operations gave a pint of his own blood as the supply of plasma had run out.[1]

Battle casualties, both British and American, resulting from patrol activities, came in in varying numbers day by day, together with a normal proportion of sick, and so life at Beja continued throughout November. Nineteen battle casualties were brought on 22nd and 23rd November.[2]

On the night of 23rd/24th November the 1st Parachute Battalion, less one company, and accompanied by the Field Ambulance Section—leaving the Surgical Team at the Hospital—moved forward to Sidi N'Sir, their immediate objective being a small hill where an Italian ' tank harbour ' was located.

The plan of attack was that a detachment of RE were to move round the hill and mine the road running away to the east, thereby hampering the enemy retreat and the approach of reinforcements, and then, following an opening bombardment with mortars, the Battalion would attack. As they approached the hill, called Gué, one of the anti-tank mines carried by the party of Sappers was accidentally detonated,

---

[1] Lieutenant Robb and Captain Haggie were both awarded the Military Cross for their work during this period.

[2] On 23rd November First Reinforcements, under command of Captain A. Percival, RAMC, and Captain D. H. Ridler, ADC, landed at Algiers. Whilst lying in the harbour their ship had been torpedoed, and the RAMC personnel were immediately engaged in dealing with the casualties on board.

exploding all the other mines which the Engineers were carrying in sandbags and killing the RE officer and men. The explosions brought the enemy to life and they opened fire, tracer bullets cutting through the darkness. The Battalion immediately attacked the enemy position which was quickly overrun, a considerable number of Germans and Italians were killed and twenty-six prisoners taken. The CO and his Adjutant were, however, shot at close range, whilst demanding the surrender of one of the enemy tanks.

Lieutenant Wright, who had been collecting the Battalion's wounded at the RAP, took the seriously wounded CO and his Adjutant back to Beja. They were laid on an Italian motor-tricycle and travelled along a railway track. It was very rough going for some four miles until they came upon a set of bogey wheels. The stretchers were laid on the carriage and pushed along by the MO and the COs batman. Later a donkey was found and hitched to the bogey to pull the trolley along to a small wayside station where they transferred to a car to rush back to the Hospital where Lieutenant Robb performed emergency operations which saved the lives of the two officers.

The rest of the Battalion's wounded were evacuated under arrangements made by Staff-Sergeant Clegg and this, in consequence of the nature of the country, involved carrying the casualties some ten miles to reach the transport to move them back. Thirteen battle casualties were admitted to the Hospital as a result of the raid.

On 26th November the 1st Parachute Battalion came under command of 'Blade Force' and was moved in Troop Conveying Vehicles (TCVs) to Mateur, some ten miles to the south of Beja. Five medical orderlies were detached from the Field Ambulance Section to accompany the Battalion. During the move they were subjected to a bombing attack, one TCV was hit, killing eight men and wounding twelve others. The casualties were taken straight back by ambulance to Beja.

The Battalion remained in the Mateur area until 11th December, when it was withdrawn to Souk el Khemis to rest. No 1 Section, 16th (Parachute) Field Ambulance and the

Surgical Team moved from Beja on 13th December to join them, being relieved by HQ and the remainder of the Field Ambulance, who took over the Hospital and accommodation in a granary at the lower end of the town.

At Souk el Khemis the 1st Battalion were joined by the remains of the 2nd, withdrawn from the action after their fighting withdrawal from Oudna.

The 2nd Parachute Battalion had been held in reserve at Maison Blanche until 28th November, when it received orders to make an airborne attack on the airfield at Depienne. They took off, accompanied by No 2 Section of the 16th (Parachute) Field Ambulance commanded by Lieutenant J. C. McGavin, in Dakotas the next night, and jumped at some 600 feet onto open ploughland where they assembled, rounded up in the darkness a few mule carts as transport for the mortars and set off for their objective, carrying their weapons, ammunition, and five days' rations. By 4.30 in the morning they had covered some twelve miles; a halt was called and the men huddled together to rest until first light. The advance was renewed at dawn and by eleven o'clock had reached the landing ground, which was found deserted, although covered by some German troops supported by tanks. As there were no enemy aircraft to destroy, and as the Battalion was then isolated some fifty miles ahead of the main British force, the CO decided to withdraw. During the day the Battalion moved cautiously back to a position at Prise de l'Eau, which they eventually reached late that evening, having been intermittently engaged with the enemy throughout the day.

On the morning of 1st December a message was received notifying the CO that the planned push through to Tunis by part of the 6th Armoured Division had been postponed. This meant that there was no hope of the Battalion meeting up with the advancing armour in their withdrawal, and the unit was practically surrounded.

During the morning the Battalion drove off two attacks and early in the afternoon commenced its withdrawal, harassed all the time by air-attacks and armour. In the space of two hours' hard fighting one company had almost ceased to exist, and as darkness came on the CO decided that each company would withdraw independently towards the village of Massicault across very rough and stony country. By that time the Battalion's casualties in killed and wounded amounted to some 150. It was out of the question to consider abandoning the wounded to the mercies of the local Arab population, who were at that time not only pro-German but openly hostile to the British, and who mutilated and killed any who fell into their hands. It was decided, therefore, to leave behind a subaltern, and what remained of his platoon, to collect the wounded and concentrate them at a small farm where Lieutenant McGavin, RAMC, and his section established an ADS, and where they could be treated until such time as the Germans would move in to take them prisoner.[1]

The companies made off during the night and made good progress, although one company was cut off, surrounded, and although fighting to the end their ammunition was eventually exhausted and they were captured. The remainder of the Battalion continued on, short of water and ammunition, constantly in action, until it reached Medjez el Bab, which was in allied hands. The Battalion had lost sixteen officers and 250 men in the withdrawal from Oudna, but even then they were called into action to take part in the defence of Medjez el Bab until 13th December, when they were taken back in TCVs to Souk el Khemis.

Whilst the 1st Battalion had been engaged in the Beja area, and the 2nd at Oudna, the 3rd Battalion had been at St Charles awaiting the launching of a number of airborne operations which did not materialise. On 6th December they entrained for Beja, and straight away moved forward to take part in the sixteen-day battle to hold Hunt's Gap.

On 6th December the 16th (Parachute) Field Ambulance, less two sections, left Rouiba and moved to Beja, where No 1

---

[1] Lieutenant McGavin and eleven ORs were captured. Five ORs were missing from the Section together with five medical orderlies from the 2nd Battalion.

Section rejoined the unit.[1] The 1st Parachute Brigade had taken part in three separate airborne operations since their arrival in North Africa, to seize key points in advance of the First Army, but had subsequently fought in a normal infantry rôle, and they were destined to continue to be so employed until the conclusion of the operations in North Africa in April 1943.

On Christmas Eve it was planned that a general advance should be launched with the axis of advance from Medjez el Bab to Tebourba, the 16th (Parachute) Field Ambulance establishing an MDS at Medjez el Bab. This was to have been the unit's first experience of service as a normal field ambulance, but in consequence of very heavy rain the advance was postponed indefinitely as it was quite impossible for the armour to function.

On 7th January the unit did move, leaving Beja and arriving four days later at Boufarik where the packing of containers into loads was reorganised as a result of the experience gained in practice since the unit's arrival in North Africa. Whilst so engaged Colonel McEwan learned that the unit was to hold itself in readiness for an air-landing operation at Sfax ; loading tables were evolved for such an operation and tried out in practice but again the operation was cancelled.

On Sunday, 24th January, the Parachute Brigade was called upon urgently ; back to Algiers they moved where

[1] During the period from 16th November to 11th December the Surgical Team of the 16th (Parachute) Field Ambulance at Beja performed a total of 162 operations—137 military cases and 25 civilians (French and Arab). Of the military cases, 37 came from the 1st Parachute Battalion and 4 from the 2nd ; 16 were American, 3 German, and 1 Italian. The other 76 came from 11 other First Army units.

The classification of the injuries treated during the same period showed a predominance of single wounds, 121 ; flesh wounds, 77 ; and compound fractures, 34. There were 15 cases of multiple wounds and 8 abdominal (colon, 2 ; colon plus small intestine, 2 ; thoraco/abdominal, 2 ; liver, 1 ; and stomach, 1). Other wounds treated were : burns, 7 ; chest intra thoracic, 5 ; eye, 4 ; joints, 3 ; simple fractures, 2 ; urethra, 1 ; testicles, 1 ; spine (laminatomy), 1 ; jaw and face (tracheotomy), 1 ; skull and brain, 1 ; Peripheral nerves, 2 ; gas gangrene (before surgery), 1 ; gas gangrene (after surgery), 1 ; amputations, 1.

the Field Ambulance embarked on two destroyers, landing at Bone two days later. The CO made contact straight away with the ADMS of the 6th Armoured Division, as a result of which one surgical team under Lieutenant C. J. Longland was sent to Gafour and the second team commanded by Major P. R. Wheatley moved to Robaa.

It was planned that the 1st Parachute Battalion would attack Djebel Mansour and Djebel Alliliga on the night of 2nd February. No 1 Section of the Field Ambulance under Captain Wright was already with the Battalion and the CO, Lieut.-Colonel McEwan, set off in a carrier on a reconnaissance of the route to be used for the evacuation of casualties. This was found to be impossible for ambulance cars to proceed very far until the Djebel Alliliga was occupied, but even then the roads would be both difficult and dangerous. It was some eight miles on to the Djebel Mansour and the intervening ground was either very rugged and mountainous, broken by steep ravines, or flat stretches of ground exposed to enemy fire, or rough and boulder strewn with patches of scrub breast high making the going dangerous and most arduous for stretcher-bearers. Captain Wright was informed of the situation and told that until the success signal was fired from Djebel Alliliga casualties could not be evacuated to Car Posts (CPs) which were to be set up on the main route.

The Section went into action carrying only standard packs and stretchers. Owing to the difficult nature of the ground, the intense mortar and machine-gun fire and the distance back to the CP, it took ten hours to bring down the wounded from the top of Djebel Mansour, by which time the stretcher-bearers too were exhausted. From the CP back to the MDS at Garfour it took another hour and a half.

Colonel McEwan fully appreciated that if all casualties were to be removed within a reasonable time of being wounded the whole Field Ambulance would have to be brought in. No 4 Section under Captain Percival was sent forward to Djebel Mansour and the remainder of the unit moved up to the CP.

On the top of the rugged Djebel Mansour the CO of the 1st

Parachute Battalion told Colonel McEwan that although his men had taken Djebel Alliliga it was impossible to hold it as he was too thin on the ground, but that he would hold Djebel Mansour. On his return to his HQ the CO established a stretcher-bearer relay post in a ravine halfway between Djebel Mansour and the CP. The intervening ground was very open, but as the route was being improved by the Sappers and it was possible to get a four-wheel-drive ambulance car up to the Post, and to protect the wounded, two carriers were obtained from a battalion of the Grenadier Guards.[1] With this organisation the time down from Djebel Mansour was reduced to three hours and two and a half hours on to Gafour.

The battle continued throughout 3rd and 4th February, and during the evening and night of 4th/5th February the Parachute Field Ambulance evacuated casualties not only from the 1st Parachute Battalion but also from the Grenadier Guards and the French troops on the left flank.

Early in the morning of 5th February Djebel Mansour was heavily bombarded, shells and mortar bombs rained down on the 1st Battalion The Parachute Regiment, which suffered many casualties. It was obvious that the enemy was launching a determined counter-attack. By this time, with the exception of the QM and two men, every man in the Parachute Field Ambulance, including the cooks and RASC personnel, were carrying stretchers. All the regular stretcher-bearers were exhausted and Colonel McEwan called for volunteers to go forward on to Djebel Mansour; Captain J. G. Cassidy and twenty men undertook the task. They had toiled halfway up the hill when Captain Cassidy learned that the 1st Parachute Battalion had received orders to withdraw from their positions, but he decided to press forward, and reaching the top of the hill was able to collect up and evacuate all the wounded.

When it became apparent to the enemy that the Djebel Mansour positions were being evacuated they lifted their fire on to the ground between the base of the hill and the CP, and numbers of grenadiers and parachutists began to pass

[1] 5th Battalion Grenadier Guards, part of the 24th Guards Brigade.

through the ravine to avoid the heavy fire. It was obvious that there were many casualties lying out on the open ground, so every available man from the Field Ambulance was organised into search parties for a sweep of the area either side of the ravine. Many casualties were found and carried in under fire.

Between 3rd and 5th February a total of 201 casualties were treated and evacuated by the 16th (Parachute) Field Ambulance.

By 15th February an enemy attack on the Parachute Brigade's front was imminent and sections of the Field Ambulance were attached to each battalion. It was five days later that the enemy moved forward but the attack proved abortive, the German advance broke against the Brigade's positions and many prisoners were taken. The battle lasted throughout the day and, as it was impossible for the ambulance cars to get forward of Arcoub, more and more stretcher-bearers were called forward until once again every available man was committed.

At five o'clock in the afternoon of 26th February enemy tanks were reported on the Brigade's left rear and a tank battle was expected. Such did develop north of El Aroussa, but did not affect the Brigade or its position. During the afternoon the 2nd Parachute Battalion repelled an attack by Italian troops. Although there were no casualties in the Battalion No 3 Section of the Field Ambulance, commanded by Lieutenant A. W. Lippman Kessel, was kept fully engaged in treating and evacuating Italian wounded.

On 3rd March the 1st Parachute Brigade was ordered up to the Sedjenane sector where the 139th Infantry Brigade were being hard pressed. All field ambulance personnel were withdrawn from the Battalions and the Parachute Field Ambulance moved forward, on the orders of the ADMS of the 46th Division, to relieve the 185th Field Ambulance at the ADS, a mile to the south of Tamera Railway Station. The rôle of the Parachute Field Ambulance was the evacuation of all casualties from the forward area, whilst the 185th Field Ambulance undertook evacuation from the Parachute MDS back to their own MDS at Tabarka.

The Parachute Brigade took up positions on high ground around Tamera to await the enemy; there was a possibility that the road back to Tamera might be cut in the forthcoming battle as the Commander of the Parachute Brigade had issued orders that there would be no withdrawal from the area. In consequence Colonel McEwan brought in his two Surgical Teams and set up an operating centre at Maison Forestière; a reserve stock of 500 blankets and 100 stretchers were brought up together with ample supplies of dressings and other stores. The French were holding the extreme left of the Parachute Brigade's positions, and arrangements were made for the reception of their casualties. Major Wheatley took command of the MDS, whilst Colonel McEwan went up to the ADS—the medical organisation was ready.

The enemy launched their attack on the 1st and 2nd Parachute Battalions on 8th March, and 108 casualties were brought into the ADS during the day. There was considerable bombing of the area, one ambulance car was dive-bombed, the medical orderly killed and the driver wounded, and the unit water-cart was hit by shellfire at the water-point at Tamera Station.

Two days later the whole brigade area was subjected to an intense and prolonged bombardment. Captain Cassidy, the MO at Brigade HQ, was mortally wounded whilst attending a wounded man, and Sergeant F. Wetherby was wounded whilst treating patients in the ADS.

On 11th March the Germans put in a determined attack against the 1st Parachute Battalion and there was some enemy infiltration into their positions. The main Djebel Abiod-Tamera road was heavily bombed and machine-gunned and Colonel McEwan sent back as many of the unit as possible to the MDS, staying behind with Captain Young and Captain Logan,[1] and fourteen ORs. During the night of 11th/12th March the Field Surgical Unit (FSU) accommodation at the Tabarka MDS was burnt out, so a surgical team under Captain Lippman Kessell was sent out to their assistance.

[1] Captain J. W. Logan, RAMC, had joined the Field Ambulance as a reinforcement officer following the capture of Lieutenant McGavin.

The severe fighting continued for a week and then, on 17th March, the area around the ADS was not only shelled continuously but dive-bombed eight times during the day, leaving not a square yard of the ADS site untouched by splinters.

Over 100 wounded were dealt with at the ADS during the day by Colonel McEwan and Captain Logan, assisted by Staff-Sergeant Stevens and with Corporal E. Hardie in charge of the reception and evacuation of casualties.

Early in the afternoon news came through that the Commandos and the French were being heavily attacked, and Captain Young went off with two ambulance cars to make contact with them. They drove through torrential rain. This led to flooding of the river, which made it impossible for the cars to regain the main road and the French casualties were diverted to the unit MDS.

At half-past eight that evening the Parachute Field Ambulance were ordered to the Tabarka area, for the Tamera position was becoming untenable. The 2nd Parachute Battalion had been ordered to hold on to their positions until all the rest of the force had withdrawn to a new line. No 4 Section of the Field Ambulance, commanded by Captain Percival, with an ambulance car, went up to the 2nd Battalion. The MDS closed and the rest of the Field Ambulance moved off to Tabarka, all stores and tentage loaded on to three-ton lorries, and the men, due to shortage of transport, marched due south across the marshes to the Tabarka road.

As soon as all casualties had been treated and evacuated the ADS closed too, moving back in two lorries, arriving at Tabarka at two o'clock in the morning of 18th March. Here Colonel McEwan discovered that only two instead of four three-ton lorries had been sent to the MDS, so the two from the ADS were hurriedly unloaded and the stores dumped; two more lorries were borrowed from the 185th Field Ambulance, and back they went through the night to Maison Forestière. Colonel McEwan had been told by the Brigade Commander that the only road up to the MDS—the main Tamera-Djebel Aboid road—would be in front of the new forward positions of the infantry by 6 am, so there was no time to be lost. The rough road, following the torrential rains of the previous evening, was almost impassable, but the small convoy pressed on through the night. It was very dark, and one lorry became so hopelessly bogged down in the deep slimy mud that it had to be abandoned. Eventually the MDS was reached at half-past four in the morning.

By this time the French troops on the left flank had given way under enemy pressure and the remnants of the 1st Parachute Battalion and No 1 Commando were fighting a desperate rearguard action to stem the German advance until the next defensive line was occupied.

The men of the MDS, together with their 'relief force', hurriedly loaded up the lorries as the first light of a grey dawn came up from the dark hills, and they finally got away at 6.30 am. The journey back to Tabarka was through a 'no-man's land'. During the journey the rear lorry, which contained the personal kits of the officers and men and all the office equipment and stores, ploughed into soft ground and became completely immobilised. This, however, was not discovered until the other vehicles reached Tabarka.

This time the QM, Captain E. D. M. Anderson, took a carrier and went back in an effort to save the vehicle and its occupants. He found it out on the marshes and was greeted by shouts and cheers from some distance off where the occupants, headed by the Orderly Room Sergeant, Sergeant J. D. Bellamy, had taken cover away from the vehicle, which would have drawn enemy fire, preparatory to making a getaway on foot. Sergeant Bellamy was humping the unit's security box, with all the unit's important papers, which he had removed from the lorry.

Despite determined efforts it was impossible to salvage the vehicle and it was set on fire. The NCO and men clambered onto Captain Anderson's carrier and back they went —one lonely vehicle crossing the 'no-man's land' back to the comparative safety of Tabarka.

During the twelve days at Tamera the 16th (Parachute) Field Ambulance had treated and evacuated 554 casualties.[1]

Then followed a short respite during which the two Surgical

---

[1] Three hundred and twenty from the 1st Parachute Brigade; 179 from other units; 11 French; and 44 Germans.

Teams operated in conjunction with the 183rd Field Ambulance.

On the night of 23rd/24th March No 1 Section, commanded by Captain Wright, went forward with the 1st Parachute Battalion in their successful assault of the feature called ' The Pimple '. Two days later the three Battalions of the Brigade were made up to their full War Establishment in medical orderlies from field ambulance personnel, the site for an ADS was selected and preparations made for an advance to be made to regain the ground yielded in the withdrawal.

On 27th March the HQ Section, under Captain J. W. Logan, moved up to join up with the RAP of the 3rd Parachute Battalion before first light at the foot of ' The Pimple ' ; later in the day Captain Wright with No 1 Section reported to the HQ of the 1st Battalion, whilst Captain Young with No 3 Section, after a difficult march over sandy country, joined No 1 Thabor (Goums) [1] of the French Force.

That night Major Wheatley, with additional stretcher-bearers from the 183rd Field Ambulance, moved up in an ambulance train to join the HQ Section at the ADS they had set up on the river bed at the foot of ' The Pimple '.

Just before midnight, whilst the artillery barrage was in progress and the 1st and 2nd Battalions were pushing in their attack, the enemy began to shell the Nefza Station area ; the shelling went on all night, several bursting in the immediate vicinity of the ADS.

Only a few casualties reached the ADS during the night, but between seven-thirty and midday of 28th March over sixty wounded, mostly from the 2nd Battalion, were carried in. At that time it was a two and a half miles stretcher carry from the Battalion position to the ADS, over ground which was constantly shelled, and at several points exposed to enemy snipers. The stretcher-bearers came from HQ and No 4 Section, although both German prisoners and mules were pressed into service. No 4 Section, under Captain Percival, had in fact followed the 2nd Battalion up the hill where they collected, treated and evacuated wounded under heavy mortar and small-arms fire.

[1] Irregular troops from Morocco commanded by French Regular Officers.

Throughout the morning large numbers of German prisoners reached the ADS and they were employed in evacuating wounded down to the relay point set up by 183 Field Ambulance.

A further fifty casualties were treated at the ADS in the afternoon and a regular evacuation stream continued back to the MDS. In the case of No 3 Section with the Goums the position was more difficult, and as it was not possible for wounded to be evacuated over open ground to 'The Pimple' ADS, an RAP had been set up at Sidi Emmbarek and casualties sent back, carried by Italian prisoners of war, to the Goums' rear HQ.

By midday, however, from the sounds of the progress of the battle, Captain Young appreciated that the 1st Battalion had seized their objectives, and so sent off another party of wounded with Italian stretcher-bearers, with an escort of two Goums, and led by Privates King and Spencer, RAMC, across the open plain to 'The Pimple' ADS. Halfway across the plain they were approached from the enemy lines by a column of almost 100 Italians who surrendered themselves to the two RAMC private soldiers. Unperturbed, they headed their now quite large body of men down to 'The Pimple' where they handed over their prisoners to a battalion of the Durham Light Infantry.

The ADS received a further twenty casualties on the morning of 29th March, before closing at midday, the HQ Section moving back to Tabarka to refit, and Captain Rutherford, the RMO of the 3rd Battalion, moved down with his RAP to deal with the remaining casualties at the ADS position.

The HQ Section, having re-equipped at Tabarka, then moved up, under Captain Logan, to the Brigade Command Post. By this time the 1st Parachute Brigade, with the Goums on their left, had taken all their three objectives and were well established in the positions occupied prior to the withdrawal on 17th/18th March. The former 'no-man's land' was, however, still mined and booby-trapped, for there had been no time for the Sappers to clear the ground. The Brigade Commander therefore ordered the Parachute Field Ambulance to open up an ADS as far forward as possible.

The HQ Section went forward and was the first unit to negotiate the road north of Djebel Abiod, and the ADS was opened at dusk. The next morning some twenty casualties were admitted; these had resulted from enemy air-attacks on convoys on the Djebel Abiod-Tamera road. In one such attack Captain Logan was wounded by a bomb splinter, and an OR from No 3 Section was also hit when a German aircraft let a stick of bombs fall on the site of the ADS.

The next day Sedjenane fell to the advancing troops, and the Parachute Brigade were relieved in their forward positions. Between 28th and 30th March the Parachute Field Ambulance had dealt with 170 casualties.

Then followed a period of respite for the Brigade, and, between 31st March and 14th April, the Field Ambulance only dealt with eighteen casualties.

On 12th May the 16th (Parachute) Field Ambulance moved to Matmore, near Mascara, to rejoin the 1st Airborne Division. Here, after a period of five months without any parachute duties, they carried out six weeks' intensive airborne divisional training, 'stick' training with container drill, trolley erection, and marching by day and night. Specialist training in post-operative nursing, resuscitation, water duties and sanitation, and parachute jumping both by day and night. On 21st June Lieut.-Colonel McEwan [1] handed over command of the unit to Major P. R. Wheatley, and on 30th June the Field Ambulance moved, with the 1st Parachute Brigade, to the area of Sousse, which was to be their operational base.

At Sousse the 16th (Parachute) Field Ambulance was joined by the 133rd (Parachute) Field Ambulance, which had been moved to Tunisia from the Middle East.

The 133rd Parachute Field Ambulance had been raised as a 2nd Line Territorial Army Field Ambulance in 1939, with its HQ at Croydon. The Unit had served with the 44th (Home Counties) Division in the BEF in 1940, and accompanied the formation when it was dispatched to the Middle

---

[1] Lieut.-Colonel McEwan was posted as ADMS 6th Airborne Division, then forming in England, an appointment he held until July 1946.

East in 1942, seeing action in the Western Desert and with the Eighth Army at El Alamein.

On the disbandment of the 44th Division after El Alamein, the 133rd Field Ambulance was moved to Syria and later to Egypt where, in January 1943, at Kabrit in the Canal Zone, it was converted to an airborne field ambulance and formed part of the newly raised 4th Parachute Brigade—then composed of the 10th and 156th Parachute Battalions.

The Field Ambulance was helped in its conversion by Major Bonham Carter, the DADMS of the 1st Airborne Division, who flew out to the Middle East to undertake this work. Initial parachute training commenced on 19th February 1943 at Quassasin and later at Ramat David, near Nazareth, using aircraft of the United States Air Force (USAF). Within four months of becoming an airborne unit, the 133rd (Parachute) Field Ambulance, as it was re-designated on 20th May 1943, embarked with the 4th Parachute Brigade on 26th May, by sea, to sail for Tripoli, under the command of Lieut.-Colonel W. C. Alford, where on landing it moved to Sousse by road to join the 1st Airborne Division. The 133rd were at that time still wearing khaki ' fore and aft ' caps and paraded so dressed on first joining the Division, but soon the red berets were issued and the 133rd took their place alongside the other airborne units ready for the invasion of Italy.

It was on 5th March 1943 that orders came to 181st (Air Landing) Field Ambulance for men to proceed on embarkation leave. On their return they were issued with tropical kit and it was soon known that their destination overseas was North Africa, where operations were drawing to a close, and that the next step would be the assualt on the ' under belly ' of Europe. In the weeks preceding their move the unit was engaged in training in tropical hygiene and officers were sent on tropical medicine courses.

On the morning of 15th May orders were issued for the move that evening, and at eight o'clock the unit embussed for Amesbury Station from where they travelled through the night to Liverpool, to embark on the *Stirling Castle*.

The convoy assembled in the Clyde and set off with an

THE 16TH PARACHUTE FIELD AMBULANCE – NORTH AFRICA NOVEMBER 1942 – MAY 1943

Map showing Mediterranean Sea coast with locations including Cape Bon, Gulf of Tunis, Bizerta, Tunis, Mateur, Tebourba, Medjez El Bab, Oudna, Depienne, Pont du Fahs, Jebel Mansour, Jebel Alliliga, Jebel Aboid, Tamera, Beja, Souk El Khemis, Souk El Arba, Souk Ahras, Bone, Guelma, and River Miliane.

PARACHUTE LANDING [a] 12TH NOVEMBER (near Bone)

PARACHUTE LANDING [b] 16TH NOVEMBER (near Souk El Arba)

PARACHUTE LANDING [c] 29TH NOVEMBER (near Depienne)

[a] 3rd Parachute Bn. [b] 1st Parachute Bn. [c] 2nd Parachute Bn.

escort composed of a cruiser, an aircraft carrier, five armed merchant cruisers, and twelve destroyers. The voyage was uneventful—although the Royal Navy destroyed two submarines *en route* and the muffled explosions of depth charges were heard—and Oran was reached on 26th May.

The Brigade, on disembarkation, was transported to the village of Fleurus outside Oran, where they occupied a camp which had been used as a temporary staging area and which proved to be quite unsuited for the housing of so many troops. The whole area had been completely denuded of grass and had become a dust-bowl. The sanitary arrangements were quite inadequate and it was quite impossible to fly-proof the kitchens. These factors, plus the fact that the men were unaccustomed to the heat, which rose to $110°$ Fahrenheit, led to an outbreak of diarrhoea, but dysentery was kept in check.

Training commenced straight away in order to accustom the men to their new conditions and within a week of landing they marched fourteen miles to Kristel, spending the day on the beaches and bathing, and marched back again to camp in the cool of the evening.

On 9th June the Brigade moved to Froha on an open plain six miles south of Mascara and some seventy miles up country from Oran, where they joined the 1st Parachute Brigade, and here final training commenced in preparation for the forthcoming airborne operation, for the 1st (Air Landing) Brigade was to play a major rôle in the invasion of Sicily.

CHAPTER IV

OPERATIONS 'HUSKY', 'LADBROKE', AND 'FUSTIAN'

THE INVASION OF SICILY

IN the original plan for this invasion all three Brigades of the 1st Airborne Division were allotted separate tasks, but it was later found unnecessary to employ the 2nd Parachute Brigade. The code name allotted to the operation was ' Husky ', and the two airborne operations designated as ' Fustian ' and ' Ladbroke '.

The objective of the 1st Parachute Brigade—Operation ' Fustian '—was the capture of the important bridge over the River Simeto to the south of Catania, after which the Brigade would take up a defensive position covering the approaches to the bridge.

The units of the Brigade [1] were the 1st,[2] 2nd,[3] and 3rd [4] Battalions The Parachute Regiment with detachments of the 1st Anti-Tank Battery, RA, the 1st Parachute Squadron, RE, and the 16th (Parachute) Field Ambulance, then commanded by Lieut.-Colonel P. R. Wheatley, RAMC.

The medical plan was dominated by the fact that the defensive position would be divided by the River Simeto, and it was decided to keep the main strength of medical services on the south bank of the river, considered to be the safer and less vulnerable area, but, at the same time, provision had to be made for medical services to be available to the troops north of the river.

In the planning stages it was decided that the RAMC personnel attached to companies should be increased to a minimum of four ; but that in the case of companies allotted

---

[1] Commanded by Brigadier G. W. Lathbury.
[2] RMO—Captain M. H. K. Haggie, RAMC.
[3] RMO—Captain R. R. Gordon, RAMC.
[4] RMO—Captain J. Rutherford, RAMC.

an individual isolated rôle this number should be further increased, and, if considered necessary in the light of the existing tactical situation, an MO should be detached from the Field Ambulance and attached to the company. It was also decided that the basic organisation by which a section of a field ambulance was attached to each battalion would be adhered to; one surgical team would be attached to the Air Landing Brigade, and two teams to the Parachute Brigade. The casualty evacuation plan was that they should all be brought into Company Collection Posts and subsequently sent to RAPs or direct to DSs.

The ADMS had made an estimate of the anticipated number of casualties at 30 per cent, of which 25 per cent would be killed or missing and 75 per cent wounded, which gave an approximate figure of 450 casualties in each Brigade.

Special attention was given to the revision of the contents of all 'Don' (Dressing) and 'Sugar' (Surgical) Packs, and finally it was considered that adequate provision had been made for the efficient treatment of the estimated casualties, plus a 25 per cent reserve to cover loss in the landings.

Provision was also made for second-line supply of medical stores, which included invalid diet packs, on a battalion group basis. These were packed in airborne panniers, marked with a Red Cross, under the supervision of the Senior Medical Officers (SMOs) of the Brigades, the main contents of each pannier being 'Don' and 'Sugar' Packs plus blankets, stretchers, plaster of Paris, plasma, and invalid packs. The packed panniers were handed over to the Commander Royal Army Service Corps (CRASC) and placed in the Brigade dumps, ready for sending forward as soon as re-supply by air was instituted.

It was at five o'clock on the afternoon of 2nd July that the officers destined to participate in Operation 'Ladbroke' assembled for briefing.

The main objective of the operation was to capture and hold the bridge—the Ponte Grande—over the rivers Napo and Cliane—until the arrival of the seaborne invading force.

The second objective was the capture of the town and port of Syracuse north of the bridge, and a number of German defensive positions to the south. It was planned that the Air Landing Brigade should land in the light of a quarter moon on the evening of ' D − 1 '—9th July.

The task of capturing the bridge and the area to the south was allotted to the 2nd Battalion The South Staffordshire Regiment,[1] whilst the 1st Battalion The Border Regiment [2] were to capture Syracuse. Landing zones for the whole Brigade were selected on the peninsula of the Cap Murro di Porco.

No two airborne operations are, or are likely to be, the same, due to the tactical plan, local and climatic conditions and the fact that the number of aircraft and gliders available may also vary according to the needs of the airborne force as a whole.

Planning for this operation had been in process since early in June, and, at that time, the 181st (Air Landing) Field Ambulance was allotted six Waco gliders. This glider had only half the load capacity of the Horsa glider, and as the movement of the unit had been planned for the use of sixteen Horsas and equipment being designed accordingly, this drastic reduction by type and numbers of gliders meant complete re-organisation, involving the cutting down of transport and the breaking down of the heavier equipment into man loads. In this the 16th (Parachute) Field Ambulance were able to advise and assist as a result of their practical experience. As the transport was to be reduced to two jeeps, one two-stretcher trailer, two handcarts, and three airborne-bicycles, the ton of medical stores was broken down mainly into individual loads of twenty-five pounds.

Many hours had been spent throughout the month of June in thinking out ways and means, paper planning and calculations, and much packing and re-packing. It had to be appreciated that it could not be guaranteed that each glider would arrive at the appointed place at the agreed time, and

---

[1] RMO—Captain J. E. Miller, RAMC, who was awarded the Military Cross for his work in this operation.
[2] RMO—Captain C. G. Black, RAMC.

OPERATIONS 'HUSKY', 'LADBROKE', AND 'FUSTIAN' 37

therefore the breakdown of stores and equipment had to be on a per glider load basis.

The whole Field Ambulance could not, as a result of the cutting down of gliders, be employed in the operation, and the medical plan for the Airborne Brigade was therefore that the 181st (Air Landing) Field Ambulance commanded by Lieut.-Colonel G. M. Warrack would detach a surgical team and two sections to operate with battalions; No 1 Section, commanded by Captain Greaves, would establish an ADS for the Border Regiment [1] and No 2 Section, with Captain Brownscombe as OC, would operate an ADS for the South Staffordshires.[2] No 1 Surgical Team was to move between these two ADSs carrying out, in succession, urgent surgery at each; Captain Graham Jones was to act as anaesthetist to the Surgical Team and his Section, No 5, was split between the two battalions, thereby providing four nursing orderlies per company, whilst two orderlies were to be responsible for the collection and evacuation of casualties from the two main landing zones. The CO, RSM and the CO's batman were to move with Brigade HQ, making a total of seventy-two all ranks.

On 27th June the unit, except for a small road party, flew the 400 miles from Froha to the air-strips at M'saken in Tunisia, from which they would make final preparations for Operation 'Ladbroke'. 'It was', it was recorded at the time, 'a bumpy but impressive flight on a perfect summer day'. The Tunisian hills to the north and the desert stretching away to the south, although bleak desolate country, made it an impressive flight.

The unit's camp was in an olive grove, free from the usual dust, the site of a former RAF ammunition dump, which was cleared by No 4 Section, commanded by Captain S. M. Frazer. The weather was such that everyone slept in the open with mosquito nets hung from the lower branches of the trees. The days which followed were full of subdued excitement, expectancy, making final preparations for the impending airborne operation, and making good use of what

[1] RMO—Captain C. G. Black, RAMC.
[2] RMO—Captain J. Miller, RAMC.

time was available for relaxation. Many took advantage of the opportunity to bathe from the clear sandy beaches at the nearby coastal town of Sousse. As ' D ' Day approached a section of the bathing beach was roped off and for security reasons all civilians excluded from the area.

On 7th July all ORs were ' briefed ' by their officers on the part they would play in the invasion of Sicily, and, on the following day, the Brigade was visited by General Montgomery, who toured the Brigade area addressing all ranks on the task they were about to carry out. Clad in khaki drill shirt and shorts and wearing his, by then, traditional beret, the General stood up in his jeep as the men gathered around him. The rest of the day passed quietly, as did the next, until 4.15 on that hot, sun-baked afternoon the unit fell in on parade, and fifteen minutes later the men clambered aboard the three-ton lorries, on the sides of which were marked in chalk the number of the glider load, and at 5 o'clock the vehicles moved off to the air-strips.

At the air-strips the order to emplane was given. The containers were collected up and humped into the gliders, the men climbed in after, off drove the three-tonners, and the engines of the ' tugs ' began to warm up.

Clouds of dust arose ; the noise of the ' tug ' engines increased in crescendo as the tow lines took the strain when the ' tugs ' taxied over the air-strips ready to take off. Glider pilots looked back around at their passengers, grinned and gave the thumbs up sign, as they waited for the ' take-off ' signal from their co-pilots, who listened intently on the ' inter-com '. Then, a few hesitant jerks followed by a surge forward into the dust clouds, particles of sand beating against the perspex. Each glider was momentarily lost to view in the fog of the dust as it pounded over the runway, then, abruptly, the rumbling ceased and was replaced by a high-pitched hiss, the gliders swayed from side to side and then, airborne at last, they climbed up into the clear blue evening sky.

For an hour after the take-off the flight was calm and the attention of all the airborne troops was focussed on the formations of tugs and gliders around them, all circling around to take up their positions for the long flight across the Mediterranean to their objective. Down in the streets, outside the cafés and houses and in the adjoining fields the population of Phillipville stood that evening, eyes shaded against the setting sun, to watch this great assembly of aircraft. At last the formation turned northwards and crossed the Tunisian Coast at Cap Bon, heading towards Pantellaria. As the evening wore on a strong wind blew up, setting the gliders weaving in the wake of their tugs. Below, the men could see, some hundred feet or so below, the sea being whipped into creamy foam by the rising wind. It became a most uncomfortable journey. Pantellaria was passed to starboard, its rocky coastline looking warm and bright in the setting sunlight. Then darkness fell, and there was nothing to do but to sit and wait ; but for the low drumming of the moving glider an uncanny stillness came over the gliders as the men did just this.

The landing was timed for soon after ten o'clock, and in most cases the men became aware of the nearness of the land by the bursting of anti-aircraft shells in the darkness ahead. The night sky was lit by the bursts of flame like exploding stars. Men peered forward into the night, surely not long now, for a building could be seen ablaze on the black outline of the coast of Sicily. A searchlight beam split the blackness, picking out in a glow of light the approaching gliders. The tugs took avoiding action, taking steep downward turns as they cast off the gliders to cruise down to land from their travelling height of some 3,000 feet. One of these gliders (No 86 in the flight) carrying No 1 Surgical Team of the 181st (Air Landing) Field Ambulance, with Captain G. Rigby-Jones, nine ORs, and equipped with a hand-cart, bore down to earth, coming to an abrupt, jarring halt. The starboard wing and undercarriage were ripped off as the glider collided with a tree ; under the strain, as they ground over the earth's surface, the port undercarriage was torn away and the glider's nose drove into a stone wall. Amid the crack of the splitting framework and fabric the men forced and struggled their way out—they were there ! [1]

[1] The only casualty being Private Martin, RAMC, whose nose was fractured.

Not so, however, were the men in the other five gliders in which the rest of 181st Field Ambulance had emplaned, for at that moment they were either struggling for life in the dark deep waters of the Mediterranean or sweeping down to crash into the sea. These gliders had been cast off their tow-lines by the American tug pilots at distances varying from ten to two miles from the coast. How far the adverse weather conditions or the inexperience of the pilots in towing was the cause of this disastrous start of the landing will probably never be known, but about a quarter of the troops being carried were drowned, and 181st Field Ambulance lost one officer [1] and sixteen men in this operation.

Only a few of the men were plunged into the sea sufficiently near to the coast to be able to struggle to the beach, but the majority of the survivors were picked up by assault landing craft and they became scattered between different ports from Alexandria to Gibraltar.

There were many amazing escapes on that dark windswept night in the raging sea. The story was later told of how the RSM of the 181st Field Ambulance rounded up the men on his side of the glider as it rocked, awash, in the sea, and marshalled them on the wing, then standing up, as best he could, called to the senior officer present, who was clinging to the other wing, saluted and reported his men as "all present and correct".

The CO, Lieut.-Colonel G. M. Warrack, together with the Brigade Commander, came down in the sea, and managed to swim ashore, but were confined to the eastern tip of Cap Murro do Porco until the arrival of the seaborne force.

The Surgical Team commanded by Captain G. Rigby Jones which landed from Glider No 86 was soon in action. They had crash-landed about 300 yards south-east of the main landing zone (LZ) allotted to the South Staffordshires. The rendezvous for the Field Ambulance was to the north of the LZ and there was a well-defined track leading to it. The party moved forward expecting to see numbers of gliders on the LZ but this was not so, and the northern limit of the area

[1] Captain Hubert Greaves, RAMC.

was reached without seeing one. The village was still in enemy hands, so the RAMC dug themselves in. Later the assault troops in the area moved forward and during the night a temporary RAP was set up in a farmhouse about a quarter of a mile from the bridge.

A platoon of the South Staffords had landed in a Horsa glider near to the Ponte Grande Bridge, and, after a short sharp engagement had captured the objective. With the platoon was Private Curnock, RAMC, a nursing orderly, who not only did magnificent work in tending the wounded, but, having had experience as a miner in civilian life, could not resist helping in removing the explosive charges the enemy had placed in position in preparing the bridge for demolition.

The immediate RAMC task was the setting up of an ADS in or near a small village, designated for the operation 'Walsall', about three miles from the rendezvous. So the party made off in that direction guided by the flashes and sounds of desultory firing in the distance. About a mile from 'Walsall' they encountered a platoon of the South Staffords, so they pressed on together to within some 200 yards of the village, when they were stopped by Major de Boulay of the Border Regiment, who had an injured ankle, with one of his sergeants, who had a flesh wound.

The following morning a road-block was set up in 'Walsall' and by midday the small mixed force in occupation of the village had rounded up some forty Italian soldiers and civilians. They had also commandeered five mule carts full of melons, which helped to quench the men's thirsts as the sun rose high in the sky to produce an extremely hot and dusty day.

By three o'clock in the afternoon there were signs of increasing activity in the area, and it was apparent that the seaborne invading troops were coming up from the south. Soon after, about three platoons of Italian troops began to fall back on 'Walsall' from the east and south, and attacked the 'Walsall' force. In the circumstances the RAMC took part in the defensive action, using captured Italian automatic carbines. The rout of the Italians was complete when a hand-cart containing the Border Regiment's reserve ammunition blew up. This loud explosion was too much for the enemy, who turned and fled; a number of them were rounded up, and work started in the ADS in treating both British and Italian wounded, although the work was hampered by the fact that the pack of surgical instruments and pressure lamps had been damaged on landing.

The next day a sweep of the nearby LZ was carried out in search of casualties, and then, about midday, the ADMS [1] and Lieut.-Colonel Warrack arrived at 'Walsall' with a large Italian ambulance. Arrangements were made for the evacuation of all casualties to the HQ of the field ambulance of the seaborne invading troops, where an advanced surgical centre had been established in a school in the hills about a mile to the north-west of Syracuse.

During the afternoon, the 'Walsall' FAP collected their equipment and together with their mule-carts and prisoners set off to join this Field Ambulance, where they joined the MDS, where a surgical team, under Captain Lewis, was already working. Captain Rigby Jones's surgical team took over two wards, and twenty-six operations were performed in the subsequent forty-eight hours.

On 13th July the whole unit marched down to the port to embark on an LCT to return to North Africa.

On the morning of 12th July the 16th (Parachute) Field Ambulance had moved down to the airfield and formed up in their 'sticks'. Every man with his small pack, two water bottles, a liberal supply of dressings,[2] and additional tea for

---

[1] Colonel A. Austin Eagger had asked to be attached to the Advanced HQ of the Division in the Advanced Seaborne Forces but permission had not been granted and he had been allotted a seat in a glider with the HQ of the Air Landing Brigade, although no accommodation could be provided for the Medical HQ staff. This glider landed in the sea approximately four miles due east of Avola. With one exception all the occupants were picked up by HMS *Mauritius* at five o'clock the following morning. The ADMS landed on 'Amber' beach at nine o'clock and made contact with the HQs of the 50th (Northumbrian) and 5th Divisions, and made arrangements for transport to clear the airborne casualties. With a number of civilian ambulances the ADMS and Colonel Warrack collected a number of wounded and later moved forward to join the 16th (Parachute) Field Ambulance.

[2] Each man carried eight Mepacrine tablets; a tin of mosquito cream; a set of water sterilising tablets; and two shell dressings.

patients. In addition a few items of essential equipment such as small surgeon's rolls, syringes, morphia, and Red Cross flags were distributed among the personnel of each 'stick', whilst each section 'stick' had six containers in which were included a trolley and a wheeled stretcher. Each surgical team carried five containers for immediate use, and one spare to be left on the DZ.

A sidelight on the work of parachute field ambulances is seen from the following administrative paragraphs extracted from the Operation Orders issued by the Medical Branch HQ, 1st Airborne Division, for Operation 'Husky-Fustian':

Rations

Every man will carry forty-eight-hour ration and one emergency ration.

It is most important that casualties bring their own rations to the DS.

Water

Two filled water-bottles will be carried on the man. No man will drink without orders from an officer. Medical officers will test water supplies and arrange for refilling of water-bottles at first opportunity. Two water sterilising tablets will be put in each full water-bottle.

One canvas three-gallon container will be carried in each aircraft for use in flight.

Anti-Malarial Measures

The area is highly malarious :—

(*a*) Sleeves will be rolled down before sunset.
(*b*) Anti-Mosquito Ointment will be applied after dark.
(*c*) Mepacrine will be taken regularly in the normal manner.
(*d*) Mosquito veils will be worn at night whenever conditions permit.

Hygiene

(*a*) Local milk is unsafe and will NOT be drunk.
(*b*) Soft fruit and local vegetables will not be eaten uncooked.

(c) Shallow trench latrines will be dug at first opportunity. It is most important that the ground should not be fouled. Until latrines can be dug 'cat hole' sanitation will be carried out and holes carefully covered.

Digging

Slit trenches will be dug at DS.

Camouflage

Movement in the open by day will be restricted to a minimum. The large Red Cross will NOT be displayed without permission of the Brigade Commander.

Relations with Civil Population

Under International Law the lives and property of the civilian population in a hostile country must be respected. Any cases of looting will be punished in an exemplary manner. Fraternisation with the civilian population during the operation will be discouraged.

Geneva Convention

No RAMC personnel will take part in any offensive action. By doing so they may jeopardise the whole of the medical service. All protected personnel will wear the Geneva Cross Armlet and carry protective cards.

Equipment

It is an operational necessity that every possible piece of equipment is salvaged for future use. If personnel are evacuated before equipment a guard will be left behind.

Patients' Kit

Haversacks of wounded men will not be removed from them. They will provide means of safeguarding men's documents and small kit and will accompany them through subsequent evacuation.

Clothing

A & D Book will be kept at the MDS. Records will be kept at the ADS of all cases evacuated direct from there.

OPERATIONS 'HUSKY', 'LADBROKE', AND 'FUSTIAN' 45

Returns

Will be rendered as follows :—

(a) Fighting strength. OC, ADS and all RMOs will inform MDS of any casualties to RAMC personnel by 0430 hours daily. Nil returns are NOT required. MDS will render fighting strength to Brigade by 0530 hours daily.

(b) State of Sick. MDS will render—

(1) Daily Signal of Sick ;
(2) Daily State of Sick ;

at midnight each night to ADMS, 1st Airborne Division.

The 'sticks' of the Field Ambulance were composed of seventeen in each 'stick'. No 3 Section with Captain J. H. Keesey, RAMC, fifteen RAMC and one RASC OR ; and No 4 Section with Captain A. Percival, RAMC, and the same number of ORs. There were two HQ 'sticks', with a surgical team in each. The first with Captain A. W. Lipman Kessel, RAMC, Captain D. H. Ridler, Army Dental Corps, and fourteen ORs including the RSM ; the second with Major C. J. Longland, RAMC, the Padre, the Reverend R. T. Watkins, Royal Army Chaplain's Department (RAChD), and fifteen ORs—eleven of which were RAMC. One MO and nineteen ORs accompanied the 1st Battalion, and an RAMC officer and sixteen ORs with both the 2nd and 3rd Battalions, whilst the SMO and two RAMC ORs went with the Brigade HQ.[1]

The Brigade took off between 7 and 8.30 pm on 12th July, and the dropping was timed to take place between 10.20 and 11.15 pm, but a number of the aircraft went off their course. No 4 Section of the 16th (Parachute) Field Ambulance—comprising Captain Percival, three NCOs, twelve RAMC orderlies and an RASC driver—approached the coast of Sicily in a Douglas C47 aircraft, and just as they were getting ready for their jump the aircraft was hit by AA fire

[1] The total number of RAMC personnel taking part in the operation was 8 officers and 110 ORs.

from a convoy of merchant ships,[1] which put the aircraft controls out of action. The pilot made a forced landing into the sea. Captain Percival detailed two men to get over through the escape hatches, and two dinghies were passed out to them, other men followed as the plane was rapidly filling with water, so the rest were ordered to file out through the jumping door, but soon the plane was completely submerged. Captain Percival and Staff-Sergeant Anderson managed to swim out, but by that time the plane was some thirty feet below the sea and two men failed to get to the surface. In all four men were lost. For half an hour the men hung on to the dinghies until they were picked up in a searchlight and rescued by the crew of a Greek destroyer. Taken to Malta, they returned to Sousse on 15th July.

As the rest of the aircraft approached the dark outline of the Sicilian coast, the enemy AA fire came up with gathering intensity and this led to considerable avoiding action by the pilots and in consequence the scattering of the 'sticks' as they came over the DZ.

No 3 Section dropped astride the River Simeto, some five miles west of the objective. Staff-Sergeant Stevens and four ORs landed on the south side of the river, Captain Keesey, with the remainder of the 'stick', on the north, where they collected the equipment from the containers and joined up with a small party of the 3rd Battalion and made their way along the bank of the river, but not meeting up with any other troops were forced to lay up as the nearby bridge was in enemy hands, and they were not able to report into Brigade HQ until the night of the 15th. Captain Ridler's 'stick'[2] dropped on one of the DZs and made their way to the farm selected for the MDS, arriving there at about a quarter to five in the morning, only to find it occupied by

---

[1] The ships having mistaken the plane for a torpedo-carrying aircraft.

[2] Less Captain Lipman Kessel and four ORs, one of whom had fainted just as he was about to jump, fouling the static line of the next man. Thirteen men had already jumped and the aircraft then started to take violent evasive action to avoid enemy 'flak'. Although Captain Lipman Kessel pressed the pilot to make a second run in, one engine had been damaged and the pilot considered it too risky, so the aircraft returned to the air-strip at Sousse.

some Italians, who were soon driven out and taken prisoner by Captain Ridler and an RASC corporal. They then set about establishing the MDS and contact was made with the 2nd Battalion. Major Longland's 'stick' also dropped on the same DZ, collected equipment from the containers and moved off, experiencing considerable difficulty with their trolley, which had to be man-handled over a number of irrigation canals. Eventually they got the trolley on to an embankment and moved along it in full view of the enemy and reached the MDS soon after Captain Ridler's party.

Captain Wright dropped some twelve miles south of the bridge, joined up with a party of Sappers and some men of the 3rd Battalion, and reached the MDS on the morning of the 15th. The CO, Lieut.-Colonel Wheatley, who had dropped in a Brigade HQ 'stick', landed on the high ground five miles to the south-west of the objective. Making his way, with the rest of the 'stick', down to the bridge, several casualties were treated on the way but left behind until they could be moved. The HQ was established by the bridge, which had been captured. Here the CO learned that the MDS had been opened, and finding a bicycle Colonel Wheatley set off thus 'mounted' to join his command.

The MDS was being set up under shelter of rising ground south of the river in the one-storied farm, which comprised seven rooms and a kitchen, standing by itself surrounded by trees; it was very dirty, but when cleaned up by a party of Italian prisoners provided a reception centre, pre-operative room, operating theatre, two post-operative rooms, three wards and a small rest room. In the stables were several carts and some horses, and these provided transport for casualties. At this time the MDS was between the British and Italian positions and there was considerable small-arms and mortar fire, although only two bombs fell in the hospital area.

The RAPs were fully engaged. Captain R. R. Gordon, the RMO of the 2nd Battalion, had dropped on 'DZ 3' with the Battalion, and soon established his RAP with twenty-nine British and a number of Italian casualties, and arranged evacuation of wounded to the MDS by horse and cart and by hand carriage by Italian prisoners.

Captain Haggie, RMO of the 1st Battalion, landed on 'DZ 1' and joined up with a party of some forty men of the Battalion. He set up an RAP in a ditch just before the attack was launched on the bridge; he soon collected fifteen casualties, but had only two stretchers and seven RAMC orderlies available.

Captain J. Rutherford, the 3rd Battalion's RMO, dropped inside the perimeter of the outer defences of the airfield, but reached the bridge at dawn, where, joined by three of his NCOs, set up his RAP by the north bank of the river, surrounded by bulrushes just west of the bridge, moving later in the morning to a 'pill-box' where he was able to keep the wounded under cover.

Staff-Sergeant Stevens and the four orderlies who had landed north of the river made their way down to the bridge by four-thirty in the morning. They set up their own FAP, collecting a number of wounded, and at daylight made their way across to join Captain Rutherford.

All the RAMC men in the area did excellent work that night, and, throughout the following day, showing considerable initiative in dealing with situations which were very different from the original plan. There was the case of Private J. Reid, RAMC, who had dropped with the 1st Battalion and found himself alone, so set up his own CAP and set about collecting casualties, whilst Corporal Scott of the ADC did most of the work in the collecting of casualties from the RAPs and the gliders on the DZs and took them in to the ADS with a horse and cart. In all he made six such journeys under fire in broad daylight.

At the MDS work continued, in treating wounded and performing operations, twenty-one being carried out in the first thirteen hours since the opening of the MDS. By ten o'clock that night there were sixty-two British and twenty-nine enemy patients in the MDS.

During the night enemy pressure forced the Brigade to withdraw from the line of the river. This left the MDS in a 'no-man's land' between the south bank of the river and the high ground to be held by the Brigade. As many RAMC personnel as possible were sent back with the Brigade, but

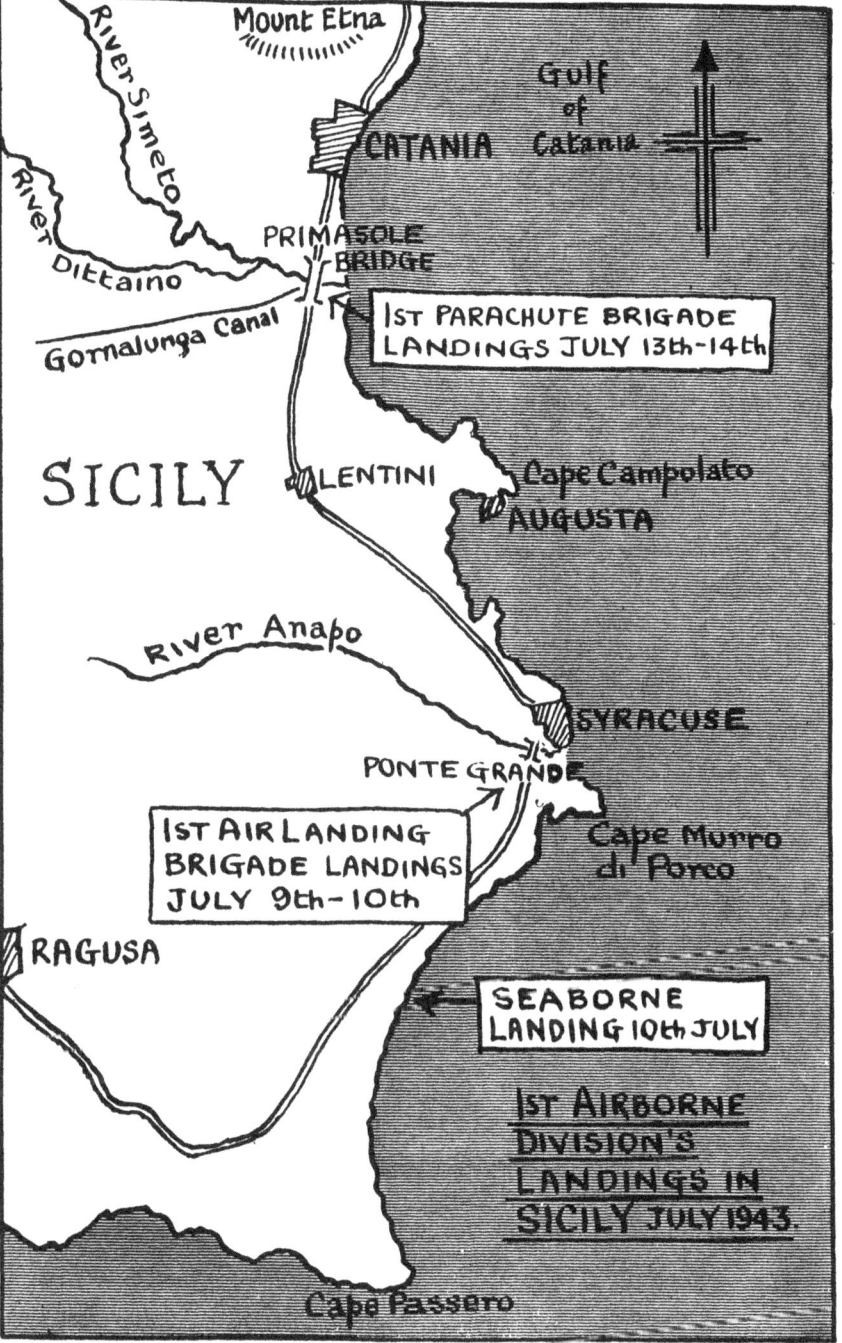

the remainder stayed behind at the MDS to treat and hold the wounded in their care.

In the early hours of the following day an Italian officer arrived, announcing that he had 'captured' the MDS, but after looking round seemed undecided what to do. He was apparently very pleased to find that the Italian and German casualties had been treated just the same as the British and wanted the complete MDS to move to Catania, but a compromise was agreed to in that only the Italian and German wounded would be moved. Soon after this a patrol of the 1st Battalion went by and, at half-past seven in the morning forward troops of the 2nd Parachute Battalion and the 50th (Northumbrian) Division advanced past the MDS. This forward movement resulted in the retention of the Italian and German casualties.

Operating continued during the day, fourteen cases being dealt with, until soon after five o'clock when the theatre and the MDS was closed after the evacuation of all the wounded had been carried out by ambulance cars. A total number of seventy-one British and thirty-eight enemy casualties had been treated. At six o'clock the order came for the MDS to move to a new position on the high ground designated 'Johnny One', where they spent the night within sound of heavy fighting during the attack on the bridge by the Durham Light Infantry.

At seven o'clock on the morning of 16th July the Field Ambulance marched down over rough country some three miles to an embussing point from where they moved to Syracuse. On the road the lorries were stopped by a military policeman, who was preceding a staff car, out of which stepped General Montgomery, who spoke to the men and handed out cigarettes. He left amid a burst of cheering and waving from the men.

The whole Parachute Brigade assembled during the day in Syracuse, and embarked on a Landing Ship Tank (LST) and remained in harbour during the night, being subjected to a two-hour air-raid; they sailed at noon, arriving at Valetta that evening, where they hove to for the night outside the harbour. Sailing again in the early hours of the

18th, the Brigade disembarked at Sousse the following morning.

During the operations in Sicily the 16th (Parachute) Field Ambulance had lost four ORs, shot down into the sea, and three ORs wounded. Six other ORs serving with the 1st, 2nd, and 3rd Parachute Battalions were missing, and one medical orderly with the latter battalion had been wounded.

A total of 109 casualties had been treated in the MDS, and in the twenty-one hours in which the Surgical Team had functioned thirty-five operations [1] had been performed, out of which there had been only two post-operative deaths.

[1] Penetrating muscle wounds, 18 ; compound fractures of long bones, 7 ; open wounds of joints, 1 ; compound fracture of skull, 2 ; wounds of jaw and neck, 2 ; wounds of chest, 1 ; wounds of hands, 1 ; wounds of foot, 1 ; infected burns, 1 ; amputations (mid-thigh), 2. Some of the cases operated on on the morning of 15th July had been wounded the previous day. The average interval between being wounded and operated on was twenty-five hours, the maximum time being thiry-four hours, and the minimum seventeen and a half, but on 15th July these intervals were brought down to an average of five hours, the maximum interval being seven and a half hours, the minimum one and a quarter hours.

CHAPTER V

INTO ITALY

WITH THE 1ST AIRBORNE DIVISION AND THE
2ND INDEPENDENT PARACHUTE BRIGADE GROUP

THE invasion of Italy was now imminent. In anticipation of the main allied attack being launched in the area of Naples the Germans made immediate efforts to reinforce the Italian mainland, and, to guard against the distinct possibility of a diversionary landing in the south, sent a force of their own determined parachute troops to defend Aipulia. Prior to May 1943 the Germans had only kept administrative troops in Italy to man the Base Supply Depots which served the Afrika Korps. After the loss of Tunisia the obvious threat to Italy was countered by the move of German divisions to Sicily, Sardinia, Corsica and the mainland. When the Germans were driven from Sicily they managed to withdraw three divisions across the Straits of Messina without serious loss of men and equipment.

The invasion of Sicily on 9th July was followed on the 25th by the fall of the Italian Fascist government and the formation of a new government under Marshal Badoglio. Towards the end of August the Italians opened up the initial negotiations with the Allies for the securing of a separate Armistice. The terms were agreed upon, and the armistice was announced on 8th September, just twenty-four hours before the assault on the Italian coast.

On 6th September the 1st Airborne Division was given orders to occupy Taranto and to hold the port against all attacks until the arrival of reinforcements, this operation being planned to coincide with the announcement of the Italian Armistice and with the landing of the Fifth Army at Salerno. There were, however, no aircraft available for the Division to be landed in its airborne rôle and so it was decided that the formation should be landed from five British cruisers,[1] a mine-layer, and the American cruiser USS *Boise*. The first part of the Division sailed at five o'clock in the afternoon of 8th September, the decks of the cruisers crammed with vehicles, guns and stores and a much greater number of men on board than had been authorised. It was not found possible to get the jeeps through the hatches of HMS *Abdiel*, the minelayer, but on the decks were carried twelve six-pounder anti-tank guns.

When the force arrived at the minefield which lay across the harbour entrance, HMS *Javelin* went through alone, and, after a wait of two hours, returned with an Italian pilot on board. At five o'clock in the afternoon HMS *Penelope* and the USS *Boise* went ahead, straight into Taranto harbour, going alongside the quay whilst the rest of the ships started to discharge men and stores by lighters.

The Division streamed ashore. It encountered no opposition and pushed straight through the port to cover the northern approaches to the town. That evening the General Officer Commanding (GOC), who had set up his HQ in the Albergo Europa Hotel, vacated, in some haste, that morning by the Germans, met the Italian military Governor and accepted the surrender of Taranto.

The approaches to the town having been secured, the 4th Parachute Brigade continued to advance throughout the night, whilst the 2nd Brigade held the port. At midnight there was a terrific explosion down by the quays as the minelayer, HMS *Abdiel*, moving into a berth struck a mine and blew up. A hundred and thirty officers and men were lost in the explosion in the dark waters of the harbour, together with all the anti-tank guns and the reserve ammunition. HMS *Abdiel* was carrying some 400 all ranks of the 6th Parachute Battalion, the 2nd Anti-Tank Battery, RA, and 127th (Parachute) Field Ambulance. The RAMC casualties included Lieut.-Colonel M. J. Kohane, the CO, two other officers, fifteen ORs, and all the unit's medical equipment.

By dawn of the following day the 9th Reconnaissance

---

[1] HMS *Aurora, Penelope, Dido* and *Sirius*. The HQ of the Division with the ADMS and the Medical Staff embarked in HMS *Aurora*.

Squadron reached the small town of Massafra where they were wildly received by the townspeople, and then the advance was continued towards Mottola. It was attacked by the 15th Parachute Battalion, which carried the town after a short, but sharp, period of resistance by the Germans before they withdrew.

From this action the first battle casualties were brought back into Taranto, where on the morning of 10th September an MDS with sixty beds had been opened at the Rendinella Hospital by the 133rd (Parachute) Field Ambulance. The Field Ambulance had also opened an MDS with eighty beds in the Ospedale Maritima—the Maritime Hospital—where their first duty had been to take over the care of the casualties resulting from the loss of HMS *Abdiel*, who had been sent to that hospital on being brought ashore, and, by the morning of the 15th sixty-seven battle casualties had also been admitted.

The Division's advance continued, facing varying degrees of opposition, for there was no doubt that the enemy overestimated the strength of the British force, and were obviously concerned by the fact that their antagonists were the Airborne forces, although had they known the strength of the Division was but some 6,600 with only sixteen six-pounder guns as their entire artillery they might well have adopted a more offensive rôle.

The advance was punctuated with brief sharp encounters. Near Cassa de Duca the Divisional HQ Defence Platoon went into action, and during the fighting the Divisional Commander, Major-General G. F. Hopkinson[1] was mortally wounded; he died at Taranto twenty-four hours later.

On the night of 12th September casualties were evacuated to HMS *Aurora* and *Penelope*, which were lying offshore. A small hospital carrier, the *Mare Chiaro*, was found in the harbour and in this casualties were taken out to sea to the two cruisers. The Italian captain of the carrier was loud in

---

[1] Major-General G. F. Hopkinson, OBE, MC, had succeeded Major-General F. A. M. Browning, DSO, in command of the Division in April 1943, on the appointment of the latter as ' Major-General Airborne Forces '. Major-General Hopkinson was succeeded by Major-General E. E. Down, CBE.

his protests at this procedure, one of his main reasons being that the exact position of the cruisers was unknown. This difficulty was overcome when the ADMS encountered a Commander, RN, who was anxious to rejoin the *Aurora* and he willingly agreed to pilot the *Mare Chiaro* out to sea. The transference of the casualties at sea was carried out without difficulty, and eventually the wounded were taken into hospitals in Tripoli.

Thereafter casualties were brought back from the RAPs to the ADS in jeeps and trucks and from the ADS into Taranto by ambulances and trucks obtained from the Italians. This system of evacuation proved very satisfactory and most of the casualties were brought into the MDS within three to four hours of being wounded. Stores were being brought by air into the airfield at Grottaglie and the evacuation of casualties in aircraft returning to North African bases commenced on 15th September.[1]

On the evening of 12th September the 181st (Air Landing) Field Ambulance [2] with the remainder of the Division landed at Taranto and thus reinforced the Division pressed on to capture Castellaneta.

The position was, despite the speed and success of the advance, somewhat unsatisfactory inasmuch as the withdrawing enemy was adequately equipped with vehicles, whereas the Division's transport was inadequate for the task in hand. The advanced troops were some twenty miles from their base, supported with little artillery, and their lines of communication were thinly held.

Despite this situation, however, Brigadier Down, who had taken command of the Division, was determined to keep the initiative, and all forward troops were instructed to be as offensive as possible with the object of pressing on to seize Gioia. It was becoming a matter of some importance that Gioia should be occupied; for its airfield could then be used as an advance base from which the RAF could operate in

---

[1] In all, a total of 123 cases were evacuated by air under the supervision of the Divisional Medical Services.

[2] Less Major Rigby-Jones, three other officers and sixty-one ORs, who formed the rear party left at Sousse.

bringing the much sought air-support to the troops battling hard in the bloody beachhead of Salerno.

The two Parachute Brigades were hard pressed to achieve this objective, at the same time holding on to Taranto; fortunately the Germans withdrew from Gioia during the night of 16th/17th September, and forty-eight hours later six squadrons of the RAF were in action from the airfield.

Two days later the 4th Parachute Brigade was relieved by the 1st Air Landing Brigade, two sections of 181st Field Ambulance being detached from Taranto to establish an ADS at Mottola in support of the Brigade, and shortly afterwards there was a general withdrawal by the enemy towards Foggia under pressure of the advance of the 1st Canadian Division from the south-west.

In the nine days since the seaborne landing of the Division the 4th Brigade had seen some sharp fighting, although the casualties had, comparatively, been light, the Brigade having lost—killed, wounded, or missing—eleven officers and ninety ORs.

There was, however, still a possibility that the Germans might attempt a counter-attack in force aimed at the recapture of Taranto. The British Command was conscious of this possibility, and in consequence from the 20th to the 24th the Division was employed in constructing a defence perimeter to supplement the Italian fortifications around the port. During this time the Divisional medical services were fully engaged in Taranto.

By 22nd September a total of 320 beds had been taken over in the Rondinella Hospital and 200 in the Maritime Hospital, and so what really amounted to two general hospitals were being run by the 133rd and 181st Field Ambulances. On 24th September the Maritime Hospital was handed over to No 8 Indian Casualty Clearing Station, and two days later No 70 General Hospital took over the Rondinella. Up to this time the Medical Services of the 1st Airborne Division had had to provide the hospital accommodation and medical treatment for the whole force in the Taranto area. Between 10th and 30th September out of the 1,023 admissions to the hospitals 424 came from units outside the Division.

The two Field Ambulances on leaving Taranto moved up into the new Brigade areas, opening up an ADS and MDSs. On 25th September the 181st Field Ambulance opened an MDS in Canossa, and twenty-four hours later another MDS at Cerignola where they were joined by 127th (Parachute) Field Ambulance.

By the end of the month the 181st Field Ambulance was somewhat scattered in consequence of operational needs. The CO with three officers and thirty ORs were running the MDS at Cerignola; Captain Taylor with four ORs were with the 4th Armoured Brigade at St Paulo; Captain Black and twelve ORs with the 1st Battalion The Border Regiment at Foggia; the QM, Lieutenant Tiernan, with the stores and thirty men were at Gioia, whilst one staff-sergeant with twelve men were with the Light Regiment, RA. During this time the Field Ambulances were temporarily under command of the 78th Division, but on 5th October the Airborne Division, which had gradually disengaged with the enemy and handed over its commitments by 30th September, started to concentrate in the Gioia area. The 16th (Parachute) Field Ambulance took over the Military Hospital at Altamura (with 150 beds); 133rd (Parachute) Field Ambulance were in a school at Gioia (with 140 beds); 127th (Parachute) Field Ambulance in another school at Acquaviva (with 100 beds); whilst 181st (Air Landing) Field Ambulance took over thirty-nine beds in the Civil Hospital at Putignano and forty beds in the Military Hospital at Brindisi. In addition the Divisional Medical Services opened up Convalescent Depots on a Brigade basis at Altamura, Noci and Putignano.

During the period from the landing on 10th September to 5th October 1,728 casualties were admitted to the MDSs of the Airborne Division's Field Ambulances, and 194 operations were performed by the Division's surgeons.

The medical organisation continued to function in this manner until orders came for the withdrawal from Italy of the Division,[1] less the 2nd Parachute Brigade Group, and the

---

[1] At the end of October General Browning visited the Division and ordered the ADMS to fly out to India to advise on the organisation of the medical services of the Indian Parachute Brigade (see page 185).

formation moved back to embark from Taranto on 20th November to return to England.

The 127th (Parachute) Field Ambulance, commanded by Lieut.-Colonel Parkinson, remained in Italy with the 2nd Parachute Brigade Group, the formation becoming an Independent Brigade [1] under the command of Central Mediterranean Force.

The advantages of having available in Italy a trained formation of parachute troops could not be underestimated, but there were no opportunities for the employment of the Brigade in an airborne rôle during the operations in the winter of 1943-44, and, located in the rear area in Southern Italy, cut off from trained reinforcement, the formation was forced to stand-by and await the opportunity of an airborne operation, should the need arise. The Brigade was also sadly short of transport, but was helped in this and other administrative problems by the 2nd New Zealand Division, to whom they were attached.

The formation maintained its standards of airborne training by the establishment of a training and parachute school firstly at Gioia and, later, after the capture of Rome, at the Lido di Roma.

In November the Brigade was called forward to action in an infantry rôle on the left flank of the Eighth Army at the battle of the Sangro.

The 127th Field Ambulance was at Gioia when it came under orders to move with the Brigade Group at forty-eight hours' notice. At the time there were some eighty sick in the MDS and, on the understanding that the Brigade would only be in the line for about three weeks, Lieut.-Colonel Parkinson decided to move with the HQ, two Sections and the Surgical Team commanded by Major McMurray, leaving the other two Sections to run the Gioia MDS. The period of three weeks in the forward area in an infantry rôle was, it transpired, somewhat of an under-estimate, for the Brigade continued in action until the end of May. However, as there

---

[1] Composed of the 4th, 5th, and 6th Battalions, The Parachute Regiment, and commanded by Brigadier C. H. V. Pritchard, DSO.

were adequate medical services in support of the forward troops it was not until April that the rear sections of the Field Ambulance were moved up to rejoin the unit, although throughout the winter and spring of 1943-44 Colonel Parkinson periodically changed over the sections so that the whole unit had tours of duty at the base and in the forward area.

For four months the Brigade saw a considerable amount of action in the Adriatic Sector, and some hard fighting.

The 5th Battalion Parachute Regiment suffered a considerable number of casualties holding a gap between the left flank of the New Zealand Division and the mountains. Relieved by the 4th Battalion, they too saw a number of sharp actions along the mountain ridges, where on one occasion Corporal Walker of the 127th (Parachute) Field Ambulance was awarded the Military Medal for distinguished service in tending the wounded under heavy fire.

The Brigade continued to hold the mountain sector along the Bianco ridge and in the Ariele sector across the Moro River, where the 5th Battalion held an entrenched sandbagged position throughout the hard winter, amid the frost, snow, and slush, until relieved at the end of March 1944, when the formation was withdrawn to rest at Guardia, in the Beneveto area near Naples.

After a short period of rest the Brigade moved up to the Monte Cassino sector where they held the line and patrolled along the banks of the Rapido under constant observation and fire from the Germans in the Monastery.

After two months the Brigade was withdrawn at the end of May to rest at Salerno, and from here three officers and fifty-seven men of the 6th Parachute Battalion carried out the last airborne operation in Italy. This was Operation 'Hasty', carried out just before dawn on 1st June, and involved a parachute drop from aircraft of the American Troop Carrier Command, behind the Germans then withdrawing towards the Pisa-Rimini line. This operation successfully prevented the enemy from carrying out their planned large-scale demolitions.

CHAPTER VI

OPERATION 'ANVIL'

WITH THE 2ND PARACHUTE BRIGADE IN THE SOUTH OF FRANCE

AT the beginning of June 1944 whilst the 2nd Parachute Brigade was at Salerno news came through that, once again, they were to revert to their airborne rôle in the forthcoming operation 'Anvil', a general attack, under the direction of the Central Mediterranean Force, on the south of France, with the object of capturing Marseilles and advancing up the Rhone Valley to link up with the Allied Armies in their advance from the Normandy beachhead into Germany.

The Brigade was to form part of the Allied Airborne Force, which was to drop inland, with the object of stopping enemy reinforcements moving down to the coast in opposition to the main seaborne invasion force. Their objective was Le Muy, a village some fifteen miles north of Frejus, where three main roads converged and met.

As soon as their rôle in the forthcoming operations was announced the Brigade was withdrawn for a period of intensive airborne training. At last, all was ready, 15th August was to be 'D' Day, and the whole Brigade moved down to the airfields at Galera and Ciampino, near Rome, to emplane in aircraft of the American Mediterranean Air Force.

The whole airborne force—all American but for the 2nd Parachute Brigade—took off on the night of 14th/15th August. The aircraft circled around above Rome to take up their assembly position before heading away into the darkness *en route* for the south of France.

The SMO of the Brigade (Lieut.-Colonel Parkinson, OC 127th (Parachute) Field Ambulance) and three RAMC ORs dropped with the Brigade HQ and it was difficult to coordinate the RAMC efforts as the medical personnel had been dropped over a wide area and, in consequence, all the reserve medical equipment dropped in containers were equally scattered and lost.[1]

No 3 Section of the 127th (Parachute) Field Ambulance, commanded by Captain Rowlands, dropped with the Surgical Team[2] and made up two complete 'sticks'. Both 'sticks' landed well off the DZ and on the wrong side of the village of La Motte.

Despite careful 'briefing', the jumping procedure was confused, for the red light failed, and without the preliminary warning on went the green light. Number One of the 'stick' —Captain McMurray—was given the order "Go!"—he jumped out into the darkness. At the same moment the crew chief let go the containers. There was an immediate collision in mid-air, and McMurray's parachute became wrapped around the containers—he sailed down to ground on the container ''chute', but in consequence sustained concussion and abrasions on his face on landing heavily. When he came to, about an hour later, he found himself being helped up by a French woman—he had undoubtedly had a miraculous escape—and then made his way across country to the Brigade HQ area.

Each man of No 3 Section and the Surgical Team had jumped carrying heavy Bergen rucksacks and neck release. Only one of these loads parted company in the descent and all the rest were collected and brought to the rendezvous, but all the other containers—there were three per aircraft—fell wide of the DZ and were either lost or looted.

The men on landing got together in twos and threes and set off to the rendezvous at Lemitan. Here at about seven-thirty in the morning they collected up the casualties from the DZ and set up a collecting point in a large barn. There were a number of severe casualties and, in consequence, the Surgical Team had to establish a theatre in a small four-

---

[1] Automatic re-supply on D + 1 also only yielded one medical pannier intact out of thirteen dropped. A further demand, dropped on D + 2 was more successful and nearly three-quarters were recovered.

[2] Major G. C. Wells and Captain McMurray.

roomed house in Le Mitan which, quite unsuitable as it was, had to suffice for the performance of operations—eight operations were carried out, seven compound fractures and one abdominal case. Conditions were extremely difficult and there was such a lack of medical orderlies that, at one stage, it was necessary for Major Wells and Captain McMurray to carry in their cases, operate on them, and then carry them out of the theatre.

By midday it became obvious that the accommodation at Le Mitan was hopelessly inadequate and, in view of the impending landings of the glider-borne element of the Force, the SMO sought the permission of the Brigade Commander to move to St Michel. This was agreed to and Captain Rowlands went off to arrange accommodation and organise the reception of the Surgical Team and all casualties. The move was successfully accomplished by seven-thirty in the evening, despite the lack of transport and the fact that the glider-borne landing coincided with the move, which entailed the withdrawal of a number of orderlies to cope with casualties on the LZ. This became necessary for no adequate arrangements had been made by the Americans to deal with their own casualties in the LZ. Eventually the accommodation left at Le Mitan was taken over by the US Medical Corps.

By half-past eight that evening the Surgical Team had set up their new operating theatre in St Michel, and they worked through until 2 am the next day.[1]

Until about 9 o'clock in the evening of 'D' Day the collection and treatment of all casualties had been carried out by the 127th (Parachute) Field Ambulance, but after that time the American Medical Corps took over the responsibility for their own casualties.

By midday on 16th August all the urgent surgical treat-

[1] During the period 15th to 18th August the Surgical Team of the 127th (Parachute) Field Ambulance performed 42 operations : Abdominal, 2 ; femur (compound fractures, 2), (simple fractures, 2) ; tibular and fibular (compound, 6 (including 1 amputation), (simple, 6)) ; Pott's fractures, 3 ; arm and wrist (compound, 7), (simple, 4) ; flesh wounds (arm, 2), (leg, 6), (neck, 1), (inguinal gland, 1). Anaesthetics used : Pentothal, 39 ; chloroform, 3 ; and 7 fresh whole-blood transfusions were given.

ment had been carried out. Sixty-three wounded were accommodated at the DS and some had already been sent to the American ADS which had moved into a site on the east of St Michel. The next afternoon it became possible to commence the evacuation of casualties to the beachhead by ambulance cars, and, early that evening, the first of the casualties sustained by the 5th Parachute Battalion began to arrive.

The 5th Battalion had been dropped well off their appointed DZ, some three-quarters of the men being scattered over a wide area between fifteen and twenty miles from the DZ, and much further inland. This had been due to the failure of the signal from the leading aircraft. In consequence the signal to jump was given by flashlight and it came much later than was planned.

The medical detachment attached to the 5th Battalion—Captain E. Morrison, RAMC, Captain Brown, ADC, and eight medical orderlies—jumped just after five o'clock in the morning on 15th August, the green light going on less then five seconds after the red warning light.

They landed about five miles north-east of Fayence, got together, and made contact with a major of the 5th Battalion. Allied aircraft were at that time putting a bombing attack on a nearby village. A rendezvous was set up in a farmhouse, where the parachutists were well received by a French family and a number of well-armed members of the Maquis who were out and about in the area. A yellow smoke signal was sent up which brought a total of some thirty men into the rendezvous. This party then set out for the Brigade HQ area, Captain Morrison and four medical orderlies carrying between them three medical packs and one stretcher bundle.

En route to Fayence the party was fired on on several occasions, but reached Tourette without casualties except for one of the French partisans who was accidentally wounded by one of his own comrades. At this village, where one RAMC orderly, injured in the drop, had to be left behind, it was learned that there was a wounded British soldier in the vicinity ; this turned out to be the Second-in-Command of the 5th Battalion,[1] suffering from grenade wounds in his thigh and calf. He was brought into Torrette and carried on with the party into Fayence, where Captain Morrison arranged for him to be admitted to the civilian hospital.

The party then broke up for their move south. At about five o'clock in the afternoon Captain Morrison's detachment encountered a German convoy, and engaged the enemy ; the fight lasting some ninety minutes, the mixed Franco-British force sustained no casualties, but two Germans were killed, three severely wounded (gunshot wounds in head, knee and buttocks), and one officer and four ORs were captured. Captain Morrison treated the wounded, administered morphia, splinting limbs and dressing the wounds, and they were left in the care of a French farmer.

Moving on, a company of US parachute troops were encountered ; and, after joining up with them, they reached a thickly wooded mountain area where they rested for the night, moving on early the next day to join up with the Brigade HQ.

No 2 Section of the 127th (Parachute) Field Ambulance, commanded by Captain A. L. Kerr, dropped with the 6th Parachute Battalion and made their way from Marchandise, where they concentrated, to St Michel, and on that evening to La Motte where they linked up with HQ of the 6th Battalion and established an ADS, which was operated until 18th August, when they rejoined the Field Ambulance.

No 1 Section with nine ORs under the command of Captain J. P. Mitchell dropped some thousand yards west of St Michel with the Medium Machine-gun (MMG) Platoon of the 4th Parachute Battalion, and by eight o'clock in the morning had opened up an ADS in a farmhouse at Goutes, where they treated thirty-three casualties arising from the glider-borne landing in addition to battle casualties before midday of D + 1, when Captain Mitchell and four ORs were ordered down to the Surgical Centre.[2]

---

[1] Major P. Dudgeon.
[2] The total casualties passing through the Surgical Centre between 15th and 18th August was 141 : 6 British officers and 93 ORs ; 38 Americans ; and 4 German prisoners.

The task of the 2nd Parachute Brigade was completed by 18th August and the whole formation returned to Italy at the beginning of September, firstly to Rome, and then to the area of Bari, where they set to work in preparing for their next operation—in Greece.

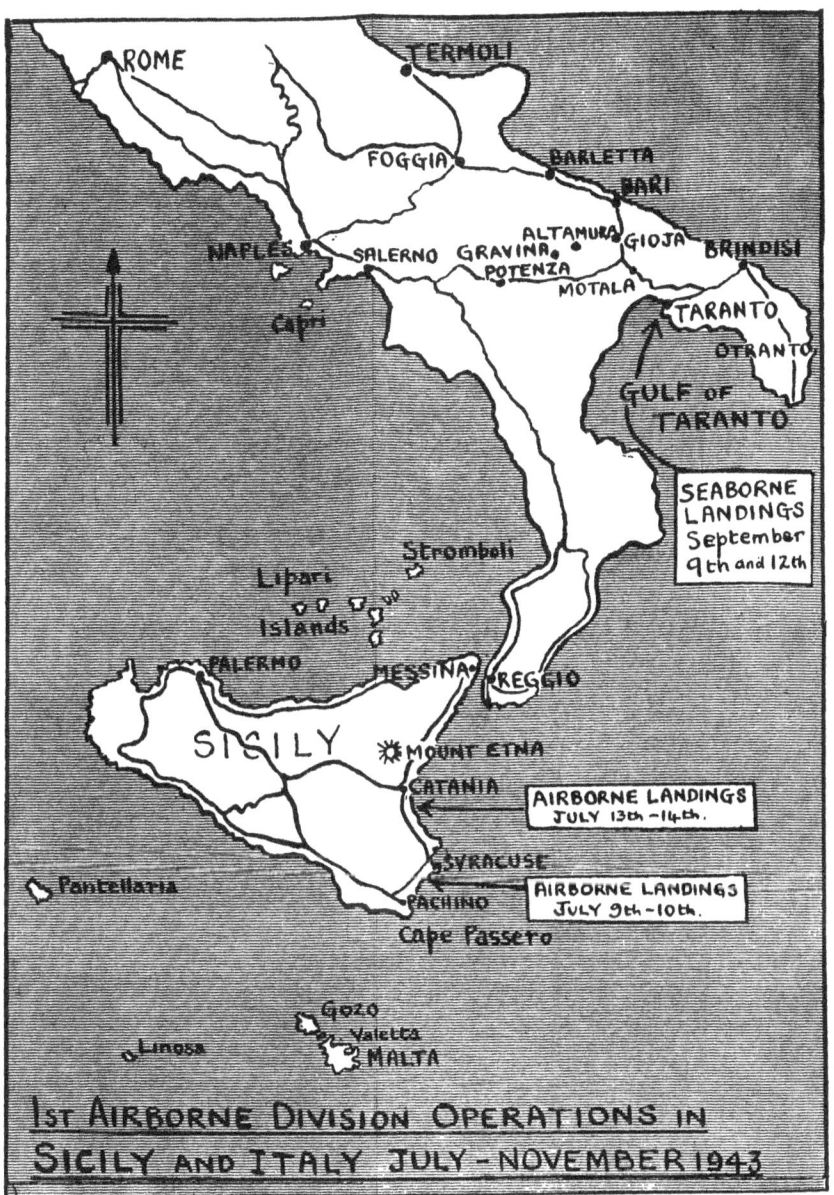

CHAPTER VII

WAR AND CIVIL WAR

THE 127TH (PARACHUTE) FIELD AMBULANCE IN GREECE

TOWARDS the end of August 1944 it became known that the Germans were preparing to withdraw from Greece and it was decided that Athens must be occupied by a British force as soon as possible after its evacuation by the enemy, with the object of preventing Greek guerilla fighters from establishing themselves in the capital, thereby preventing civil disturbances and the probability of civil war. The task of the British force was to maintain order, organise food distribution and be present 'in aid of the civil power'. It was planned that the 2nd Parachute Brigade should establish a beachhead in an airborne landing and that the main seaborne body of the force would land at Piraeus.

At the beginning of September the 2nd Parachute Brigade had moved from Rome to Bari and thence to a tented camp at San Pancrazio midway between Taranto and Brindisi, and here the Brigade prepared for its part in operation 'Manna', the code name for the airborne landing in Greece.

By 1st October the Brigade was ready and waiting when torrential rain swamped the camp, and the formation moved into buildings scattered over a wide area, the Brigade HQ, together with the 127th (Parachute) Field Ambulance, moving into the Ordinance Depot in Taranto.

The original plan was for the Brigade to land on the Kalamaki Airfield, south of Athens, and the task of securing the DZ was allotted to the 4th Battalion The Parachute Regiment.

The medical plan for the operation was for a detachment of the Field Ambulance, composed of one officer and nine ORs, to drop with each Battalion, and two complete 'sticks' each of seventeen all ranks—including the Surgical Team and one complete section—with the Brigade HQ block in the first air-lift, and one ' stick ' in the second lift.

Two jeeps filled with medical equipment were to follow by glider. In addition to the equipment carried by the men twelve containers were to be filled with reserve stores, to be dropped by parachute and collected on the ground as soon as possible. All ranks of the Brigade were equipped with two shell dressings and one tubonic of morphine.

On 11th October the operational plan was suddenly changed and the DZ was altered from the Kalamaki Airfield to a landing strip at Megara, twenty-eight miles west of Athens. The Brigade Commander received orders to put the formation into the air as quickly as possible and the next day, 12th October, the Battalion HQ, one Company of the 4th Battalion, with additional mortar detachments, took off from the airfield at Brindisi, the intention being that the main air-lift of the Brigade, including the Field Ambulance, should follow the next day. The weather on the 12th was bad, the flight bumpy and the force jumped on to their DZ in a wind estimated at over thirty miles per hour. This resulted in a considerable number of casualties on landing and some forty men were injured, including the Battalion MO.

An ADS was set up in the village hall at Megara, and here one officer and two ORs died from their injuries. The casualty rate among the company of the 4th Battalion was 27 per cent, most of the casualties were orthopaedic cases, but the majority did not require urgent operative treatment.

The news of this disastrous landing reached the Brigade HQ by wireless together with reports of bad weather in Greece. Further, similar reports concerning the weather reached the HQ early in the morning of the 13th and continued throughout the morning. This caused a postponement of the main air-lift, and that evening the Brigade Commander informed the SMO that if the high winds persisted it was very doubtful if the main drop could take place the next day, although the winds might not be too high to send in the glider-borne part of the force. In consequence it was decided to transfer a surgical team, composed of the surgical specialist, two medical officers and thirteen ORs, into gliders in the hope that some medical assistance would reach the 4th Battalion's company at Megara the next day.

On 14th October the weather reports were good and the main Brigade air-lift commenced. Very bad weather was, however, encountered over the Gulf of Corinth. This forced the gliders to turn back but the parachutists went on, and the jump was made into a fairly strong wind on to very hard ground, resulting in more casualties.

The Field Ambulance detachment with the 6th Parachute Battalion set to work in collecting the casualties on the DZ.[1]

As soon as they landed the 4th and 6th Parachute Battalions formed up to march on Athens, the gliders had not arrived and, in consequence, the medical services were very scattered. The Field Ambulance Section Officer with the 4th Battalion was acting as RMO, leaving only the SMO and one section officer with twenty-four ORs to look after the ninety-four casualties at Megara.

The next day, the weather had improved and the 5th Parachute Battalion parachuted down on to the Megara airstrip sustaining only three casualties. On 16th October the gliders were able to come in and land safely, bringing with them the remainder of the Field Ambulance, and the surgical specialists were soon at work, mainly engaged in setting broken limbs and putting them into plaster.

The 4th and 6th Parachute Battalions were, on their arrival in Athens, greeted by dense crowds of enthusiastic Athenians. It was a tumultous welcome, bursts of cheering and shouting, women grabbing the troops to kiss them, men embracing them and wildly shaking them by the hand. The crowds were so thick that it was with difficulty that the Brigade continued its march into the city, but, beneath the surface of this great welcome there was an obvious feeling of unrest, and sections of the crowd were antagonistic to one another.

[1] Between 12th and 16th October the total number of parachutists who dropped at Megara was 1,900, out of which there were 100 casualties—3 died, and 97 were treated by the Field Ambulance. Of these casualties 20 were head injuries (concussion); 15 broken upper limbs; 40 broken lower limbs; 8 multiple injuries; 4 abrasions; and 10 miscellaneous injuries ranging from lacerated scalps to severe bruising.

The situation rapidly became critical but was saved by a cloudburst which effectively drenched and dispersed the mobs. It was soon evident, however, that the situation in Athens was one which gave rise to considerable apprehension.

The Parachute Brigade was soon after reinforced by the arrival from Italy of the 23rd Armoured Brigade,[1] and the British force became responsible for policing the city and for providing guards for the main government offices and installations. The British control of these vital points became a matter of open dispute with the guerilla force, known as ELAS,[2] the left-wing political 'army' of the EAM.[3] These two organisations started to move about the city in strong columns, and whenever they met rioting occurred. The British force was ordered to avoid becoming involved with these internal troubles, but nevertheless the tension became acute.

On 17th October the 4th Parachute Battalion [4] was withdrawn from Athens and ordered to Thelses in pursuit of German forces, who were still withdrawing from Southern Greece, with the object of harassing their rearguard. The 4th Battalion, and attached troops, was designated 'Pompforce', and No 3 Section of the 127th (Parachute) Field Ambulance, commanded by Captain L. S. Bruce, was ordered to join the column. In the medical plan it was assumed that at the outset any serious casualties would be evacuated by road to Athens, but from a study of the map this did not appear to be a practical plan, and it was proposed that evacuation should be by air from Lamia, Larissa or Grevena. The next day the Field Ambulance moved into Athens from Megara and was established in the Evangelismos Hospital, to which all casualties were transferred.

On 22nd October No 3 Section left Athens at eleven o'clock in the morning to join 'Pompforce' and, as no further infor-

---

[1] 40th, 46th and 50th Royal Tank Regiments and the 11th Battalion The King's Royal Rifle Corps.
[2] Ellinikos Laikos Apelœutherotikos Stratos (Greek Peoples Liberation Army).
[3] Ethnikon Apeleutherotikon Metopan (Greek National Liberation Front).
[4] The RMO was Captain D. R. Rowlands.

mation had been received concerning the evacuation plan, as much surgical and MDS equipment as could be loaded into the available transport (one jeep and a trailer, one ambulance, and two 15-cwt. trucks) was taken, but even then it was kept at a minimum for this same transport had to carry a total of twenty-two all ranks with their personal kit.

Levedia was reached at six o'clock that evening and billets were found, but the town was full of ELAS ' troops ', and the Section's reception was far from enthusiastic. It had already become obvious that no assistance would be forthcoming from the Greek partisans. In fact, the ELAS forces regarded the British troops as intruders in their domestic affairs.

The next day the Field Ambulance Section moved on towards Lamia. The conditions generally, both geographical and political, were such that it was then obvious that no serious cases could be sent back to Athens by road. The roads were in an appalling state and the lives of casualties would most certainly have been endangered by their being transported in such vehicles as were available. A demand for additional medical supplies was sent back to Athens, for both the Section and the Battalion, for the RMO had sufficient to last two to three days only, because he had only one jeep in which to carry all his requirements.

During the day it was decided that a hospital should be set up in Lamia while the force continued its advance, which might well be up to 200 miles, but it was pointed out that it would be impossible to evacuate casualties over these distances over such appalling roads. In the circumstances, therefore, it was agreed that the Section should move further on at 9 am the next day towards Trikala.

The move forward was over loose stone roads, with deep ruts and holes, but good progress was made and, just before reaching Larissa, it was discovered that the Section was the foremost unit of the whole force, but on they went, crossing a broad river and making a detour of some fifteen miles, both of which it was learned would be impassable after rain, to reach a hill just outside Trikala, where they spent a bitter night in bivouac.

On 25th October the Section moved on through impressive rugged country, but again over very bad roads, and reached Grevena at six o'clock in the evening, where with the help of the British Military Mission a small hospital was established. Soon after it was learned that the 4th Battalion anticipated going into action at dawn the following day in the area of Kozani, some fifty miles further north. The Mission also gave the information that there were five detours on the route between Grevena and Siatista, although the road on to Kozani was clear. Leaving Lance-Corporal D. C. Hibbert and three medical orderlies in the hospital at Grevena, Captain Bruce and the rest of the Section repacked, and set off at eight-thirty that evening to make the thirty-mile journey to Siatista. The detours were poorly indicated, and the small convoy was soon lost. At one point they drove along a dried-up river bed, where the ambulance was almost tipped on its side in the steep rocky ascent of the banks.

On reaching Siatista in the early morning of 6th October a surgical unit was set up in a building already in use as a hospital by local partisans. At dawn, however, it was discovered that the only water supply came from a nearby well, with a latrine sited but three feet away; this, together with the fact that the partisans were helping themselves to the Section's kit and equipment, necessitated yet another move into two houses some distance away, where again preparations were made to receive casualties from the impending action which, for tactical reasons, had been postponed until dawn the next day.

At first light on the morning of 27th October 'C' Company of the 4th Parachute Battalion advanced towards a mountain above Kozani, which the Germans were still holding, and after a sharp engagement cleared the enemy from their positions, holding the ground they gained against all counter-attacks throughout the day. The Company withdrew in accordance with their orders that evening, carrying their wounded with them. Some of the casualties from the first attack were carried down to the Battalion RAP, but it was four o'clock in the afternoon before they could be got back to the Field Ambulance Section's 'hospital' at Siatista. Twenty-one wounded were brought in for treatment,[1] the most serious case being the Second-in-Command of the Assault Company.[2] In treating the wounded Captain Bruce was helped by Staff-Sergeant Cargill, who organised the reception of casualties, and the 'ward' was run by Private Christensen. Corporal Thomas acted as C.R.A., and Private Ure operated the pressure sterilising unit, which had been borrowed from the partisan's 'hospital', as well as assisting in the theatre.

In this manner the small, isolated section, with only one medical officer, carried out its task, under almost primitive conditions, in this small undeveloped Greek township, saving all lives, except for the severely wounded officer, who had been admitted twelve hours after receiving his injuries and who died the next day.

From 27th to 30th October Siatista was cut off from Grevena by the flooding of the rivers following heavy rain, which also put Grevena Airfield out of action, but this was all to the good, for by 1st November, after a period of crisis, all the wounded were fit for evacuation.

Medical supplies were by then very low and demands for stores were wirelessed back. On the afternoon of 1st November news came through that two aircraft had landed at Grevena, and so sixteen cases were loaded into the ambulance, two three-tonners and two fifteen-cwt. trucks. The convoy left Siatista at midnight, humping their way over the rough roads to Grevena, which was reached at five o'clock the next day, and the wounded were evacuated to Barletta in the two DC3 planes.

The Section continued to function at Siatista until 10th

[1] The casualties included 3 with haemothorax; 2 penetrating FBs of the eye; a double gun-shot wound in the neck; and 1 fractured mandible with displacement. Most of the cases were treated by excision and debridgment, chest and neck injuries receiving prophylactic sulphathiazole, and one case with penicillin.

[2] This was a severe gun-shot wound entering below and anterior to the left acromio-clavicular joint and leaving lateral to the right border of the right clavicle at the level of the third rib, the injuries to the right lung causing haemorrhage into the bronchial tubes.

November, evacuating some more cases on the 5th, but all the time they were receiving medical cases for treatment, including a number of Greek civilians.[1]

When the HQ of ' Pompforce ' retired from Siatista the RAMC Section returned to Grevena, and on the 13th started the return journey to Athens, a slow and dangerous journey —the fifteen-mile detour between Trikala and Larissa taking eight hours. Passing through Thermopylae, Larissa was reached late on the 14th and, at last, back to Athens.

Whilst ' Pompforce ' had been engaged in the operations up to Kozani, the 6th Parachute Battalion moved out of Athens to occupy Thebes and some other small towns in that area and the Brigade HQ and the 5th Parachute Battalion were ordered to move to Salonika by sea. The Field Ambulance was to move with Brigade HQ. The unit handed over its accommodation and casualties at the Evangelismos Hospital to the 150th Light Field Ambulance and embarked with the small force at Piraeus on 4th November. This disembarked at Salonika on the 8th, having been delayed twenty-four hours whilst a channel was swept through the minefield outside the port. They found the town controlled by ELAS forces. An MDS was established in the Hirsch Hospital, and the SMO selected a site for a 400-bed hospital which was due to arrive.

On 28th November the 5th Battalion accompanied by one section of the Field Ambulance and the Surgical Teams was despatched into Thrace and Northern Macedonia, where ELAS forces were causing trouble with the 7th Brigade of the 4th Indian Division, with the object of maintaining the peace between the Nationalists and the ELAS forces. Although every effort was made to keep the situation under control, within a month civil war had broken out across the whole of this area to the Bulgarian frontier. On 2nd December the force was withdrawn from Salonika to embark on HMT *Worcestershire en route* for Italy. At that time, however, the situation in Greece had become so serious that it was

---

[1] The prevalent diseases among the Greek population were scabies, impetigo, malaria, tuberculosis with purulent infections.

decided that the Brigade should return to Athens, where the 5th Parachute Battalion landing at Piraeus on the 5th came under fire from ELAS patrols. This saw the start of a difficult period for the Parachute Brigade and for the whole British force, with open fighting with the fanatical well-armed ELAS forces up and down the streets of Athens.

The 127th (Parachute) Field Ambulance (less No 3 Section) assembled in the Rouf Barracks on the evening of the 5th, where the critical situation was discussed at a conference held at midnight, and at which it was decided that the British force [1] would hold the Acropolis and the vital points of the city as the most effective way of maintaining control.

During this time the Acropolis, its dominating position overlooking the crowded streets of Athens, was occupied and held by troops of the 2nd Parachute Brigade, and less than fifty yards from the steps of the ancient Parthenon, Lieut.-Colonel Parkinson with a surgical team established an ADS in the Acropolis Museum.

In the absence of a firm medical plan, the Field Ambulance established an ADS in the barracks the following morning, whilst Captain D. R. Rowlands with a small detachment set up a CP at the Hotel Grand Bretagne, and soon after the first casualties from the street fighting were brought in. The next day Captain A. L. Kerr, acting as OC of the Field Ambulance, decided to try and make contact with the RMOs with the battalions in the Piraeus area in order to make arrangements for the evacuation of casualties back to the ADS in Rouf Barracks. It was a difficult task in a city under the tense atmosphere of civil war. He passed through several road-blocks guarded by heavily armed ELAS ' troops ' but was unable to get through to the Battalions. Later in the day, whilst crossing Omonias Square, he was fired on by ELAS men, despite the Red Cross markings on his jeep. On 8th December Major Wells, the Second-in-Command, rejoined the Field Ambulance, having flown in from Italy, and that day orders were received that all surgical cases from the British force were to be sent either to 127th (Parachute)

---

[1] Composed of the 2nd Parachute and 3rd Armoured Brigades commanded by Brigadier Arkwright and designated ' Arkforce '.

Field Ambulance or to 97th General Hospital. There was a steady flow of wounded into Rouf Barracks from the 4th and 6th Parachute Battalions, and from other units in the Piraeus area, but those from the 5th Battalion, which was concentrated in the centre of the city, went to the General Hospital.

Fighting was spasmodic, and flared up every now and again as ELAS 'troops' tried to force their way into or past the points held by ' Arkforce '.

On 11th December the 4th Parachute Battalion was engaged on and off with the enemy, for so they could then be called, because on 7th December war had been officially declared on ELAS. Casualties resulted from the periodical clashes in the suburbs between Athens and Piraeus. As Captain Phillip Irwin, the RMO of the 4th Battalion, stepped out of an ambulance to attend some wounded, ELAS men opened fire from some nearby buildings and he was killed. Later in the day Captain Rowlands, with a medical orderly, similarly engaged in tending wounded, were descended upon by a heavily armed ELAS party and were captured together with two ambulances and their drivers.

On 14th December the Parachute Field Ambulance moved out of Rouf Barracks into the University buildings in the centre of the city ; the convoy being escorted by armoured vehicles, which kept up a steady and constant fire, sweeping the buildings on either side of the route as they passed. In Piraeus Street all the houses were sandbagged and occupied by heavily armed ELAS men and fire was exchanged all the way. All but a few of the wounded were moved in this way, Captain Bruce remaining behind in Rouf Barracks with those who could not be got away. The move, hazardous as it had been proved, was fully justified, for shortly afterwards the barracks and 97th General Hospital were competely cut off. In consequence the 127th (Parachute) Field Ambulance became the only unit capable of effecting major surgery in Athens and the Piraeus area, and the University took on the appearance of a small general hospital. Beds, sheets and screens were acquired from various sources, and a number of Greek Red Cross nurses were temporarily taken ' on the strength '. On 16th December the SMO of the Brigade, Lieut.-Colonel Parkinson, arrived at Brigade HQ at Phaliron. The road from Phaliron to Athens was held by ELAS so, waiting until nightfall, the SMO rode into Athens in an ammunition lorry to join the Field Ambulance.

By 20th December the road to Phaliron was cleared of the enemy and evacuation of casualties by air was recommended. Rouf Barracks was still cut off, but on that day Colonel Parkinson, carrying some medical supplies, accompanied the Brigade Commander in a tank which fought its way down to the Barracks, and later communications were re-established.

This difficult situation obtained until Christmas. In the University Hospital the Greek sisters put up decorations and carol services were held in the wards, despite the sound of spasmodic small-arms fire.

On 27th December the Field Ambulance was visited by Field-Marshal Alexander [1] who toured the hospital and spoke to many of the wounded.

At that time arrangements for the air evacuation of casualties was not entirely satisfactory. Owing to the uncertainty of the arrival of aircraft, casualties had to be held by the medical units of the 4th Division, whose resources were already strained by the attention needed by the wounded awaiting evacuation from the airfield at Kalamaki. The situation was eased, however, by an arrangement whereby the first two aircraft to land would be set aside for evacuation of wounded and held until casualties arrived on the airfield.

There had been no air evacuation since 26th December, and the numbers of wounded were beginning to strain the hospital resources. By six o'clock in the evening of 2nd January forty-two new cases had been admitted and every available bed was in use. In consequence stretchers were used to bring the ' bed-state ' up to 170, of which by midnight 133 were occupied. The theatre was engaged all day, likewise the resuscitation team, in carrying out blood trans-

---

[1] Who had arrived in Greece with the Prime Minister, Mr Winston Churchill.

fusions. During the day a number of civilians were carried in for treatment following shelling by ELAS artillery of the Brigade HQ area ; after first-aid most of those were evacuated to the civil hospital.

On the morning of 3rd January the SMO was told that the 2nd Parachute Brigade was to put in a full-scale attack on the ELAS positions. As many cases as possible were got ready for evacuation, but again air transport was not available, neither was it possible to get casualties to the hospital ship at Piraeus. The situation was such that the SMO had to tell the ADMS that unless at least forty cases could be transferred to the Indian Casualty Clearing Station (CCS), then the ADS would have to close, as further expansion was impossible ; because the ADS was the only medical unit in Athens capable of performing any surgery this was a serious situation, but it was relieved by the acceptance, by three o'clock in the afternoon, of some forty wounded by the Indian CCS.

The 4th January was the peak day of the Brigade effort in dislodging the ELAS guerillas. By 11.30 am thirty casualties had been admitted to the ADS, and in all over sixty major cases were brought in during the day. Minor casualties were dealt with by the 150th Light Field Ambulance, and the CCS were able to absorb a further forty cases. The operating theatre was opened at nine o'clock on the morning of the 4th and contrived to function right through until three o'clock the following morning. Despite the fierce fighting the RAMC personnel with the Battalions were able to compete with the situation, making outstanding efforts to get the wounded back to the ADS with the minimum of delay.

The period from 5th to 23rd January, when the ADS closed, was in comparison quiet, the admissions being in the main ' sick ' personnel and a few wounded ELAS prisoners.

During the period from 14th October to 22nd January 628 cases had been admitted to the Field Ambulance and 214 operations had been performed. During the heaviest period of the fighting practically all the blood used for transfusions had been taken from donors within the Brigade, 112 bottles having been taken between 1st and 4th January alone.

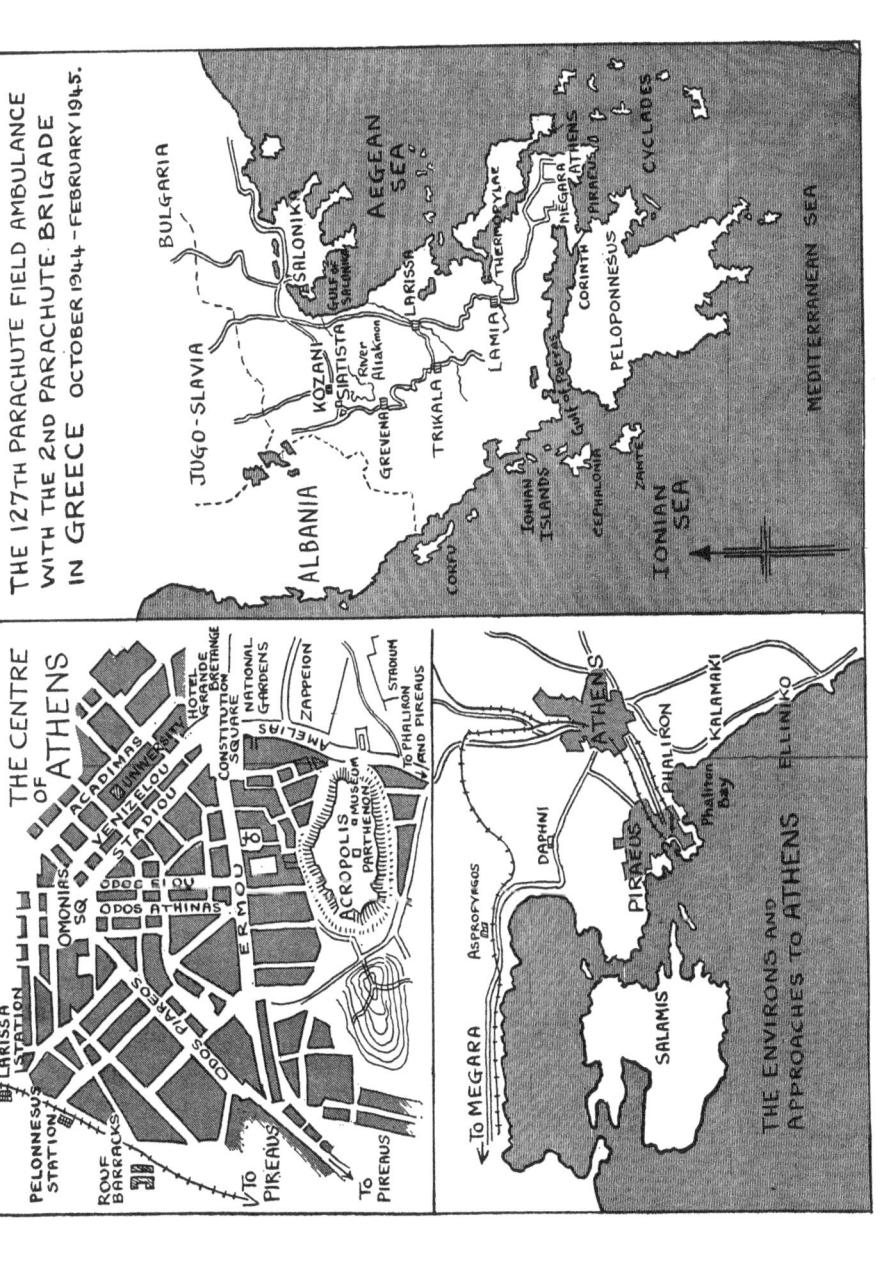

The smooth running of the ADS had been due to the teamwork of all ranks, and to a great extent to their ingenuity in improvisations, whilst the first-aid rendered at, and the speedy evacuation from, Battalion RAPs had without doubt been a major factor in the saving of many of the seriously wounded.

Early in February 1945 the 2nd Parachute Brigade was withdrawn from Greece, and returned to Italy. Here, after two weeks' rest, the Brigade was put into a state of readiness to participate in the Eighth Army's spring offensive—the plan aimed at forcing the crossing of the River Po and the final destruction of the enemy forces in Northern Italy. From mid-March until 'VE' Day the Brigade was constantly on the alert, ready for action. Some thirty operations were planned, and on five occasions the men actually emplaned, but these airborne operations were all cancelled and the Brigade was not called upon in the final stages of the war in Italy.

In May the Brigade returned to England to join the 6th Airborne Division, then preparing to move to Palestine as part of the strategic reserve.[1]

---

[1] See Chapter XVI.

CHAPTER VIII

THE NORMANDY BEACHHEAD

WITH THE 6TH AIRBORNE DIVISION FROM 'D' DAY ONWARDS

IN May 1943 the 6th Airborne Division was formed under the command of Major-General R. N. Gale.[1] Training and expansion was limited by the availability of aircraft because many of the aircraft and crews of No 38 Wing RAF were still in North Africa. It was not until the late summer that the Wing could be fully employed in the training of the men for the great event of the war, the invasion of Europe.

The medical units of the new 6th Airborne Division [2] were the 224th and 225th (Parachute) Field Ambulances, and the 195th (Air Landing) Field Ambulance.

It was in October 1943 that the 195th Field Ambulance was converted into an Air Landing Unit. A strenuous period of training followed to accustom the men to travelling in gliders and a number of them qualified as parachutists. The whole training was designed to ensure physical fitness, and also to anticipate and practise every possible situation envisaged in future airborne operations.

Both parachute and glider training went forward steadily. By November some forty gliders were being put into the air on exercises, and methods of routing and landing were practised. The 9th US Troop Carrying Command had arrived in the United Kingdom and played a major rôle in this training. A number of Stirling and Halifax bombers were diverted from Bomber Command to airborne training and such progress was made that on 24th April 1944 the complete Division

---

[1] Now Lieut.-General Sir Richard Gale, GCB, KBE, DSO, MC—appointed vice Major-General R. E. Urquhart, DSO, who had been appointed to command 1st Airborne Division vice Major-General E. E. Down.
[2] The ADMS was Colonel M. McEwan, OBE, DFC, TD.

was airborne by the united effort of the RAF and the US Troop Carrying Command. The exercise lasted for three days. It was, in fact, the dress rehearsal for the invasion of Normandy just six weeks later.

As far back as August 1943 the use of airborne forces in the Caen-Bayeux area of Normandy had been considered and studied. The first plan was for airborne troops to land immediately in front of the seaborne assault divisions, but this was changed by Field-Marshal Montgomery, when, fresh home from his triumphs in command of the Eighth Army, he took command of the invasion forces. His plan was for the airborne formation to land, hold and protect the left flank of the British sector, and this was the rôle finally allotted to the 6th Airborne Division.

The part of Normandy which was to be the scene of the airborne landing comprised high ground interspersed with valleys, through which flowed the Rivers Dives and Orne, both rivers being bordered with reeds and long grass. Between these rivers lay agricultural ground, with lush meadows on the slopes of the valleys, and above, belts of woodland, the largest of which was the Bois de Bavent.

It was planned that the first men to land in Normandy would be the 22nd Independent Parachute Company, their task the marking, with lights, of the dropping and landing zones.

The 3rd and 5th Parachute Brigades would drop together.

The task of the 3rd Brigade, under the command of Brigadier S. J. L. Hill, DSO, MC, was firstly to capture and destroy the German battery at Merville, a little over a mile from the coast; they were then to demolish four bridges over the River Dives, and finally they were to hold, and deny to the enemy, all roads leading into the British sector from the east and south.

The 5th Parachute Brigade, commanded by Brigadier J. H. N. Poett, DSO, also had three tasks. Firstly they were to seize the crossings over the River Orne and the Caen Canal near Ranville and Benouville; secondly to secure and hold the area around these two villages and that of Le Bas de Ranville, and finally to clear and hold the LZs near these villages on which the gliders of the Air Landing Brigade would touch down.

The medical plan for the operation was that the 224th (Parachute) Field Ambulance, commanded by Lieut.-Colonel D. H. Thompson,[1] would drop with the 3rd Parachute Brigade and establish an MDS in the area of Le Mesnil as ordered by the Brigade Commander. It was planned that casualties would be collected, held and treated at this MDS until such time as it was possible for them to be evacuated to the 3rd British Infantry Division, the spearhead formation of the seaborne assault.[2] The 225th (Parachute) Field Ambulance, commanded by Lieut.-Colonel E. I. B. Harvey, was to drop with the 5th Parachute Brigade and would establish their MDS in the area of Le Bas de Ranville. The 195th (Air Landing) Field Ambulance, commanded by Lieut.-Colonel W. M. E. Anderson, would land with the 6th Air Landing Brigade and would set up their MDS in buildings to be selected on landing by their own liaison officer. Sections from each Field Ambulance were to land with each battalion of the Division, but were to come under command of SMOs after landing.

At last all was ready. June 5th was to be *the* day, but, on the 4th, the meteorological forecast was unfavourable and the order for the launching of the invasion was postponed. Although the conditions on the night of 5th/6th June were not as good as was desired the order was given for operation ' Overlord ' to be launched. . . .

The rôle of the 3rd Parachute Brigade was such that it was necessary for the formation to be dispersed into two Battalion Groups, and in consequence the 224th (Parachute) Field Ambulance, comprising 129 all ranks, was similarly dispersed. The CO's party of five all ranks and the main MDS party, sixty all ranks, were to drop with the Brigade HQ, whilst

---

[1] Lieut.-Colonel Thompson was dropped wide of the DZ and, after nearly three weeks of gallant attempts to reach his unit, was taken prisoner.

[2] A liaison officer from the 6th Airborne Division Medical Services—Major D. S. Clark, the DADH—accompanied the 8th Field Ambulance, RAMC, of the 3rd Division in order to effect this link-up of the medical services of the two formations.

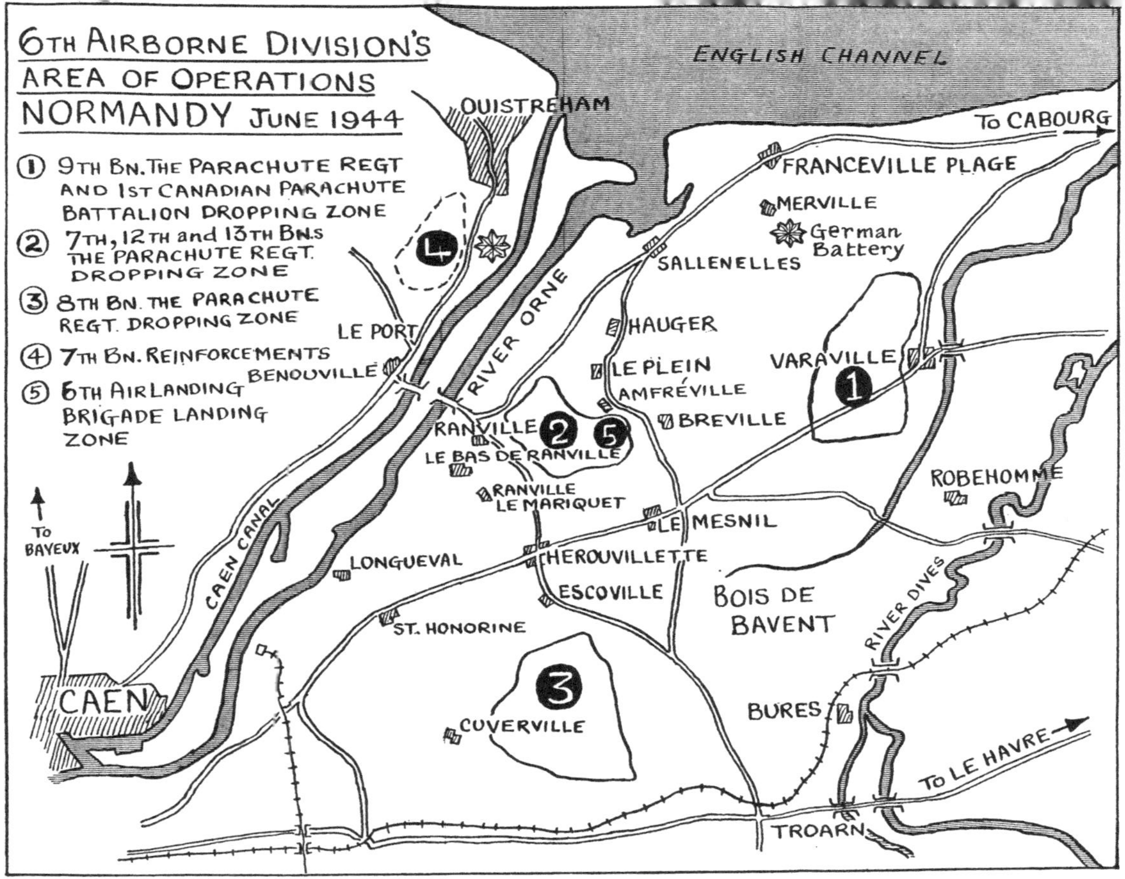
6TH AIRBORNE DIVISION'S
AREA OF OPERATIONS
NORMANDY JUNE 1944
① 9TH BN. THE PARACHUTE REGT AND 1ST CANADIAN PARACHUTE BATTALION DROPPING ZONE
② 7TH, 12TH and 13TH BNS THE PARACHUTE REGT. DROPPING ZONE
③ 8TH BN. THE PARACHUTE REGT. DROPPING ZONE
④ 7TH BN. REINFORCEMENTS
⑤ 6TH AIRLANDING BRIGADE LANDING ZONE
ENGLISH CHANNEL
TO CABOURG
OUISTREHAM
FRANCEVILLE PLAGE
MERVILLE
German Battery
SALLENELLES
HAUGER
LE PLEIN
AMFRÉVILLE
BREVILLE
VARAVILLE
ROBEHOMME
LE PORT
BENOUVILLE
RIVER ORNE
RANVILLE
LE BAS DE RANVILLE
RANVILLE LE MARIQUET
LE MESNIL
HEROUVILLETTE
ESCOVILLE
BOIS DE BAVENT
RIVER DIVES
LONGUEVAL
ST. HONORINE
CUVERVILLE
BURES
TO LE HAVRE
TROARN
CAEN CANAL
TO BAYEUX
CAEN

Nos 1, 2, and 3 Sections, each of twenty all ranks, were to drop with the 1st Canadian Parachute Battalion [1] and the 8th [2] and 9th [3] Battalions of the Parachute Regiment.

The air passage from the departure airfields of Down Ampney, Blake Hill Farm and Broadwell was uneventful although the moon was overcast and the weather generally unfavourable, and there was a certain amount of AA fire as they crossed the coast.

The 224th (Parachute) Field Ambulance dropped into Normandy at one o'clock in the morning of 'D' Day, some of the 'sticks' landing several miles from the DZ. Among these were Major A. D. Young's, who on landing was unable to make contact with any of the other members of his 'stick'. However, he judged the position of Varaville by the amount of machine-gun fire, and set off to make a wide detour in order to reach the RV. Half an hour later he encountered an officer and a party of ten ORs of the 9th Battalion; they went forward together, and during the next two miles of their march Major Young collected up ten men of the Field Ambulance, one of whom had a broken arm. At about three o'clock in the morning he decided that they were moving in the wrong direction, and after discussing the position with the 9th Battalion officer the party split up. Major Young and the RAMC personnel going off northwards, on their move they found a further five RAMC ORs. Eventually they reached the DZ where they found and treated several casualties. Moving on the party arrived at the RV of the 1st Canadian Parachute Battalion, where they were joined by Lieutenant G. C. A. Philo, RASC, with another twelve ORs of the Field Ambulance.

The sound of firing still came from Varaville, and it became obvious that the drop had not gone according to plan. Moving on, in the early hours of the morning, the Field Ambulance party reached Le Mesnil and occupied a farm,

[1] RMO—Captain C. Brebner, RCAMC. (The Canadian battalion arrived in the United Kingdom on 28th July 1942, and in the summer of 1943 took the place of the 7th (Light Infantry) Battalion in the 3rd Parachute Brigade when that battalion joined the then newly raised 5th Brigade.)
[2] RMO—Captain R. E. Holden, RAMC.
[3] RMO—Captain W. E. Church, RAMC.

where they dug in. At about eleven o'clock Lieutenant D. J. C. Cunningham and the Reverend A. L. Beckingham, CF, reported, and at midday the CO of the 8th Battalion The Parachute Regiment agreed with Major Young that it was advisable to open up the MDS. The Regimental Sergeant-Major—RSM G. M. Green—had dropped with five ORs in swampy ground south-east of Varaville. They had no idea where they were and marched and struggled for three hours through swamps and ditches in the direction of the sound of the fighting, reaching the scene of action soon after four o'clock in the morning, where they waited until dawn, when the RSM recognised, from his briefing, Varaville Church. He pressed forward and found Captain Nelson, Lieutenant (QM) Horder and fourteen ORs of the Field Ambulance in a chateau where they had opened an ADS. The RSM made his way back to his party, meeting Major Darling, also of the 224th (Parachute) Field Ambulance *en route*. He directed him to the chateau and carried on.

On his return to the chateau with his own party the RSM found that the ADS had been abandoned. An enemy patrol had, in his absence, reached the chateau from the cover of a nearby wood, taking prisoner Major Darling, Captain Nelson and their party. There were some sixteen wounded lying at the chateau in the care of Private H. H. Harris. Harris had landed with Captain Nelson and helped in opening the ADS, but had been sent off in an attempt to find a handcart. During the time he was away German infantry had cleared the chateau, so Harris, finding himself alone with the wounded, set to work collecting up all the medical equipment he could find, and established his own RAP. RSM Green left his five men with Harris and made his way to Le Mesnil, where he reported, that evening, to the MDS.

Lieutenant R. Marquis, with the section of the Field Ambulance allotted to the 8th Battalion The Parachute Regiment, had dropped very wide of the DZ in the vicinity of Dozule, and it was obvious that they would be unable to join the Battalion before its primary objectives of destroying the two bridges over the River Dives at Bures and the bridge immediately to the east of Troarn had been completed. They therefore made off across the dark countryside towards the Battalion's final position. At four o'clock in the morning they reached the village of Robehomme, which was being held by some 150 men of the Canadian Parachute Battalion, this force being cut off from the rest of the Division. That night the officer in command decided to attempt a breakthrough, so the whole force moved at midnight, and after two brisk clashes with the enemy reached Le Mesnil at dawn.

No 3 Section, commanded by Captain I. F. B. Johnson, which was allotted to the 9th Battalion The Parachute Regiment, also dropped very wide of the Battalion DZ, landing in flooded, marshy ground east of the River Dives and northeast of Robehomme. There was confused fighting in the area, but by two-thirty in the morning Captain Johnson had collected his ten men in a wood together with a number of combatant personnel, but there were no other officers, so he took command, and having realised that there was no hope of reaching the Battalion, which by then was fully committed to its primary task of destroying the coastal battery at Merville, decided to make his way to Le Plein, which was the 9th Battalion's second objective, *via* Robehomme and Bavent. The party of some twenty-five all ranks moved off across country and joined the Canadians who were holding the Robehomme area. Here he handed over the infantry to the Canadian Commander, established an ADS in the village and organised the evacuation of wounded in a horse and cart which he took over from a French farm. It was here he was later reinforced by the arrival of Lieutenant Marquis and his party.

The manner in which these members of the Field Ambulance came together was typical of many similar instances, and there were, on that dark, historic night, many individual deeds of initiative, perseverance and personal bravery.

By the time 3rd Brigade had consolidated its position—from just south of Bréville to the tip of the Bois de Bavent at Mont des Gondes—the medical strength of the battalions had been depleted. The RMO of the 8th Battalion, Captain Holten, had been killed and only nine of its medical section remained, for, apart from those missing since the drop, two men had died from wounds. In the 9th Battalion only the RMO, Captain Watts, Corporal Tottle and Private Anderson were able to reach the RV at the Bois de Mont, although the Corporal was killed on a minefield shortly afterwards. The 9th Battalion medical strength was, however, increased by the arrival of two medical orderlies from the 12th Battalion and one from the 7th.

As soon as was possible the battalion medical sections were reinforced from the Field Ambulances.

The 225th (Parachute) Field Ambulance had taken off a quarter of an hour before midnight, crossing the French coast at Cabourg just after one o'clock, and at one-twenty the green lights went on and the unit dropped into the darkness.

By two-thirty in the morning most of the unit had reached the RV; there had been some enemy opposition, and the unit was under mortar fire. They moved off in rear of the 12th Battalion The Parachute Regiment to Le Bas de Ranville and on arrival they occupied a chateau, where the French occupants gave them an enthusiastic welcome and three German officers of the TODT organisation were captured in their beds. The MDS was established at 4 am and half an hour later casualties began to arrive.

At first light on the morning of 6th June the CO, Lieut.-Colonel E. I. B. Harvey, set off to find No 3 Section. They had established an RAP in the church at Ranville, where Captain Tibbs[1] was treating casualties his section had brought in from the DZ. The section had been constantly under shell and mortar fire, four men had been wounded and two killed, but the men carried on with their task of sweeping the area for wounded up to two o'clock that day.

From Ranville Church, Colonel Harvey went on about a mile to a point near the bridge over the Caen Canal, where Captain Jacobs had set up an ADS in a big open ditch by the track leading to the bridge. The position was the target of enemy snipers and there were some fifteen wounded and a number of dead at the RAP. Arrangements were made to get the wounded away to the MDS.

During the time the CO was away, Lieutenant L. Hill,

[1] For gallantry and devotion to duty on ' D ' Day Captain D. J. Tibbs was awarded the Military Cross.

RASC, the Transport Officer, captured a German supply vehicle and brought back welcome supplies of bread, cheese, tinned meat, sugar and tobacco. He also brought in a number of enemy trucks, mostly small Citroens, in various stages of disrepair found in the vicinity of the MDS, and they had been put into running order for use in carrying casualties. During the morning three of the glider-borne jeeps and trailers arrived, but were off-loaded and withdrawn for the urgent transport of ammunition until the evening.

Casualties began to flow in from the Battalions, and the Surgical Teams were constantly at work,[1] although the situation was such that it was not possible for many to be evacuated to the MDS. No 2 Section, commanded by Captain Wagstaff, had established an ADS at Benouville with ' A ' Company of the 7th Battalion The Parachute Regiment and were cut off altogether. Captain D. R. Urquhart set up an ADS near the second Caen Canal Bridge and was tending casualties from the rest of the 7th Parachute Battalion and ' A ' Company of the 2nd Battalion Oxford and Buckinghamshire Light Infantry.

The whole Field Ambulance worked under constant sniping and mortar fire throughout the day. By nine o'clock in the evening Major McDonald of the 8th Field Ambulance from the 3rd Infantry Division had established contact and began the move of casualties back to the Field Dressing Station (FDS) in the beach area. Some sixty wounded were taken away in this manner within an hour, but by then the bridge on the route back was being heavily mortared, so Major MacDonald set up a CCP at a farm not far away and the evacuation of the MDS, which by this time had admitted some 280 wounded, continued.

Fierce fighting continued in the area throughout the night and the MDS was under fire all through the day. At five o'clock it was nominally closed, having up to that time admitted a total of 380 casualties, but still the wounded came in.

The 9th and 10th June were regarded as ' fairly quiet '

[1] During the first 40 hours the surgeons performed 43 operations : face and neck, 3 ; upper limbs, 5 ; upper limb amputation, 1 ; lower limbs, 1 ; lower limb amputation, 3 ; abdominal, 8 ; chest, 3 ; back and buttocks, 5 ; multiple, 4 ; 4 of the 8 abdominal and 1 of the chest cases subsequently died.

and the MDS was only occasionally shelled and mortared; but by this time all ranks were getting accustomed to this form of bombardment and were digging in well, for they had soon realised the value of deep slit trenches. During these days the 152nd and 153rd Infantry Brigades of the 51st (Highland) Division crossed the River Orne, thereby covering the area in which the MDS was located.

Between 10th and 13th June the 6th Airborne Division drove off a number of enemy attacks and held their ground. On the 12th the 12th Battalion The Parachute Regiment, the 1st Special Service Brigade and 'B' Company of the 12th Battalion The Devonshire Regiment (of the 6th Air Landing Brigade) launched an attack on Breville. This was preceded by a heavy artillery concentration on the enemy positions, but some of the shells fell short in the Parachute Battalion assembly area, causing a number of casualties, including the CO, who was killed. The attack went home and was successful, Breville was captured, but at great cost. Major John Bamfield, OC 'B' Company of the 12th Devons was killed in action, and among the wounded brought into the MDS were Brigadier Kindersley of the 6th Air Landing Brigade and Brigadier Lord Lovat of the Commando Brigade.

From 14th to 18th June there were few casualties from the 6th Airborne Division and the MDS was mainly engaged in admitting wounded from the 51st (Highland) Division, and on the 18th the 175th Field Ambulance of the 51st Division took over the MDS, the 225th (Parachute) Field Ambulance being moved back into the rest area, where they bivouacked in an orchard by the banks of the River Orne, but having by this time became seasoned soldiers the men immediately started to dig themselves in.

The 195th (Air Landing) Field Ambulance, carried to Normandy in ten Horsa gliders,[1] landed soon after eleven

[1] Six gliders were allotted to the MDS party and 2 to each of Nos 3 and 4. Each section comprised 1 officer and 21 ORs (19 RAMC and 2 RASC with 2 jeeps and 1 trailer), and HQ consisted of 9 officers (8 RAMC and 1 AD Corps) and 60 ORs (48 RAMC, 6 RASC, 1 AD Corps, 4 ACC, and 1 RE), making a total of 11 officers, 102 ORs, 9 jeeps, and 5 trailers in the airborne party.

o'clock on the night of 5th/6th June. One glider was hit by 'flak': one man was killed and Sergeant Torrens was wounded.

The CO and No 3 Section landing on LZ ' N ' and the MDS and No 4 Section on LZ ' W '. All the glider tails were successfully detached and by 11.30 pm the MDS party had assembled. After a sweep for casualties over the DZ the party was met by Captain West who had dropped with the 225th Field Ambulance, who guided them to Bas de Ranville where they bivouacked for the night. No 3 Section had moved off with the 1st Battalion The Royal Ulster Rifles to Longueval and No 4 Section accompanied the 2nd Battalion The Oxford and Buckinghamshire Light Infantry to Herouvillette.

Early the following day a site for the MDS was found in a large building in Mariquet, previously occupied by a German Regimental Headquarters. The MDS was open and fully functioning by eleven o'clock in the morning and casualties were coming in from most of the units in the Division. By midnight there had been 154 admissions and twenty-three surgical operations had been performed.

At seven o'clock in the morning of D + 2 evacuation of casualties across the bridges commenced in co-operation with the 8th Field Ambulance of the 3rd (British) Division. In the afternoon the seaborne party of the Air Landing Field Ambulance came up from the beaches having lost two men as they had moved up. That evening the MDS became a target for mortar fire. There was one direct hit and three men were killed. Conditions were becoming difficult and the operating theatre was moved into the basement of the building. Some measure of the work of the MDS can be assessed by the fact that during the day there were 102 admissions and twenty-eight operations. The next day, during which the MDS sustained another direct hit, there were a further 156 admissions and eleven operations.

No 3 Section was still with the Royal Ulster Rifles, and as the evacuation of casualties was difficult from the battalion area an ADS was opened at Longueval and casualties were sent back to the MDS by jeeps.

Evacuation from the Oxford and Buckinghamshire Light Infantry RAP was, however, quite straightforward, and No 4 Section was withdrawn to reinforce the MDS.

The MDS at Le Mesnil operated by the 224th (Parachute) Field Ambulance was fully functioning at midday on 6th June. Soon afterwards Captain Chaundy of the ADC and another three ORs reported in. Still some two-thirds of the 224th Field Ambulance were unaccounted for and there was no definite news from the 9th Parachute Battalion engaged in the assault on the battery at Merville. In this bloody battle the whole of the attached RAMC section which was with the Battalion became casualties. On the capture of the Battery the close and dangerous nature of the country decided the move of the Battalion back to Salenelles, from where the task of collecting the wounded was carried out later during the day.

The 8th Parachute Battalion was still some distance away and were in action without a MO, so Major Young detached Lieutenant Cunningham from the MDS to join them. The MDS was thereby left with only two officers, and during ' D ' Day they received and treated fifty-three all ranks, and two civilian casualties, and carried out ten operations.

By the next day the enemy were within 300 yards of the MDS on three sides, there was spasmodic sniping and machine-gun fire throughout the day, and although the roads were under mortar fire evacuation of casualties to the beaches in captured enemy transport commenced. Casualties flowed in, nineteen operations were performed that day, and there were a number of casualties among the RAMC personnel, three men were blown up on a minefield whilst collecting wounded, and others did not return from their missions in searching for battle casualties.

In the face of all the difficulties of nursing and evacuating casualties the MDS of the Field Ambulances worked efficiently according to the plans which had been evolved during the pre-invasion training period in England. The one problem, the extent of which was unforeseen, was the proximity of the Germans. As far as the 224th (Parachute) Field

Ambulance was concerned it was the first occasion on which a MDS had been set up so close to the front line. Throughout 6th June the MDS had been surrounded by Germans, and during the following two weeks it sometimes functioned within 300 yards of their positions, and even when the Le Mesnil area was not the objective of any concerted attack, sniping and stray bullets and mortar bombs restricted movement at the MDS.

Such a situation was, however, to be expected. The Brigade HQ was in the vicinity and in the circumstances no protection could be justly claimed for the Red Cross. At one time, the command post was at the end of a building in which serious casualties were being attended to ; the Brigade Signals Office was functioning alongside the stores ; a tall fir tree near the gate leading into the farmyard was in use as an observation post and, on one occasion a tank was ' harboured ' right in the farmyard.

At two o'clock in the morning of 8th June the 9th Parachute Battalion came under command of the Brigade, and the RMO, Captain H. P. Watts, established an RAP in the chateau St Corone at Le Mesnil, where they were joined by Captain Johnson, Lieutenant Marquis and sixteen ORs, reporting into the MDS after their somewhat hazardous route from their DZ.

Soon after first light the enemy launched an attack against the 9th Battalion and the Canadians, the attack was driven back, as were three others during the day, during which sixty-eight wounded were treated and seventeen operations performed. The RAP of the 9th Battalion, manned by No 3 Section of the 224th (Parachute) Field Ambulance, was in a solid stone villa standing on high ground which sloped gently away from a terrace down to the River Orne. It was surrounded on three sides by a wood where the Battalion was dug in. A short drive through the trees led to the main Breville road, along which casualties were evacuated to Le Mesnil whenever the road was open. Except for one small room occupied by the Battalion Commander as his office the whole house was used as wards where wounded awaited evacuation. Casualties brought in were taken into a small backyard and their wounds dressed in a tool-shed. At times when the fighting was heavy there was no time to clear up, the entrance and floor was red with blood, and bits of bloodstained clothing and boots lay about in grim disorder.

Later, when sniping made the yard and shed unsafe, casualties were brought round to the front of the house and wounds dressed in the hall with its pictures and ornaments still as they were when the house suddenly became the centre of a battalion position.

The evacuation of casualties on the Breville road to Le Mesnil was a hazardous operation. On one occasion Staff-Sergeant Brown and Private Irvine on their way to collect wounded at a nearby cross-roads turned a bend and drove straight among a German patrol, the men scattered and plunged for the ditches, and then turned and gazed with astonishment at seeing a British Ambulance Car in their midst, the driver braked with a jerk and shot back in reverse round the bend, just as several of the Germans opened fire.

On another occasion Major Young with Driver Buffin passing the same spot heard cries from the adjoining field. They halted and traced the source of the voices and found two Germans lying face downwards; one had a serious wound in his back, and the other, a mere boy, also complained of back injuries, but when Major Young slit his tunic he found no wound and ordered the boy to his feet. He obeyed sulkily and slowly, and, when he turned to face the Major, held an automatic pistol in his hand. " Unload and hand it over ! " demanded Major Young, which the boy did.

The situation continued in this manner for the next three days, the enemy continuing to attack. There was heavy machine-gun fire, bullets whining around the MDS and mortar bombs falling all around. The MDS was, however, reinforced by the arrival of the seaborne parties from the beaches, just in time, in light of the increasing casualties.

At half-past four on the morning of 11th June the 5th Battalion The Black Watch, then under the command of the 3rd Parachute Brigade, supported by the tanks of the 13th/18th Hussars, launched an attack on Breville, during which they sustained 104 casualties, which were all treated at the

MDS and, the following day, there were another 114 casualties in the same battalion when their positions were heavily shelled and mortared. During the day the main road was so constantly under heavy fire that all wounded from the combined RAP of the 9th Parachute Battalion and the Black Watch had to be carried out by hand carriage, yet this continued throughout the night, under most difficult conditions, so that by five o'clock in the morning all the Black Watch casualties had been evacuated. In the carrying out of this task Corporal Cranna had played a leading part in organising and directing the stretcher-bearers as they traversed the fire-swept ground between the Battalion positions and the MDS.

The fighting throughout the day was close, neither side was able to disengage and in the early evening the MDS was twice attacked by Typhoons of the RAF with 20 mm cannon and rockets. At two o'clock in the morning of the following day the MDS and surrounding area was heavily bombed by enemy aircraft, but the work at the MDS continued uninterrupted.

The 15th June was, for the first time since the landing, a comparatively uneventful day, although soon after four o'clock in the morning of the 16th the MDS was heavily shelled and mortared for nearly an hour. The buildings were hit on several occasions but no casualties were sustained.

Three days later the MDS was again the target for a battery of 105 mm guns. There were three direct hits and all the unit transport except for one ambulance car and two German trucks were put out of action, and one of the RASC drivers was killed. Soon afterwards orders came from the Commander of the 5th Parachute Brigade that the Field Ambulance should evacuate its position, and move further back; the move was completed by half-past five the following morning, Captain Johnson and nineteen ORs remaining behind at Le Mesnil until 21st June as an Ambulance Car Post.

During that day the unit was moved to the reserve area at Ecarde. Here it had to be reorganised in consequence of its own casualties and the fact that two officers and twenty-five ORs were needed to make up the medical services casualties in the battalions of the Brigade. It was decided that it was of primary importance to make battalions up to strength in RAMC personnel and only to run an Ambulance Car Post with what was left of the unit.

Between the period 6th to 19th June a total of 822 casualties had been treated by the 224th (Parachute) Field Ambulance and 112 operations performed.[1] ' The effect on morale of the immediate treatment this Field Ambulance [2] was able to give, as well as the saving of life which resulted from the Surgical Team being right up in the foremost of the fighting, is just immeasurable ' wrote General Gale, the GOC of the Division.[3]

At Le Mariquet the MDS of the Air Landing Field Ambulance was still functioning under enemy fire, as was also the ADS run by No 3 Section at Longueval, which had come under close range small-arms fire. Two men were killed, and the CO, Lieut.-Colonel W. M. E. Anderson, DSO, and two ORs wounded. Both the MDS and ADS carried on and, during the day 156 casualties were admitted and eleven operations were performed, and the wounded were evacuated as soon as they could be got away.

D + 5, the 10th June, was quiet and uneventful, during which stocks of plasma, plaster and glucose saline were obtained from No 16 CCS, a re-supply pannier and container were located, and a special ' abdominal ' ward was opened at the MDS.

On 11th June the attack was launched against Breville, No 3 Section of 181st (Air Landing) Field Ambulance taking part in the action with the Royal Ulster Rifles.

The evacuation of the increasing flow of casualties was

[1] Toilet of penetrating wounds (single), 22 ; simple fractures, 8 ; compound fractures, 16 ; toilet of penetrating wounds (multiple), 16 ; penetrating wounds of abdomen, 28 ; acute appendicitis, 1 ; penetrating wounds of the brain, 5 ; facio-maxillary, 2 ; wounds, large vessels, 4 ; amputations, 5 ; burns, 1 ; extraction of bullets, 1 ; reduction of dislocation, 1 ; suprapubic cystotomy (paraplegia, 1, and urethral injury, 1), 2.
[2] 224th (Parachute) Field Ambulance.
[3] ' With the 6th Airborne Division in Normandy ' by Lieut.-General R. N. Gale, CB, DSO, OBE, MC (Sampson Low, Marston & Co., Ltd.). (1948.)

eased by the arrival of the D + 1 and D + 2 seaborne transport, together with five Motor Ambulance Column cars, which helped, during the next week, in establishing an MDS car shuttle-service in conjunction with a CP at Benouville and in the collecting of whole blood from the advanced 'Blood Bank' at Le Deliverande, forty-five minutes' drive away.

After stormy sea crossings and rough handling in transit quite a high proportion of the plasma received in the early stages was unfit for use. In any case plasma did not always fully resuscitate the patients before they entered the operating theatres, but once whole blood became available many severely wounded men were saved, some of whom were in a far worse state than other less serious cases who died earlier before the whole blood supply was available. In some urgent cases blood was taken on the spot from volunteers. One donor at the Le Mesnil MDS was a captured German medical orderly, Unteroffizier Hans Kehlenbach; for this and other services Major Young wrote out a citation for the award of the Iron Cross Class II and gave it to a senior wounded German officer, who on evacuation took it down the line.

Eight German medical orderlies and a Russian were employed at the MDS; they were all hard workers who fitted into the general organisation and became an integral part of the unit; their behaviour was most correct and they were particularly punctilious in their dealings with the British MOs.

Between 18th and 20th June the whole Divisional area was shelled continuously,[1] resulting in a continual flow of casualties—275 in all, of which seventeen needed immediate operations. From then until the end of June the Le Mariquet MDS settled down to a regular pattern of work, and had time

[1] Not for the first time, for it had its full share of enemy bombardment since landing. At the outset so heavy and concentrated was the artillery fire on the position occupied by the Divisional Headquarters that by the end of D + 2 all the medical personnel had become casualties with the exception of the ADMS and three ORs. The DADMS, Captain Maitland, was mortally wounded whilst attempting to rescue wounded men lying out in the open.

to devote to sanitation throughout the Brigade area; and during the latter ten days opened up special 'exhaustion' wards where cases could be 'sedated' and kept for forty-eight hours, by which time about a quarter of these men were fit to return to their units.

By the end of the month, a total of 1,687 cases had been admitted to the MDS, and 127 surgical operations were performed.

From 23rd June until the first week in August the 224th (Parachute) Field Ambulance was at Ecarde, although the unit continued to provide medical personnel for the Battalions of the 3rd (Parachute) Brigade, and during this time opened up a Divisional Skin and VD Clinic. Although Ecarde was designated a 'rest area', the unit lived in slit trenches. Half of the personnel were away continuously with the battalions, and those whose turn it was to remain behind were subjected to constant air-raids nearly every night, during which the surgeon, Captain T. G. Gray, was seriously wounded and two ORs were killed.

On 17th July the CO was told by the ADMS that three Armoured Divisions were about to put in an attack, through the 6th Airborne Division, crossing the River Orne over pontoons. It was anticipated that the crossing would be subject to concentrated attack by enemy aircraft. The 224th Field Ambulance set up four FAPs. No 33 FDS with an FSU and FTU under command moved with the unit. The next day there was a four-thousand-bomber raid on Caen, elements of the 7th, 11th, and Guards Armoured Divisions went through the Divisional area, the attack was successfully launched, and the FAPs of 224th Field Ambulance withdrawn.

On 7th August the unit moved to Rivabella, the newly selected Divisional rest area. Three days later a JU88 was shot down over the camp where it crashed, killing thirteen men and wounding another twenty, whilst in the days which followed the whole area was subjected to considerable shell-fire.

By 20th August the unit was again in action, having been hastily re-organised on the 18th as a Field Ambulance with reinforcements from 195th (Air Landing) Field Ambulance. It moved at nine o'clock in the evening to 'leap frog' the 225th (Parachute) Field Ambulance and to open an MDS at Dozule by the evening of the following day, with the task of evacuating casualties from the 3rd and 5th Parachute Brigades, the 6th Air Landing Brigade and the 1st and 4th Special Service Brigades. The MDS received thirty-three British and three German casualties soon after opening.

On 24th August the unit prepared to move forward in support of the 3rd Parachute Brigade, but on reaching St Gatien at half-past seven the next day the CO found that the Brigade had pressed on, so he went on to the small village of St Andre d'Herbetot where the MDS had opened in a chateau at two o'clock that afternoon to receive casualties from the two Parachute and two Special Service Brigades as well as the Royal Netherlands Brigade—by nightfall eighty-six casualties had been admitted. In consequence of these numbers and further anticipated casualties the CO sent a message to the ADMS asking for a surgical team. Major N. A. Miller and four ORs from the 195th Field Ambulance reported the following afternoon. Forty-seven casualties were treated that day and another thirty-nine on the next.

After 28th August the unit ceased to receive further battle casualties and became responsible for the treatment of the sick from the four brigades.

On the morning of 20th June the 225th (Parachute) Field Ambulance received a warning order to move again and set up an MDS in a quarry in the forward area to receive casualties which would result from an attack about to be launched by the Division.

The site chosen for the MDS was unfortunately adjacent to an important cross-roads which was subject to intermittent mortar and shell-fire. In consequence the Commander Royal Engineers (CRE) was asked for help in the building of a splinter-proof operating theatre and a 'ward'; shelters and tarpaulins were also borrowed from other units. At nine o'clock the following day the Field Ambulance moved into the quarry and started to dig in. They 'shared' the new position with a French family who were living in a 'lean-to'; they were, it was noted at the time, 'extremely dirty and their conditions most insanitary'. It took three days to get them moved out by a Civil Affairs detachment.

In the week preceding 30th June the Divisional Engineers built a splinter-proof theatre and resuscitation ward, both with electric light, and the Field Ambulance settled down to a regular routine. There was a continual flow of casualties, most of which were as the result of mortar fire, and small-arms wounds arising from patrol activity in the sector of the bridgehead held by the Division and the Special Air Service (SAS) Brigades. On 6th July the casualties rose to sixty. They came from the 5th Parachute and 6th Air Landing Brigades, resulting from an attack by two companies of the 7th Parachute Battalion, supported by two Field Regiments. The enemy response was a two and a half hour bombardment. The casualties were all brought back by hand carriage, and during the peak of the shelling Captain Urquhart, the Brigade MO, went out to supervise the evacuation from a collecting point.

Just after six o'clock on the morning of 18th July 1,000 heavy bombers attacked the enemy positions between Cuvreville and Demouville. Bombs were rained down on the target area until seven o'clock, when an artillery concentration was delivered for half an hour, which preceded an attack by the 11th Armoured Division.

The 225th Field Ambulance was in readiness to receive casualties, which started to come in before midday, these were mainly wounded Germans.

At eleven o'clock that night enemy aircraft attacked the area. Three ammunition lorries just near the MDS were hit, set on fire and exploded—the MDS was showered with antipersonnel bombs, over a hundred falling in the camp in the quarry. All the tents were riddled by fragments and a pile of blankets was set on fire. Some forty-five casualties were brought in from the area, Sergeant Thomas and Private Flynn doing fine work in organising stretcher-bearer parties to collect the wounded.

Throughout the month there were frequent night air-raids

and a considerable number of bombs fell in the vicinity of the MDS. After one heavy raid it was seen, at dawn, that the entrance to the MDS had been cratered. An unexploded bomb was suspected but, after much searching, it was discovered that the bomb had ricochetted over the MDS to explode, harmlessly, in a field some hundred and fifty yards away.

At first light on 7th August the 5th Parachute Brigade moved into the La Plein sector to relieve the 1st and 4th SAS Brigades. Immediately the German artillery started to shell the sector and about eleven o'clock the RAP of the 7th Parachute Battalion received a direct hit from an 88 mm self propelled (SP) gun.[1] An RAMC orderly was killed and there were a number of other casualties.

The following day orders were received for the 225th Field Ambulance to take over the MDS of the 195th Air Landing Field Ambulance at Le Mariquet when that unit moved to the MDS at Ecarde. Hardly had the 225th settled in on their arrival the following day when casualties came in from the 3rd Parachute Brigade, some thirty-five wounded were brought in that day, their injuries being mainly from mortar bombs.

A warning order was received on 12th August for a general advance along the whole sector held by the Division. In this operation, which had the code-name 'Paddle', the Royal Netherlands Brigade and the Brigade Peron[2] were placed under command of the 6th Airborne Division. The advance commenced on the 17th.

The Field Ambulance was responsible for the collection and evacuation from the 3rd Parachute, 1st and 4th Special Service Brigades and the 5th Parachute Brigade in Divisional Reserve, although the SAS Brigades had the responsibility of transporting their casualties to the nearest medical installation.

The MDS at Le Mariquet was to remain open for surgery.

[1] 'There is no doubt that houses, unless they have cellars, are unsuitable for RAPs, which should always be " dug in " when in the front line, as one direct hit on a house causes more casualties than one in a dugout or trench.' (Comment of the CO of 225th (Parachute) Field Ambulance, referring to this event.)
[2] The Belgian Brigade.

Captain Johnson from 224th (Parachute) Field Ambulance with a jeep and three ambulance cars were attached to the 3rd Brigade.

Transport presented a difficult problem and there was an acute shortage of RAMC personnel. By the time each battalion had been made up to fourteen stretcher-bearers the unit was left with sixty ORs to form an ADS and at least two CCPs. These CCPs were established by No 4 Section at Le Mesnil, commanded by Captain J. M. G. Wilson, and another by Captain MacPhearson with No 2 Surgical Team in a battle-scarred pottery; each CCP being allotted a jeep, a two-seater ambulance car, and two four-seater ambulance cars, in which they were to carry all equipment and personnel.

By nine o'clock in the morning of 17th August it was evident that the Germans had withdrawn their line facing the Divisional Sector and had evacuated the coastal area back to Troarn. All the roads had been hastily obstructed by felling of trees, and some mines had been laid along the verges. None of this, however, held up the forward move and no contact was made with the enemy until reaching the line of the River Dives where all bridges had been blown and the Germans were covering the crossings.

Throughout the advance the CO was with the Commanders of the 3rd Parachute and 1st SS Brigades, and the MDS was at four hours' notice to move. At four o'clock in the afternoon the order was given for the CCP at Le Mariquet to move to Bassenville, east of the river, in support of the 3rd Parachute Brigade, then in the area of St Samson-Goustrainville, the 1st SS Brigade around Robbehomme, and the 4th in the area of Troarn. The only available crossing over the Dives was by a jeep ferry at Bures. Seeking the ferry the CO made a reconnaissance of a bridge east of Bavent, where he made contact with an NCO and a Sapper from No 6 Commando, and together they had a brief encounter with a party of Germans covering the bridge, which had been demolished.

Captain Johnson's CCP crossed the river at Bures, and at midnight opened up again at Bassenville. The civilian population had completely evacuated the village, and the majority of farms and houses were intact.

Early the next day Captain Wilson's Section was moved up from Le Mesnil where they had an RV with Lieutenant MacPhearson's Surgical Team, and together they established an ADS, where they were reinforced by Captain Cunningham and twenty ORs from the 224th (Parachute) Field Ambulance.

A few casualties were admitted to the ADS during the night for the 3rd Parachute Brigade launched their attack at 11 o'clock, there was severe fighting in the early hours of the morning, but by 4 am all objectives had been captured and the CO went forward with the Brigade Commander to contact the advanced unit, the 9th Parachute Battalion. They made their way through the half light and morning mist, through country still full of enemy posts and patrols. They came upon the 9th Battalion under heavy mortar fire at a railway station, and there were a considerable number of casualties. The Battalion MO and the RAP had been left behind at Goustrainville, and the CO and Company Commanders were all calling up medical transport and organising evacuation which caused a somewhat difficult situation which took some time to reorganise.

From five o'clock in the morning of 19th August casualties poured into the ADS, and in the ensuing thirty-six hours 310 wounded were admitted. There was no question that the ADS was inadequate and understaffed. The three MOs [1] and all ranks of the Field Ambulance worked incessantly, often under shell-fire from which there was but little protection, and there was no labour available for digging in.

During the afternoon Captain Tibbs, the RMO of the 13th Parachute Battalion, was wounded by a sniper during a gallant attempt to bring in two wounded men hit during the assault on Putot en Auge, and Captain Urquhart was sent up to take over. By the early hours of the next morning he too had been wounded whilst out searching the ground for casualties who were still lying where they fell during the

[1] Captain J. M. G. Wilson, Captain Cunningham, and Lieutenant MacPhearson.

attack on the previous afternoon. Lieutenant Atkinson went forward to take his place as RMO to the 13th Battalion.

During the battle evacuation of wounded from forward RAPs was by hand carriage back to a CP from which two jeeps and two ambulance cars were operated by Lieutenant Hill, Staff-Sergeant Hodgson and eight ORs.

Later in the afternoon orders were sent to the MDS to move up to the area of Butte de Bois L'Abbe. In an effort to overcome the difficulties of the move, which was a matter of urgency, Major Hewlings organised the MDS into two echelons, A and B, the latter being the QMs echelon with all the heavier stores. The MDS went forward and was established at Goustrainville.

During that evening the 5th Parachute Brigade was ordered to capture Dozoule. The attack was delivered at one o'clock in the morning and the village cleared of the enemy, but, by dawn the next day, it had been heavily shelled by both sides, rubble and burning buildings in the main street were causing delays, so it was decided to evacuate Dozoule, and both the 3rd and 5th Parachute Brigades advanced on Pont L'Eveque. Captain Holland, ADC, remained on the outskirts of Dozoule with a CP, and at seven o'clock in the evening an ADS was set up in the ruined village by 224th (Parachute) Field Ambulance. Throughout the day casualties had been passed back to the MDS at Goustrainville, where 479 cases were admitted.

In the early hours of 21st August the CO and Captain Holland went forward to select a site for an ADS west of Pont L'Eveque. They decided upon the Chateaux de Reux, which had been used by the Germans as a formation HQ, but on joining up with the 5th Parachute Brigade they heard of the existence of a German hospital at Mont Gassard. This proved to be a chateau used as a permanent hospital. It was clearly marked with the Geneva Cross and there were 350 beds.

It had been evacuated forty-eight hours before, the Germans leaving behind six British and six German wounded in the care of a British RAMC orderly and four Wehrmacht medical orderlies. The hospital was in good order, all the wounded spoke well of the treatment they had received. The Germans had left a message to the effect that they would respect the hospital and requested that no fighting troops should be placed within a thousand yards of the chateau.

The CO sent Captain Holland back straight away to bring up the ADS and the CO went off to make contact with the 13th Parachute Battalion in Pont L'Eveque, which was under heavy shell-fire. The bridge had been demolished, houses on either side were ablaze, the RMO was running his RAP in a small hospital and was treating casualties from the attacks being launched to force the crossing.

The CO went on to the 12th Parachute Battalion, which was also experiencing stiff opposition, and many men were lost in the attack across the river. It was during this time that Private Shelly, one of the RAMC orderlies, ' volunteered to cross 200 yards of open ground to reach wounded men to alleviate their sufferings. This he did with great gallantry '.[1]

By the early afternoon an MDS had been opened up in the captured hospital. None of the Corps medical units had, at that time, been moved up on the Divisional maintenance route—the nearest RAMC unit was then thirty-five miles from the MDS. Evacuation of casualties was still to Deliverande, some five and a half hours' journey by car, which entailed three river crossings. In view of this long turn round of ambulance cars the CO instructed the Surgical Teams to carry out major surgery as necessary.

There was severe fighting along the River Touques throughout 23rd August. Pont L'Eveque was ablaze, the Germans having planted incendiaries in the houses when they withdrew, and then subjected the town to heavy shell-fire. The troops in the open in the forward area were heavily mortared and over a hundred casualties were received at the MDS in the first twenty-four hours.

During the day arrangements were made for 1st Corps to take over the hospital, and No 20 FDS and a surgical team moved in. Casualties requiring operations, it was ordered,

[1] 'The Red Beret' by Hilary St George Saunders. (Michael Joseph, Ltd.) (1950.)

were to remain at the hospital for twenty hours until the arrival of a CCS at Lisieux.

In the evening the CO was called to a conference with the Commander of the 4th SS Brigade, who had been ordered to put in a brigade attack involving an assault crossing of the river at Piere Fitte, whilst the 1st SS Brigade were to cross the river higher up and secure the high ground around St Julien. At one o'clock in the morning the attack was called off, but at first light the enemy pulled out from the Pont L'Eveque area and the 7th Parachute Battalion set off in pursuit. No vehicles could cross the bridges, so a Car Collecting Point was set up in the nearby house of a local doctor. Evacuation of casualties to this house was by hand carriage, from there by ambulance car to the east bank of the river. Here the wounded were ferried across to another CCP. Some twenty-five wounded were evacuated in this manner until the Sappers had constructed a class 40 bridge over the river at Touques.

The battle raged for the next two days, and by dawn on 27th August there were no enemy left west of the River Risle. The 6th Airborne Division had successfully completed all its tasks, and the formation was withdrawn into 21st Army Group's reserve. At four o'clock in the afternoon of the previous day the 225th (Parachute) Field Ambulance had received orders to move to the rest area at Trouville, which was reached two hours later.

From 1st to 16th August the 195th (Air Landing) Field Ambulance had remained in the Le Mesnil area. At nine-thirty in the evening of the 16th the code word ' Paddle ' was received, and at half-past ten the next day the MDS moved to the Chateau de Nuxon at Le Plein. No 2 Section commanded by Captain West was attached to the 2nd Battalion Oxford and Buckinghamshire Light Infantry, and opened an ADS at Merville at five o'clock in the evening. No 3 Section under command of Captain Shaw was first attached to the 12th Battalion The Devonshire Regiment, but was transferred to the 1st Battalion Royal Ulster Rifles at four o'clock in the afternoon. By first light on the 18th the forward platoons of the RUR, having advanced up the coastal road, were on the outskirts of Cabourg, but were pinned down by machine-gun and shell-fire from the enemy positions across the River Dives.

The coast road had been cratered by the German Pioneers in three places at one-mile intervals. The diversions round the craters were over loose sand which only permitted, and then with difficulty, the passage of empty jeeps. Evacuation of casualties was therefore arranged by jeeps running between each crater, the wounded being carried round each crater to the next jeep on the other side, and this arrangement continued until nine o'clock in the evening when proper by-passes round the craters, built during the day, permitted a direct run through from the RAP to the ADS; and about the same time the road from Le Plein to Salenelles *via* Merville was clear of mines and four stretcher ambulance cars were put into use.

The next day No 3 Section rejoined the Unit HQ but No 2 Section's ADS remained open to receive the casualties from the 1st RUR [1] and the 12th Devons.[2] This ADS closed on 20th August, having passed over seventy wounded through the DS.

That night Captain Prentice and twenty ORs were detached to the 1st SS Brigade to accompany them in their infiltration during the night into the higher ground west of the River Dives. This detachment also dealt with some seventy casualties up to eight o'clock on the 21st, some of which they had had to hold for up to fifteen hours.

The MDS at Le Plein was closed on that day, spending the night 'on wheels', standing by in a harbour area ready to move. They crossed the River Dives the next day and opened up an MDS at three o'clock in the afternoon in the Chateau de Villers on the line of the Division's forward route to the River Touques. No 3 Section again went forward with the RUR and set up an ADS at Deauville in a German

---

[1] The RMO of the 1st Battalion The Royal Ulster Rifles was Captain D. Rees, RAMC.

[2] The RMO of The 12th Battalion The Devonshire Regiment was Captain J. S. Binning, RAMC.

hospital evacuated by the enemy. Moving the next day the Section was engaged in the evacuation of wounded from the patrols of the RUR, then operating in the area of Cour Carrel au Cerf, across the River Touques.

On 24th August the whole of the 6th Air Landing Brigade advanced across the Touques and two RAMC sections went with them on foot to bring back wounded in stretchers down to the river bank, where they were ferried across to two Casualty Points on the west bank. The MDS was closed that evening and further casualties were redirected to the Light Field Ambulance of the Belgian Brigade Group at Villiers-sur-mer.[1] The MDS divided for the move, a marching party moved through Touques and the vehicles went *via* Pont L'Eveque, the unit concentrating to open up at St Gatien at nine o'clock.

The following day a casualty post was opened up at Honfleur to evacuate wounded from the 12th Devons, and in the evening Captain Shaw with No 3 Section rejoined the Oxford and Buckinghamshire Light Infantry near Malhortie with orders to go forward with the Royal Ulster Rifles when they moved against Berville.

By 26th August the 6th Air Landing Brigade had cleared the enemy from the whole of the sector from Berville-Foubec up to the Rivers Seine and Risle. In the late afternoon of that day the MDS moved again, re-opening some three hours later in the Brigade area at the Manor de la Pommeraye. On the 28th only fifteen wounded were admitted, these casualties resulting from the shelling of the forward troops in the Foubec area, and that evening the MDS was finally closed.

Between 1st and 16th August 397 casualties had been handled by the 195th (Air Landing) Field Ambulance; 149 were admitted between the 17th and 21st during the advance to the River Dives; a further seventy-three between the 22nd and 24th during the attack on the River Touques, and for the attack on the Rivers Seine and Risle between the

---

[1] During the advance an NCO and a small party of men of the 195th Field Ambulance rescued three badly injured Belgians from a burning tank, filled with explosives. For this gallant action the Corporal was awarded the George Medal and three privates received Belgian decorations.

25th and 28th 110 casualties were treated, and nineteen surgical operations performed.

On 29th August the ADMS held a conference at which the withdrawal of the Division from Normandy was announced, and preparations commenced for the return of the formation to England. Thirty-three further casualties were admitted to the 224th Field Ambulance MDS up to 31st August and on the following day all ambulance cars were returned to the MAC, all equipment, ordnance and medical stores, other than certain specialist airborne equipment was handed into the Corps dumps, and the advance parties of the Divisional Field Ambulances left for England.

September the 2nd was marked by a grand tea party, at which 224th Field Ambulance entertained some seventy children from the area, and on the following day a Thanksgiving Service was conducted, on this National Day of Prayer, by the Reverend A. L. Beckingham, Chaplain to the Forces.

Moving down to the beachhead Transit Camp on 4th September the three Field Ambulances of the 6th Airborne Division embarked from the Mulberry Harbour in Tank Landing Craft (LCTs) to be ferried out to HMS *Invicta* lying off Arromanches.

Sailing at nine-thirty on 6th September the *Invicta* anchored off Calshot Castle that evening, disembarking the units at Southampton the following morning. Welcomed by the Band of the Hampshire Regiment [1] and each man given a bag of food and twenty cigarettes, the units entrained for Bulford and they were back in Gordon Barracks late that afternoon.

During the seventy-seven days that the 6th Airborne Division had been actively engaged in the assault and subsequent operations in Normandy a total of 6,722 casualties had been admitted to the Field Ambulances of the Division [2]

[1] The Regiment was granted the title 'Royal' in November 1946.
[2] 293 officers and 4,557 ORs of the 6th Airborne Division were treated, 101 officers and 1,781 ORs of other formations. 4 officers and 38 ORs of the Royal Netherlands Brigade, 3 German officers and 284 German ORs, and 62 French civilians.

and 397 operations had been performed.[1] The Divisional medical units 224th (Parachute) Field Ambulance; 225th (Parachute) Field Ambulance; 195th (Air Landing) Field Ambulance; and RAMC personnel attached to the Battalions, had themselves sustained casualties of thirteen RAMC officers and 182 RAMC ORs, of which three officers and twenty-eight ORs had been killed; and of attached personnel—Royal Army Service Corps (Drivers), Army Catering Corps, Army Physical Training Corps, and Royal Army Chaplains Department—there had been a total of seventeen casualties.

In step with the Normandy landings a considerable number of SAS troops were dropped into France well south of the beachhead to carry out sabotage missions to delay the movement of German reserves. In a number of cases the SAS parachute troops made contact with the 'Maquis' (the French resistance movement) and operated together on the German lines of communication. During operation 'Houndsworth', June-August, the 1st and 2nd SAS Parachute Battalions were engaged and RAMC personnel accompanied them (Lieutenant M. McReady, RMO, 1st Battalion; Captain Miln, RMO, 2nd Battalion, and Captain Patterson).

[1] Multiple penetrating wounds 16
Single penetrating wounds 22
Simple fractures 11
Compound fractures 108
Penetrating wounds of abdomen 63
Acute appendicitis 1
Penetrating wounds of brain 6
Facio maxillary 8
Wounds, large vessels 4
Amputations 72
Burns 1
Extraction of bullets 1
Reduction of dislocations 1
Supra pubic cystotomy 2
Flesh wounds, including arterial haemorrhage 39
Intra thoracic wounds 6
Penetrating joint wounds 7
Spine 4
Miscellaneous wounds 4

397

Many were the lessons learned from the operations in Normandy, and a number of recommendations were made in consequence of the experience gained.

It was considered that the establishment of the Surgical Teams was adequate except that it was advocated that a graded anaesthetist should work with each surgeon as many of the cases presented technical difficulties beyond the scope of the Dental Officer or a General Duties Medical Officer.

It was also suggested that the surgical personnel and equipment should be detached from the Field Ambulance to constitute FSUs as it was considered desirable to establish a surgical centre as soon as possible, pooling the surgical resources and establishing post-operative facilities at the most conveniently sited Field Ambulance. Furthermore, greater flexibility and economy of manpower would be achieved if Surgical Teams could be attached and detached from medical units as the tactical situation demanded. Finally one observation was that once contact with the main force was established there was no necessity for more than two surgeons in the Divisional area.

Quite apart from experience in action resulting in official recommendations concerning organisation and equipment, the medical units of the 6th Airborne Division had gained invaluable personal experience in Normandy, and this was taken into consideration in their training on their return to England, and well fitted them for the work that they had before them.

CHAPTER IX

'NOT LEAST IN THE CRUSADE'

THE AIRBORNE MEDICAL SERVICES AT ARNHEM

THE object of the airborne operations in Holland was the capture and holding of the crossings of the rivers and canals on the main axis of the advance of the Second Army from Eindhoven to Arnhem.

The operation was carried out, under the orders of First Allied Airborne Army, by the 1st British Airborne Corps, which was composed of the 1st British Airborne Division; the 82nd and 101st (US) Airborne Divisions; and the 1st Polish Parachute Brigade.

The medical organisation of the 1st British Airborne Division was comprised of two Parachute Field Ambulances —the 16th and 133rd—each with two surgical teams; one Air Landing Field Ambulance, the 181st, also with two surgical teams; and with medical detachments with each battalion. The general medical plan was that casualties were to be held and treated in Divisional areas until such time as contact was made with the medical units of the supporting ground force.

Each medical unit carried with it, in the initial lift, sufficient stores to deal with the estimated number of casualties for a minimum of forty-eight hours and all gliders carried two airborne stretchers and a supply of blankets.

The plan for the maintenance of the medical units was that medical supplies were to be pre-packed for a daily maintenance supply for five days by parachute drops and later a detachment of an Advanced Medical Stores Depot was to be flown in, in eight Dakota aircraft, loaded with medical stores,[1] additional medical supplies being held available at base supply aerodromes to meet demands. The British Airborne Medical Services destined to participate in the airborne operation comprised a total of forty-seven officers and 545 ORs, thirty officers and 348 of whom were serving with the 16th and 133rd (Parachute) Field Ambulances and the 181st (Air Landing) Field Ambulance.[2] The ADMS had one officer and seven NCOs and men on his staff, whilst the remainder were serving with units.[3]

In addition, each RAMC unit had a ' seaborne tail '.[4] This comprised the bulk of the unit transport, including seven ambulances for each unit, all the available drivers, and five days' supplies of medical and ordnance stores and equipment. (These stores being in addition to one month's Medical Inspection (MI) room stores in the ' seaborne ' tails of the battalions.)

It was planned that the Field Ambulances should, in the opening stages of the operation, be under command of the Brigades.[5] They were to be responsible for clearing their own DZs and evacuation of early casualties to the DSs in the

[1] It was intended that this Medical Stores Depot should be flown in to Deelen Airfield to the north of Arnhem, but due to the situation which developed it was flown in on 26th September (D + 9) to the Ood Keeut Airfield, south of Grave.

	Officers	ORs
[2] 16th (Parachute) Field Ambulance, RAMC	10	125
133rd (Parachute) Field Ambulance, RAMC	10	119
181st (Air Landing) Field Ambulance, RAMC	10	104
Reserve Section (181st Field Ambulance)	1	23
[3] Six Parachute Battalions (1st, 2nd, 3rd, 10th, 11th, and 156th Battalions The Parachute Regiment) (each with a Medical Officer and eighteen ORs, RAMC)	6	108
Two Parachute Brigade HQs (1st and 4th Parachute Brigades) (each with one officer and three ORs, RAMC)	2	6
Three Air Landing Battalions (1st Battalion The Border Regiment, 2nd Battalion The South Staffordshire Regiment, and 7th Battalion The King's Own Scottish Borderers) (each with one officer and thirteen ORs, RAMC)	3	39
21st Independent Parachute Company	–	4
1st Airborne Reconnaissance Squadron	1	4
HQ Royal Artillery	1	2
1st Airborne Light Regiment Royal Artillery	1	4

[4] Under the command of Major Richards, DADH of the Division, assisted by Captain Willard and Captain (QM) J. Tiernan.

[5] 1st and 4th Parachute Brigades and 1st Air Landing Brigade Group.

Landing and Dropping areas. It was the task of the 181st (Air Landing) Field Ambulance to establish for the treatment and care of the early casualties a temporary DS in the vicinity of Wolfhezen, and it would then move, when the situation stabilised, into the area of the Municipal Hospital in Arnhem, for it was intended that the Division should occupy the town at an early stage of the operation.

It was also planned that the other two Field Ambulances should function in, or at least adjacent to, two other Dutch hospitals. The St Elizabeth Hospital was allotted to the 16th (Parachute) Field Ambulance, whilst the 133rd would operate in the hospital, and other adjoining buildings, located in the Brigade area.

As soon as the Division's medical units were so established they would revert to the control of the ADMS. Dressing Stations would be opened in rotation and plans made to commence the evacuation of casualties as soon as possible by both road and air.

The reserve section, composed of one officer and twenty-three ORs of the 181st (Air Landing) Field Ambulance, was from the outset to be under the direct control of the ADMS of the Division [1] and would be available, ready to open and operate a Casualty Air Evacuation Centre (CAEC), as soon as the airfield at Deelen had been seized and was fully functional.

Two days prior to the launching of the operation the ADMS discussed the Brigade medical plans with the SMOs; they were simple and practical and followed the routines practised on exercises.

It was between ten and eleven o'clock on the morning of Sunday, 17th September, that the 1st Parachute Brigade,[2] with the 16th (Parachute) Field Ambulance under command, emplaned at airfields in Lincolnshire, whilst the 181st (Air Landing) Field Ambulance under command of the 1st Air Landing Brigade,[3] went aboard their gliders at Oxfordshire

[1] Colonel (now Brigadier) G. M. Warrack, DSO, OBE, TD.
[2] 1st, 2nd, and 3rd Battalions The Parachute Regiment.
[3] 1st Battalion Border Regiment, 2nd Battalion South Staffordshire Regiment, 7th Battalion King's Own Scottish Borderers.

airfields. The weather was good and the flight across the North Sea from the quiet British countryside over the flat Netherlands was uneventful.

The air landings and the parachute drop took place between a quarter-past one and two o'clock—the air landing preceding the parachute drop by nearly an hour—by which time all section commanders detached by the SMOs to battalions had reported their safe arrival.

By four o'clock in the afternoon 181st (Air Landing) Field Ambulance were established according to plan in the area of Wolfhezen, about two and a half miles north-west of Oosterbeek and the same distance north of the Lower Rhine. A DS was opened up in four small houses near the railway line from Arnhem to Utrecht by half-past four in the afternoon, and the first operation was performed an hour later, and by the evening some sixty casualties had been admitted and one of the surgical teams was fully functioning. Eight operations were performed during the night.

The 16th (Parachute) Field Ambulance dropped with the 1st Parachute Brigade successfully and intact, just north of Heelsum, two miles north of the river and about four and a half miles west of Arnhem. The unit moved straight through Oosterbeek and the western outskirts of Arnhem into the St Elizabeth Hospital, where casualties were already awaiting them. By ten o'clock that evening the unit surgical team started to operate under ideal conditions.

So it was that by nightfall of 17th September the medical plan had gone without a hitch. There had been virtually no opposition from the enemy during the flight or the actual landing and casualties in the Division had been considerably lighter than had been anticipated.

At seven o'clock on the morning of Monday, 18th September, the Divisional HQ, which had been dug-in for the night on the outskirts of the LZ, moved in towards Arnhem and Lieutenant Randall, the RMO attached to HQRA, established a RAP for Divisional HQ near their temporary HQ on the Waginen-Arnhem road and reported for duty to the ADMS. Shortly after, Colonel Warrack went out to the DS at Wolfhezen where everything was running smoothly, although a formation of German fighter aircraft had just swept the area machine-gunning a number of the positions, leaving behind a trail of wounded.

Casualties were, however, increasing in numbers. By eight o'clock there were 180 patients at the DS, which was then moved across the railway line to better accommodation in a former Dutch mental hospital which had housed a unit of the German Women's Services. Going on to Jonkershoeve the ADMS visited the RAP of the 1st Battalion The Border Regiment, which was located in the middle of the Dropping and Landing Zones for the second air-lift. The RAP was working under considerable pressure, it was under fire from small-arms and mortars and casualties from the landing of the second lift were pouring in. The enemy had vigorously opposed this landing and Captain J. Graham Jones, the RMO, his orderlies and his driver were working without respite, unperturbed by the constant fire in their direction, and the explosions around the RAP. Casualties were detained for the minimum period and they were being evacuated to the DS by jeep.

Just after five o'clock in the afternoon the DADMS [1] reported to Divisional HQ with the rest of the ADMS staff; and, shortly after, the Divisional Commander issued orders for the Air Landing and 4th Parachute Brigades, together with all Divisional troops, to concentrate for the night nearer to Arnhem. This move involved a change of location for the 181st Field Ambulance, for Wolfhezen would then be outside the perimeter. The CO [2] drove into Divisional HQ to discuss the move with Colonel Warrack. Together they went off to reconnoitre the area of Oosterbeek to select a suitable site. The reconnaissance was, however, somewhat hampered by spasmodic bursts of fire arising from minor engagements in the locality, and in particular from the houses in the vicinity of the selected site, the Hotel Schoonhord. This was a large building situated some 300 yards from the position selected for Divisional HQ, on the main road into the town. The Hotel, however, was only selected as a temporary loca-

[1] Major J. E. Miller, MC, RAMC.
[2] Lieut.-Colonel A. Marrable, RAMC.

tion, for it was still intended that as soon as the Division moved into Arnhem the 181st Field Ambulance would, as originally planned, occupy the Municipal Hospital.

The situation that developed, however, was such that this move never took place and, in consequence, the Hotel Schoonhord subsequently became the main 'hospital' building in the area, and as such, in its very central position, seriously interfered with the battle.

By six o'clock in the evening Lieut.-Colonel Marrable, CO of the 181st (Air Landing) Field Ambulance, had driven back to Wolfhezen where he found the DS to be holding over 150 casualties, and, in consequence, it had moved into a larger building near the original position of the ADS. Explaining the position to his Second-in-Command, Major S. M. Frazer, Colonel Marrable left him to organise the move, which he did, evacuating the wounded in jeeps and in requisitioned vehicles. Returning to Oosterbeek Colonel Marrable set about the organisation of the new ADS. Looking around the Hotel Schoonhord for additional accommodation he discovered a nursing home about 200 yards from another nearby hotel, the Taffelberg, and here he decided to install his surgical teams.

About eight o'clock Colonel Warrack went across to Wolfhezen where he found that No 5 (the Reserve) Section of the 181st (Air Landing) Field Ambulance, under the command of Captain Doyle, had arrived intact. He was instructed to remain at Wolfhezen for the night with those casualties that were not transportable and to move to Oosterbeek in the morning. Half an hour later some of the NCOs and men of the 133rd (Parachute) Field Ambulance reported to the ADMS. The unit had met with considerable opposition on landing and had dropped, scattered, over a wide area. More men of the unit came into Wolfhezen as the evening wore on and finally the CO [1] arrived, reporting that his Brigade (the 4th) were remaining in the area for the night, so he was put in command of what remained of that DS.

The close of the second day thereby found the ADMS at Divisional HQ at Hartestein; the 133rd (Parachute) Field

[1] Lieut.-Colonel W. C. Alford, OBE, RAMC.

Ambulance, still concentrating following their landing, at Wolfhezen, with the Reserve Section, the 181st (Air Landing) Field Ambulance operating the DS at the Hotel Schoonhord at Oosterbeek. Part of the 16th (Parachute) Field Ambulance, although captured, was still functioning at the St Elizabeth Hospital at Arnhem.

The HQ of 16th (Parachute) Field Ambulance, commanded by Lieut.-Colonel E. Townsend, MC, together with No 2 Section, had taken off, on the morning of Sunday, 17th September, from Barkston Heath Airfield, together with units of the 1st Parachute Brigade, and had floated down in their parachutes, seven miles west of Arnhem without incident at two-fifteen in the afternoon. All the RAMC personnel, together with all the equipment and stores except one surgical pack, assembled at their rendezvous, and moved forward with the Brigade HQ towards Arnhem, the equipment being carried on trollies pulled by German prisoners sent for this work by the Field Security Section. By eleven-thirty that night the Field Ambulance had reached the St Elizabeth Hospital which was situated in the western part of Arnhem, not far from the north bank of the Rhine, off the main road leading from the west into the centre of the town.

A few casualties from the Rhine bridge area had already been brought into the hospital by Captain Tobin, RAMC, and arrangements were immediately made with the Dutch civilian hospital staff to take over accommodation,[1] which it was agreed would be a reception area, two operating theatres, one large and several smaller wards, every facility being extended by the helpful Dutch doctors and nurses. During the night a few more casualties arrived, together with a number of Germans who were taken over by the Dutch, who also undertook to receive and treat any civilian wounded.

At eight o'clock on the Monday morning, after a heavy exchange of fire in the neighbourhood, German troops were seen moving forward past the hospital, which was then recaptured.

After some argument with the Wehrmacht they agreed

[1] The hospital had a capacity of 300 beds.

that the two surgical teams—comprising the two surgeons, two anaesthetists, a nursing sergeant orderly and fourteen ORs [1]—could remain at work in the hospital, but the CO, all other officers and other ranks were not permitted to stay and were marched away as prisoners of war. Fighting was continuing around the hospital area and at about eight o'clock in the evening an officer of the Schutzstaffel (Nazi Blackshirts) (SS) marched up with a body of troops with the object of taking all the British away. Grenades, it was alleged, had been thrown from the hospital. With the help of a Dutch Red Cross interpreter, however, the situation was saved, and the surgical teams were left to carry on, but it was insisted upon that they should give their parole, which was given on condition that it applied only to the period of the battle.

The SS troops occupied the hospital, and two guards were even placed at the door of the operating theatre, but they soon left after Captain Lipmann Kessel performed a particularly unpleasant amputation in front of them.

Dawn of Tuesday, 19th September, found the greater part of the 133rd (Parachute) Field Ambulance concentrated at Wolfhezen. Both surgical teams had reported in during the night but there were still three officers,[2] and a number of NCOs and men missing. They had been 'lost' during the scattered drop the previous day and in the confused and hard fighting in which the 4th Parachute Brigade had become involved on landing.

It was planned that the Brigade would move into Arnhem along the route north of the main railway line. Colonel Alford was still under command of the 4th Brigade and decided that he would keep the Wolfhezen DS open during the move, manned by the 133rd (Parachute) Field Ambu-

---

[1] Major C. J. Longland ; Captains D. H. Ridler, MC, and A. W. Lipmann Kessel ; Lieutenant P. Allenby ; Sergeant Tennucci ; Corporals E. J. M. Thompson and D. Meakin ; Lance-Corporal J. G. Wallace ; and Privates W. B. Corris, J. H. Butcher, J. Gaskell, J. H. Hill, E. F. Horton, G. Myers, J. A. Maidens, E. F. Mumford, G. Pleasance, J. Reid, and W. Roberts.

[2] The Second-in-Command, Major T. R. B. Courtney and Captains Cliff and Redman.

lance, and would in turn move into the town as soon as it was possible and practicable. At half-past eight the Reserve Section of the 181st (Air Landing) Field Ambulance left Wolfhezen for Oosterbeek with all the remaining casualties which could be moved.

Meanwhile the fighting in Arnhem was becoming confused and heavy. The GOC on returning from the scenes of house-to-house fighting to Divisional HQ told Colonel Warrack that 16th Field Ambulance was hard at work in the St Elizabeth Hospital and that it might be possible to make contact with them by phone. This was eventually achieved at about ten-thirty by the use of a civilian line from the house of a Dutch doctor. The telephone was answered by the Dental Officer of the 16th (Parachute) Field Ambulance,[1] who told the ADMS that he was standing in a telephone booth by the main entrance to the hospital and that it was rather difficult to hear! This, it would appear, was one of the understatements of the day, for there was, in fact, a pitched battle going on in and around the hospital grounds, the conversation between the ADMS and Captain Ridler being punctuated by the crash of shell-fire, the staccato rattle of light automatics, and the crack of an SP gun from a position just outside the hospital entrance. Despite the difficulties, Captain Ridler was able to give the ADMS a good picture of the position, he said he had been left with the surgical teams, about twenty all ranks, to deal with almost a hundred casualties, the majority of whom needed urgent treatment.

The telephone conversation ended with a particularly loud explosion being transmitted over the line and an assurance from Captain Ridler that " the detachment was in good heart " and that, " comparatively speaking, all was well ! "

On Tuesday, 19th September, the 1st Parachute Brigade had launched an attack towards the Rhine bridge. Good progress was made towards the centre of Arnhem, and once again the hospital was in the Brigade area, the German withdrawal under pressure being quickly followed up by the advancing Parachute Battalion, which sent in their wounded.

The Germans made determined efforts, however, to oust

---

[1] Captain D. Ridler, MC, Army Dental Corps.

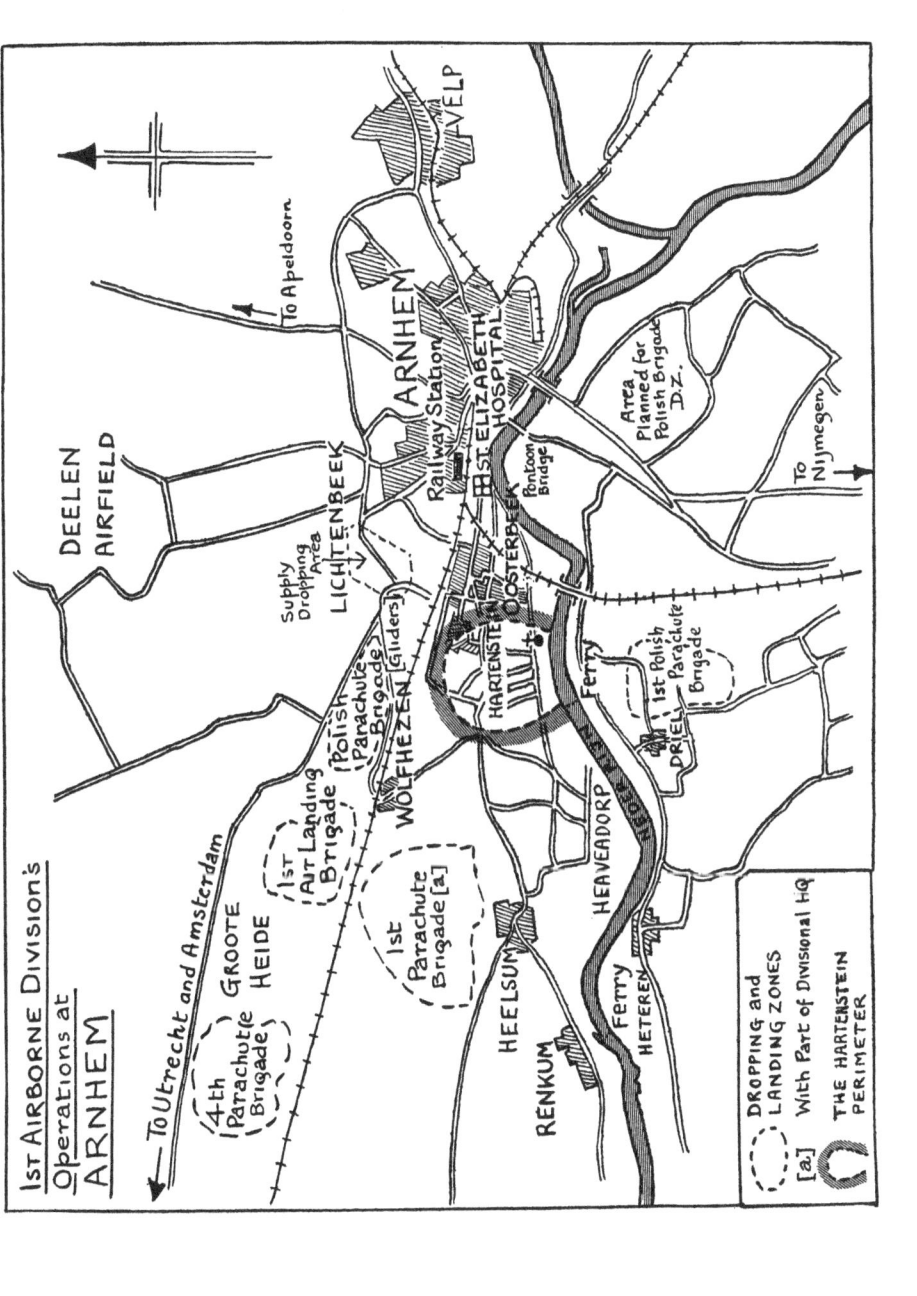

the parachutists from this area, and the hospital became the centre of some heavy fighting, and sustained a number of hits from mortar fire and shells from SP guns. Several bursts of small-arms fire went through the windows. Patrols of both sides passed through the ground floor of the hospital, some in close contact, and bursts from brens and spandaus were even fired along the corridors.

As soon as the fighting had started there was a constant flow of casualties into the hospital and several further casualties resulted from flying broken glass and the exchange of fire in the building. Prompt action by Sergeant Tennucci, the nursing orderly sergeant, however, prevented further casualties by his moving of all the patients into the corridors. Some of the civilian cases who had been in the hospital at the outset were killed, and except for those on essential duties the civilian staff had been sent to cover in the cellars. The fighting died down towards the close of the day, for the ground gained in the morning by the 1st Parachute Brigade had to be given up, and from then onwards the hospital was isolated from the main Divisional area around Oosterbeek and the force holding the northern approaches to the Rhine bridge, and there was no communications with either.

Before the hospital was cut off, two medical officers and several RAMC ORs managed to reach the building and they were taken on to the ' staff '.

The situation at Oosterbeek worsened during the morning of 19th September. Casualties were coming into the Hotel Schoonhord at such a rate that it became impossible to accommodate them. More buildings were taken over as annexes to the MDS, one big house on the opposite side of the main road and another in a school about a hundred yards away, where Captain Doyle and the Reserve Section of 181st (Air Landing) Field Ambulance were running a secondary DS for the lightly wounded, which by eleven o'clock totalled some 300. Fortunately the school provided adequate cover, and there were ample stretchers and medical supplies. The SMO [1] had called in all the commanders from the sections on detachment and in consequence there was quite a large

[1] Lieut.-Colonel A. T. Marrable.

medical staff to compete with the constant stream of casualties. The staff was further increased by the arrival of Corporal Cooling with the glider-borne element of the 16th (Parachute) Field Ambulance, which had been unable to link-up with their own unit. The medical supplies they had kept with them were taken over by the DS and the Corporal was sent to the building across the main road, where he remained as NCO in charge throughout the battle.

Throughout the day, under fire, amid the constant rattle of small-arms, the medical organisation worked to full capacity as the casualties came in ; unconscious men carried on jeeps, their camouflaged smocks stained with great smudges of dark blood ; still, white-faced bodies lying on the stretchers ; and the limping but inevitably cheery walking wounded.

At seven-thirty in the evening the GOC, accompanied by Colonel Warrack, visited the DS and its annexes. The sight of General Urquhart's burly figure making his way around the ' wards ' had a great effect on the morale of the wounded, who were in good spirits. In response to the General's question to one young heavily bandaged private of The South Staffordshires as to how he felt, the reply was typical of the attitude of the men—" I'm OK, sir," said he, heaving himself on to his elbow, " but they got me pretty quick wiv a bloody mortar and I'd only 'ad time to get a couple of the bastards ". " Just my luck, sir," added a Corporal on the next stretcher, pointing to his bandaged foot, " it's a bit 'ard getting knocked out in the first 'arf."

It was about this time that Lieut.-Colonel Alford, Captain Mawson, the RMO of the 11th Battalion The Parachute Regiment and some forty all ranks of the 133rd (Parachute) Field Ambulance came into Oosterbeek. The 4th Parachute Brigade's attempt to push through into Arnhem along the route to the north of the railway had been unsuccessful and they were, at that time, attempting to force their way along the main road. The medical ' reinforcements ' from the 133rd, which included the two surgical teams, were then absorbed into the combined divisional medical services in Oosterbeek, which then comprised the complete 181st (Air

Landing) Field Ambulance; part of the 133rd (Parachute) Field Ambulance; and the Reserve Section. With the exception of the surgical teams which were still functioning in the St Elizabeth Hospital the whole of the 16th (Parachute) Field Ambulance were prisoners of war.

The neighbourhood of the hospital in Arnhem was quieter during the next two days, although there was a constant stream of casualties. The reception of the wounded was handled by Captain Lawson of 133rd (Parachute) Field Ambulance, whilst the wards were supervised by Captain Keesey. The surgical teams continued to function under the leadership of Major C. J. Longland, with the assistance of Captain Lipmann Kessel. The responsibility for running the wards and giving treatment rested with Sergeant Tennucci, who was assisted by the Dutch nurses who, despite the conditions, had all volunteered to stay, and as the number of casualties grew it would have been almost impossible to have carried on without their help.

The main water supply and lighting had failed which added to the considerable difficulties of catering by the civilian staff, which contained a number of German nuns. Fortunately emergency lighting was available in the operating theatres, but the X-ray equipment could not be used owing to lack of current.

On 21st September the German ADMS arrived at the hospital and gave warning of the arrival of several hundred more wounded. Major Longland made a tour of the building with the Dutch Dr Siemens, and together they arranged for the movement of the civilian cases to a place of safety in a basement corridor, and earmarked further accommodation for the reception of the fresh casualties.

Early morning of Wednesday, 20th September, saw enemy activity building up in the vicinity of the Divisional HQ at Hartestein. At ten o'clock mortar fire was directed on the Oosterbeek area. This preceded an attack in force, and after some violent action clusters of men in field-grey uniforms came doubling through the drifting smoke up to the DS, which fell into the enemy's hands together with the adjoining houses where wounded were resting. The Germans were quick to tackle the situation, they hurried round shouting at and jostling all the walking wounded and medical orderlies into a straggling column to be hurried off along the route that they had fought their way into Oosterbeek. Practically all that was left of 133rd (Parachute) Field Ambulance were captured in this attack. Lieut.-Colonel Alford, together with his two surgeons, dental officer, and about ten ORs remained with the more seriously wounded, although their operating theatre, the surgery of a Dutch dentist, was deliberately wrecked by a small party of German infantrymen.

In the confusion following the arrival of the German troops, who began to crowd into the area sweating, truculent, small-arms at the ready, watching every move, the ADMS, Colonel Warrack, determined not to be captured at the outset, slashed off his tabs and rank badges, and joined in the work of the orderlies. In this rôle he was able to see the Germans take over, and watch how Lieut.-Colonel Marrable handled the difficult situation. He found the senior German officer and pointed out to him that he had some 400 wounded on his hands, including a number of Germans, insisting that he must keep the whole of his staff if the wounded were not to suffer. The German agreed to this, but went to some lengths to point out that everyone in the area was a prisoner, and underlined this by leaving a guard with Colonel Marrable, albeit a somewhat undersized and nervous youth, who fingered his rifle uneasily.

Shortly after this a minor counter-attack developed and a duel between a German SP field-gun and a six-pounder anti-tank gun took place in the DS area. The SP gun slewing round about twenty yards from the main DS put four shots through the building—although it was clearly marked with the Red Cross—it was fortunate that the 'wards' in which the round exploded had only two wounded in them at the time, and they were carried out between the shots, although one of the padres [1] and the Orderly Room Sergeant of 181st (Air Landing) Field Ambulance were both wounded by this fire.

The firing then slackened as the engagement tailed off.

[1] The Rev. B. J. Benson, CF(RC), who died of his wounds on 28th September.

German infantry doubled down the road, or hugged the walls of buildings as they moved towards the sound of the firing, which was then drawing away. A German officer clumped into the DS, went straight to German wounded demanding if they were receiving proper treatment. He was evidently assured that the treatment was the same for all, for he saluted meticulously and stalked out. Although indeed the standard of treatment was the same for all casualties, there was one case of an ardent Nazi youth, about twenty-five years of age, who was carried in with a shattered knee-joint, he was obviously in great pain, but refused any treatment, help, or morphia, for about four hours, when he finally broke down, shouting " Kamerad! Kamerad! " and allowed himself to be treated.

Mortaring of the area continued and several casualties were wounded again by mortar fragments. There were about 300 wounded in the hotel. As many as possible were kept on the ground floor, only the ' walking wounded ' were taken upstairs, for at this time there was great danger of the hotel being set alight—a building but fifty yards away was blazing furiously with a crackle and splutter as flames leapt through the blazing roof, and smoke and sparks blew across the DS.

By three o'clock in the afternoon the battle had died down and the firing had become desultory. At this time word got through from the two surgeons [1] of the 181st Field Ambulance in the Hotel Taffelberg—200 yards away—they were all right, were carrying on, and so far had not been overrun by the German infantry ; the same situation also obtained at the aid post operated by Captain Doyle in the school about a hundred yards away in a side road. These facts give a good indication of the outcome of street and house-to-house fighting in a built-up area where all troop movements are cautious and hampered and a ' line ' must be established at some point.

In the Hotel Schoonhord Lieut.-Colonel Marrable had organised minor treatment and resuscitation wards and an emergency operating theatre (his surgical team being in the Taffelberg) where he and his staff did a number of amputa-

[1] Major G. Rigby Jones, MC, and Captain James.

tions and other essential surgery. One young soldier, whose foot had been shattered, had the remains amputated at the ankle. The unit's amputation saws were, of course, with the surgical teams, and in consequence the tibia was eventually sawn through with an escape file produced by the DADMS which was cleaned and sterilised and worked very satisfactorily.

At eight o'clock in the evening Captain Doyle walked in from the school, he had come past several German posts and when challenged had answered " Arzt ! ".

Half an hour later the ADMS decided to return to Divisional HQ, the German guard being engaged in conversation while he got away. Here he found that the Assistant Adjutant and Quartermaster General (AA and QMG) had been acting for him and had sent casualties to an RAP in a house next door to that in which the Border Regiment RAP was operating.[1] The MO of the Recce Squadron [2] was in charge, assisted by Lieutenant Randall and the Senior Chaplain.[3]

At nightfall on 20th September the lay-out of the Division's medical services was the same as on the previous evening, although the main DS at the Hotel Schoonhord was in enemy hands and the only RAMC personnel still free were the two surgical teams of the 181st Field Ambulance in the Hotel Taffelberg [4] and the Reserve Section in the school. The RMOs and their staffs with the battalions were also free, except for those of the 1st Parachute Brigade, of whom nothing had been heard, except for an SOS from the bridge asking for ammunition and a surgical team.

During the night part of the 4th Parachute Brigade moved forward, passed the Hotel Schoonhord, and the MDS was back in the divisional perimeter, so it became possible to evacuate casualties from the outlying RAPs. The Light

[1] Captain J. Graham Jones, RAMC, RMO.
[2] Captain T. D. V. Swinscow, MC, RAMC.
[3] The Reverend A. W. Harlow, RAChD, the SCF.
[4] Here the surgical teams were assisted by a Dutch doctor, Dr Giesbert, and Mr Bauman, ' an electrician from Oosterbeek,' rearranged all the lights so that an efficient operating theatre could be established. He then made splints out of pieces of scrap iron or wood ' (vide ' The Red Beret ').

Regiment's RAP [1] had been moved when the building became untenable. Nearly 100 casualties were held there at the time and they were evacuated under almost impossible conditions. The area was under constant enemy fire but the walking wounded made their way through to the Hotel Schoonhord and some of the more seriously injured were taken through the smoking streets in a jeep. Casualties were, however, still arriving, and arrangements were made whereby the RMO, who held adequate medical supplies and food, could send wounded on to the MDS as soon as the situation eased.

The small DS in the school was also then being subjected to heavy cross-fire by small-arms and mortars. There were about 100 lightly wounded men at this DS, which was hit repeatedly. Captain Doyle was killed, together with five men, and a number of casualties were wounded again.

It was soon apparent that the building must be evacuated, and the Reserve Section of 181st Field Ambulance, together with all its wounded, moved down the lane and across some gardens to a large house to the rear of the Hotel Taffelberg, where a new DS was established by Captain Scott.

The medical services were, by this time, nearly all concentrated in this area. The office of the ADMS was moved to the 'Hospital Area'. A house opposite the Hotel Taffelberg was taken over as another DS and, in a very short space of time, ninety wounded were accommodated there. Casualties continued to pour in during the afternoon and yet another DS was opened up about 100 yards from the Taffelberg, staffed by Lieut.-Colonel Alford, the surgeons, a dental officer [2] and about twelve ORs of 133rd (Parachute) Field Ambulance.

By the evening there were well over 1,000 patients in the 'Hospital Area'. It was no longer possible to continue surgery in the Taffelberg DS. The ceiling of one 'operating theatre' had come crashing down, littering doctors and patients with plaster; the windows of the other 'theatre'

[1] RMO—Captain R. Martin, RAMC.
[2] Major P. Smith and Captain W. I. S. Hudleston, RAMC, and Captain A. S. Flockhart, Army Dental Corps.

had been blown in, and although Captain James carried on he was forced to cease operations soon after five o'clock, when the second ceiling collapsed. By this time the surgical team had performed over sixty operations, and they were then forced to turn their hands to routine nursing of the large number of casualties in the DS and its subsidiaries.

All the RAPs [1] were continuing to function and news came through that the 16th (Parachute) Field Ambulance surgical teams were still at work in the St Elizabeth Hospital at Arnhem, with the RAP of the 2nd Battalion Staffordshire Regiment [2] in the vicinity and the 2nd Battalion Parachute Regiment's RAP [3] still in action near the bridge.

Early on Friday, 22nd September, the MDS at the Hotel Schoonhord was recaptured by the German infantry, the senior officer of which delivered an ultimatum that a certain six-pounder gun must be moved from a position covering the HQ of the 4th Parachute Brigade, if not, the 'hospital' would be knocked down—the gun was withdrawn.

During the day the situation, from the medical viewpoint, gradually deteriorated. The nine 'hospital' buildings were constantly under fire and it was only possible to evacuate casualties during the infrequent lulls in the battle. The buildings were hit time and time again, and a number of the wounded were killed and wounded again while lying in their beds.

'It was one of the most tragic experiences', wrote Colonel Warrack after the battle, 'to see these men who had been wounded in the battle coming to the medical services for help and protection and finding themselves still in the front line and even more exposed than in their slit trenches. There was never a murmur even when mortar bombs burst in the wards. One cannot speak too highly of the courage and fortitude shown by the wounded, or of the coolness of the staffs of the various Dressing Stations under these extremely trying conditions.'

[1] 1st Airborne Light Regiment, RA, RAP (Captain Martin); 1st Battalion The Border Regiment, RAP (Captain Graham Jones); 7th Battalion The King's Own Scottish Borderers, RAP (Captain Buck—who had taken over earlier in the day following the capture of Captain Devlin).
[2] RMO, Captain B. Brownscombe, GM, killed outside the Hospital on 24th September.
[3] RMO, Captain J. W. Logan.

The dawn of Saturday, 22nd September, saw no change in the situation. Major Rigby Jones went round the RAPs in a jeep to give orders that all casualties must be held where they lay as evacuation was extremely hazardous, if not impossible, and medically nothing could be done in the hospital area, which, at that stage, could not be done in the RAP, whilst the risk of re-wounding was as great in one locality as in another. Fortunately medical supplies were still adequate, although food was getting short, and although the extra sugar and milk carried by the Field Ambulances were invaluable,[1] steps were already being taken to ' live off the land '. The Dental Officer [2] of the 181st Field Ambulance killed two sheep with a sten gun, and they were made into stew, and shops in the neighbourhood were systematically searched for supplies. Water supply, however, began to present a difficulty. Nearly all the 10-cwt trailers had, by this time, been holed and were of no further use as containers; however, early morning rain and water from central heating systems overcame the immediate problem.

The ' line ' of the perimeter nearest to the hospital area was held by the Independent Parachute Company, who were in action in the neighbouring houses, whilst men of the Glider Pilot Regiment were dug in, in slit trenches, around the area.

Communication between the DSs was of an extremely hazardous nature. All ranks of the RAMC carried Red Cross flags tied to sticks when they moved about in the open —and officers were ordered to discard their pistols—despite this, bullets often whined dangerously near or sent up spurts of dust and plaster in their paths; disconcerting and unnerving as it was, the shots appeared, however, to be in the nature of hasteners.

During that night the ' hospital area ' suffered a loss. The house near the Taffelberg, in use by Captain Scott and his team, which had been hit by mortar fire had begun to smoulder. Major Rigby Jones, with Captain Scott and Captain Griffin, assisted by Staff-Sergeant Saunders and

---

[1] Each Field Ambulance carried a case (120 lb) of tea; a sack (112 lb) of sugar and 96 tins of milk.
[2] Captain P. Griffin, Army Dental Corps.

what was left of No 5 Section quickly evacuated the building. By eight o'clock in the morning all the patients had been carried out and the stores removed, and within two hours the house was a gutted wreck.

Early that morning the ADMS discussed the position, and the increasing medical problems with the GOC, for the removal of casualties from the outlying RAPs would, he said, have to stop as the loss of both personnel and vehicles was too great. At that time there were over thirty wounded in the Divisional HQ RAP, and it was becoming increasingly difficult to conduct the battle under these conditions. Similar situations obtained at all the other RAPs.

Finally it was decided that the ADMS should try and make contact with the SMO of the German force with the object of arranging the evacuation of the wounded to a safer area into German-held territory—for it was quite impossible to attempt evacuation across the river. General Urquhart, however, made it quite clear to Colonel Warrack that under no circumstances whatsoever must the enemy be allowed to think that this was the beginning of a crack in the formation's position, and it must be made clear that this step was being taken purely on humane grounds and between the protected personnel of both sides for the benefit of the many wounded. The ADMS was to ask that fire on the medical area and RAPs be lifted for a period during that afternoon to allow the battlefield to be cleared of wounded ' so that both sides could get on with the fight '.

So it was that at ten o'clock in the morning of Sunday, 24th September, Colonel Warrack, accompanied by a Dutch liaison officer and the local doctor approached a young German Medical Officer, Captain Skalka, who was then in the DS at the Hotel Schoonhord, and asked if he might discuss the medical problems with the senior doctor of the German force. Skalka stated that *he* was the SMO. The ADMS, however, realised that little could be achieved at this level, and in the battle area, and asked to see the German Commander. He and Skalka climbed into a Red Cross jeep and, accompanied by the Dutch interpreter, drove off down the main road into Arnhem. All the way into the town the route was littered with wrecked guns and vehicles of all types, and most of the houses shattered or gutted.

At the German Divisional HQ word was sent to the Commander that the Senior British Medical Officer had arrived and Skalka sent word to his superior officer [1] asking for all available ambulances to be made ready to start evacuation of what he called " Der Kessel "—" The Cauldron ". The German GSO1 then appeared, and the position was explained to him ; finally the German Commander arrived, and opened his conversation by stating that he was " very sorry that there should be this fight between our two countries ". He agreed to the proposals of the ADMS and that every help would be given in the matter of the wounded of both sides. Colonel Warrack and the interpreter were then offered sandwiches, allowed to help themselves to the stocks of captured morphia, given a bottle of brandy to take away, and finally sent off in the jeep with an armed guard. Before returning to Divisional HQ they drove into Arnhem and visited the St Elizabeth Hospital. Here Captain Lipmann Kessel reported that everything was under control, as indeed it was, the casualties there were in beds—with sheets—and were being very well cared for, and the Dutch doctors and nurses were doing all in their power to help. Everyone was desperately anxious for news.

During the morning of Friday, 22nd September, Major Longland accompanied by a German MO went to Oosterbeek to visit the DSs which had fallen into German hands, to try to make the necessary arrangements to evacuate the casualties to the St Elizabeth Hospital.

Many of the men had been wounded several days before, and had only, by force of circumstances, received first-aid. They had lain in ordinary houses, under constant fire, with both food and water in short supply and tended by medical orderlies, a number of which were themselves wounded. ' The spirit of these wounded ', wrote Major Longland, ' was beyond all praise '.

The local armistice arranged two days later with the

[1] Thought to be the area 'ADMS'.

Germans by Colonel Warrack, the ADMS, permitted the evacuation of some hundreds of casualties back to the Arnhem Hospital. Most of the walking wounded were, after what treatment was possible, evacuated further back by the Germans the same evening, but nearly 300 lying cases remained at the St Elizabeth Hospital.

The HQ of the British Airborne Corps had landed on 17th September with the 82nd American Airborne Division in the area between Nijmegen and Grave. The 82nd US Division seized the bridges over the Maas at Grave, and the bridges over the Maas-Waal Canal were also captured intact, but the Americans met with considerable opposition before Nijmegen and did not capture the bridge until three days later.

The 101st US Airborne Division landed in the area of Zon, north of Eindhoven on 17th and 18th September and gained all their objectives. The 326th Medical Company of the Division with a surgical team set up a Clearing Station, and a platoon of the Field Hospital with another surgical team opened up at Vechel. Between them the medical units of this Division admitted a total of 2,990 cases.

On the 19th, Brigadier Austin Eagger, the DDMS of the British Airborne Corps, made his way to the St Canisuis Hospital in Nijmegen—the only civil hospital still functioning. Here he was met by the Dutch Director and his medical staff, who were most co-operative and willingly agreed to straight away take in fifty of the most serious casualties from the 82nd US Division. The Brigadier then carried out a reconnaissance of the area, earmarking suitable buildings for hospital accommodation. He came upon the Berchnanium College, and took it over at once. It was in the process of conversion by the Germans into a ' Hitler Mother ' obstetrical unit and had accommodation for 450 cases. The American CCS moved into the College on 20th September, and another CCS was opened up at Jonkersbosch two days later.

Signal communication with 1st British Airborne Corps was, from the outset, unreliable and intermittent and it was not until the 22nd September that the first message was received from the ADMS of the 1st Airborne Division. It was then that Brigadier Eagger learned that the Division had sustained some 2,000 casualties and were in urgent need of medical supplies. Arrangements were made straightaway for the dropping of two and a half tons of medical stores in the Divisional area.

It was at this time that the 163rd Field Ambulance, from the Second Army, was placed under command of the DDMS of the Airborne Corps and was moved forward, with the object of establishing a casualty evacuation point on the north bank of the Neder Rijn if the attack during the night of 23rd/24th September by the 43rd (Wessex) Division achieved its objective.

On the afternoon preceding this attack Lieut.-Colonel M. E. M. Herford, MBE, MC, the CO of the 163rd Field Ambulance, accompanied by Captain Louis, of the Airborne Corps Medical Staff, and a small detachment, crossed the river in a boat loaded with medical stores, in an effort to make contact with the 1st Airborne Division. They crossed into German-held ground near Arnhem, but were not fired on.

As soon as the boat came alongside the river bank Colonel Herford left the party and made off to make contact with the Division. Captain Louis and his small party of ORs were, however, quickly captured by a German patrol, but were soon released and given a safe conduct back to the British lines, taking the stores back with them.

That night Captain Louis and the Quartermaster of the 181st (Air Landing) Field Ambulance, Captain (QM) J. Tiernan, accompanied the 4th Battalion The Dorset Regiment during the attack across the river west of Arnhem in another attempt to get medical supplies through to the Airborne Division.

The 4th Dorsets made a determined and gallant assault, but the Battalion was overwhelmed and the break-through failed. Captain Louis was lost [1] and Captain Tiernan swam back across the river under heavy small-arms fire.[2]

By the time the ADMS returned to Oosterbeek from Arnhem at midday on 24th September the Germans had

[1] Presumed killed in the battle.
[2] For his gallantry in this action Captain J. Tiernan was awarded the MBE.

I

launched an attack in strength on the south-eastern sector of the perimeter and were in occupation of the Taffelberg area, from which they were attempting to launch an attack on Hartestein. The Independent Parachute Company were, however, keeping them ' pinned down ' from the adjoining houses ; they were getting desperate, especially on being refused entry into the hospital buildings, although they did occupy fire positions in the grounds protected by the Red Cross where they could not be shot at by the Parachute Company for fear of hitting the wounded and the RAMC personnel.

At the Schoonhord end of the hospital area the visit of the ADMS to the German force HQ was beginning to have effect. Ambulances and lorries flying the Red Cross flag were coming up from the rear, taking away firstly the German wounded and then the British.[1]

Jeeps started to go direct from the RAPs to the St Elizabeth Hospital. The German reaction to this was somewhat surprising, although, having unloaded their wounded, the regular RAMC jeeps—with Red Crosses *painted* thereon— were permitted to return. All others diverted to this work and marked only by Red Cross flags were captured and their drivers marched off.

During this time the Germans moved up in force to the Schoonhord, apparently with the plan of launching an attack under cover of the evacuation of the casualties. They tended to infiltrate round and through the position and any forward movement brought down a hail of fire from the Polish troops who had moved up to reinforce the Division. Lieut.-Colonel Marrable adopted a firm approach to the Germans. It was a strange situation to see a British officer determinedly ordering heavily armed German infantrymen out of the hospital buildings and to see them go, albeit hesitantly, as they went out into the bullet-swept garden. Eventually,

[1] The commander of the 4th Parachute Brigade—Brigadier Hackett (now Lieut.-General J. W. Hackett, CB, CBE, DSO, MC)—was taken off in this manner. He had been wounded in the abdomen. In the St Elizabeth Hospital he was operated on by Captain Lipmann Kessel within twelve hours of being wounded.

and at considerable risk, Colonel Marrable crossed the road to explain the position to the Poles and managed to temporarily restore peace in the area.

By the evening the whole of the hospital area was occupied by the enemy. All the combatants were, however, kept outside the buildings. Colonel Warrack found it rather surprising to note how quickly a tough-looking SS Corporal with a spandau and a garland of bullets round his neck ' jumped to it ' when told, in English, to " get the hell out of here, and be quick about it ", accompanied by an angry look and a gesture to the Red Cross brassard. The ambulances and lorries evacuating the casualties ceased to operate as dusk fell and the DSs began to suffer periodic mortar and small-arms fire. This, plus the fact that there was still no news of 30th Corps, began to have an effect on the morale of the wounded. All through the battle Padre Harlow, the Senior Chaplain, had played a great part in the work at the DSs, but during the afternoon he had been sent away with about 250 walking wounded, although Major Maguire and his party of some 30 lightly wounded had been overlooked by the Germans, and had to be visited clandestinely by a MO and his orderly.

It was about nine o'clock on the morning of Monday, 25th September, that the ADMS on his visit to Divisional HQ was told of the decision to withdraw what remained of the British force to the south of the Rhine, but that it would in the circumstances be impossible to take the wounded. It was decided, therefore, that the medical services would stay behind and do all that they could to help those who would shortly become prisoners of war. The withdrawal was planned to take place under cover of a barrage that night, and during the day the strictest secrecy was to be maintained, particularly in the hospital areas which were already almost fully occupied by the enemy.

Colonel Warrack took his leave of General Urquhart and his Staff and agreed to sweep the Divisional area for casualties early the following day ; he also went over to HQRA and gave the CRA the positions of all the RAPs and DSs, asking if they might be transmitted to the supporting gunners.

By ten-thirty the Germans made an all-out attack on the Independent Parachute Company in the Taffelberg area, the DS being constantly under fire, and heavy fire. One direct hit in the Hotel killed four, wounded a Dutch nurse and two orderlies, whilst Captain James and about ten patients were wounded. Many German troops sheltering from the fire around the DS were also killed and wounded.

All the wounded had been evacuated by the Germans from the Schoonhord DS and they now had to compete with the wounded from all the outlying DSs and the 300 from the Taffelberg. The casualties were moved by men of the 181st Field Ambulance, on carts, by hand carriage and in jeeps under fire all the time. During the evacuation the hospital buildings were hit again and again and even more casualties were sustained.

By six o'clock in the evening the Schoonhord DS had been filled up again with the wounded from all the outlying DSs and RAPs, except for about eighty men in the house 'Petersberg' a few hundred yards south of the Taffelberg, and the last big stretcher-bearer party organised by the 181st Field Ambulance moved down to move as many wounded as possible in readiness for the night's activities. Colonel Warrack sent a message to the GOC by hand of his ADC, who had been treated at the DS, reporting the medical situation and also arranged for the DADMS [1] to return, with the Independent Parachute Company in their withdrawal, in order to report on the medical aspects of the battle to the DDMS of both the Airborne Corps and 30th Corps.

The medical situation at the time of the Division's move down to the banks of the Rhine was that some 400 wounded would be left behind [2] in the care of the Divisional RAMC personnel. As soon as darkness fell what sounded like a pitched battle opened up, but it was under cover of the gun-

---

[1] Major J. E. Miller, MC, RAMC.
[2] 200 at the Hotel Schoonhord Dressing Station; 30 in the house 'Petersberg'; 100 in the RAP of the Light Regiment RA, and 70 at the RAP of the Border Regiment.

fire, and the constant rattle of brens, stens and spandaus, that what remained of the Division effected their withdrawal across the Rhine.

The fire slackened during the night, and as the first streaks of the pink and grey dawn tinged the ruins of Oosterbeek with a pale light only spasmodic bursts of small-arms fire broke the silence. By eight o'clock a strange stillness lay over the Divisional area, and parties of German infantry could be seen, cautiously moving around, rifles at the ready, searching for stragglers. They moved in, slowly, over the Divisional HQ area, which was an utter shambles, a battalion of crouching field-grey figures. At the HQ they found only a small party of wounded in the care of Lieutenant Randall and his orderlies.

As German transport moved in, jeeps and motor cycles, the ADMS stopped a German driver, took over his vehicle, and drove down the routes taken by the Division during the night. German medical personnel were already tending wounded. There were still some British wounded about, hidden in houses, and Dutch people beckoned from doorways to indicate where they were.

His 'recce' over, the ADMS made contact with Captain Skalka and the junior medical officer the German had put in charge of the evacuation, who had brought up some forty ambulances and lorries. It was then learned that all casualties were going to be sent to Apeldoorn, about thirty miles away.

Colonel Marrable and Major Frazer took control of the evacuation, the latter starting a plaster clinic in order to immobilise as many fractures as he could for the journey, and worked all day, saving without doubt many lives and limbs. The German evacuation officer drove the ADMS in his side-car on a complete tour of the whole area, Colonel Warrack taking him to all the RAPs and small CCPs which had sprung up during the withdrawal.

At the Petersberg they found the DADMS, whom it had been hoped should have got away with the Independent Parachute Company, but he had been wounded and had stayed behind with a number of men wounded during the withdrawal.

At the Gunners' RAP they found the RMO, Lieutenant Martin, who had been wounded two days before, but who had carried on. ' He was absolutely " out on his feet ", and described by Colonel Warrack as ' keeping himself going by sheer determination and guts '. There were over 100 casualties in the RAP and the area was still under fire from three-inch mortars on the other side of the river. Captain Griffin of the Army Dental Corps was sent to supervise the evacuation and he went down to the river bank to bring in about twenty wounded lying there.

The evacuation continued throughout the day. In the afternoon Captain Skalka again took Colonel Warrack round the whole area in a jeep. The German took in the scene, with a strange look of wonderment on his face, he was obviously very impressed with the terrific fight which the Division had put up ; it was, he said, a much tougher battle than Caen, as indeed it would appear to have been. They drove past anti-tank guns, wrecked, and with the gunners lying dead by the breeches and across the trails ; burnt-out tanks and SP guns ; shattered and gutted houses ; groups of British and German dead lying as they had fallen in the close and hard fighting. German patrols were everywhere, still searching for British soldiers—they found some, and more Germans fell, as the exchange of small-arms fire was heard, for the determined men of the Red Beret refused to give up or give in.

By six o'clock in the evening all the wounded and medical personnel, except for a small party on the river bank, had been evacuated from the area. What was left of the HQ of the 181st (Air Landing) Field Ambulance, the ADMS, DADMS, and six Dutch nurses who insisted on accompanying them, climbed on board the last lorry, the armed guard climbed in too and the convoy rumbled off through the shattered streets of Oosterbeek and Arnhem on the road northwards to Apeldoorn.

At seven o'clock that evening the last lorries from Oosterbeek drove through the entrance of the large modern Dutch

barracks—The Caserne William III—on the outskirts of Apeldoorn, and the guard shut and locked the gates behind them.

It was these barracks that were destined to become, for the following four weeks, the 1st Airborne Division's Military Hospital in German-occupied Holland.

CHAPTER X

AFTER ARNHEM

THE 1ST AIRBORNE DIVISION'S MILITARY HOSPITALS IN OCCUPIED HOLLAND

THE arrival at the Caserne William III at Apeldoorn was organised by an efficient but very truculent Oberfeldwebel of the Hermann Goering Division. It was later discovered that he had fought against the Division in Sicily and Italy and no doubt felt that this was *the* opportunity for him ' to get his own back '. He barked and shouted, demanding all weapons, knives, torches and maps. Although his meanings were obvious, misunderstanding and near stupidity was the order of the day and his methods did not produce much result.

The timely arrival, however, of Lieut.-Colonel Herford, commanding 163rd Field Ambulance, and Captain Redman of 133rd (Parachute) Field Ambulance, who both spoke fluent German, restored a reasonable position of understanding, and permitted the arrivals to settle in.

Lieut.-Colonel Herford had come across the Rhine from 30th Corps with stores for the relief of the Division, but as he had arrived on the north bank under a Red Cross, and not a white flag, he had been made a prisoner. It was some time before Colonel Herford was accepted, as no one was quite sure whether or not he had been ' planted ' by the German Intelligence Service to keep the British Medical Services under observation. He was the only non-airborne officer present and was not personally known to anyone. In the course of time, however, it became quite clear that he *was* genuine, and he was of the utmost help in every way, particularly in his quick thinking and thorough knowledge of German, which helped to surmount numerous administrative problems.

The German medical plan, which had been decided upon by General-Arzt Meyer, the Deputy Director of the German Medical Services in Holland, and Lieut.-Colonel Zingerlin, the German equivalent of an ADMS of the area, was that the Airborne Medical Services should run their own hospital, behind barbed wire and under guard. To this hospital all British wounded would be sent until they were considered fit to travel, when they would be sent to the British Prisoner of War Hospitals in the Reich.

Throughout this period the flow of wounded had continued into the hospital at Arnhem, and the Germans had set up an evacuation service by ambulances and trucks from Arnhem to Apeldoorn. Although the German medical services provided a number of items of medical equipment and supplies,[1] including plasma, they seemed incapable of providing rations, and one truck was borrowed from the Germans to collect food from a ' Dump ' known to the Dutch.

It was on the evening of 23rd September that Lieut.-Colonel Herford had arrived in Arnhem, having been passed through the German lines, under a Red Cross flag. He asked Major Longland for as much assistance as he could spare to help him in the establishment of a hospital for British wounded at Apeldoorn, to which casualties were already being sent in large numbers. Equipment was collected up, and Major Smith, Captain Keesey and some twenty RAMC ORs went off with Colonel Herford to Apeldoorn.

Between 24th and 26th September wounded from the battle arrived at the St Elizabeth Hospital at Arnhem in diminishing numbers—although on the 25th some 400 casualties from the 181st (Air Landing) Field Ambulance DS at Oosterbeek had passed through the hospital—and on Thursday the 27th all wounded fit to travel were moved to Apel-

---

[1] The equipment of the field ambulance had proved most satisfactory. The accumulator-operated spot lamps particularly proved their worth, as did the paraffin pressure-lamps which gave a good general light. The penicillin supply lasted a week although it was carefully conserved, and plasma, of which, in addition to that provided by the German medical services and the supply drop, was always sufficient in quantity.

doorn, leaving behind only about thirty cases in the care of 16 (P) Field Ambulance surgical team, supplemented by one RMO, Captain Devlin, Father D. McGowan, CF, and a number of ORs, who in turn were sent on to Apeldoorn on 13th October, at very short notice, and despite the strong protests of Captain Lipmann Kessel—one soldier operated on that morning and still under the anaesthetic.

Between 700 and 800 British wounded had passed through the hospital since the first day of the battle; nearly 150 operations [1] had been carried out, but under twenty wounded had died during this time, the majority of whom had been so badly injured as to be inoperable, and death from their wounds was inevitable.

The medical situation as a whole following the withdrawal of the 1st Airborne Division presented a major medical problem. There were 2,000 British wounded plus practically the whole of the Divisional medical services—twenty-five officers and some 400 RAMC personnel and unit stretcher-bearers—together with their equipment. Some 2,500 German wounded had been admitted to hospitals in the Apeldoorn area—the German Military Hospitals, the St Joseph's Kreigs-Lazarett and a six-hundred-bedded hospital at Het Loo were both full, and the two Dutch civilian hospitals, the Algemina Zikenhause and the Catholicha were rapidly filling with casualties, both British and German, and wounded Dutch civilians.

It was to the St Joseph's Kreigs-Lazarett that the first

[1] During the period of the battle (17th to 26th September) Captain A. W. Lipmann Kessel performed over 100 operations, most of which were Priority I or II cases categorised as follows :—

Abdomen (including 2 negative laparotomies), 5 ; thoraco-abdominal, 2 ; head (open fracture, penetrating), 1 ; urethra and bladder, 2 ; thorax (open), 3 ; jaw (upper only), 2 ; femur (open fracture), 14 ; miscellaneous fractures and flesh wounds, 70.

Following the battle he performed a further 40 operations as follows :—

For empyema, 1 ; skin grafting, 8 ; suture, secondary or delayed primary, 12 ; secondary amputations, 2 ; excision of popliteal aneurysm, 2 ; 3 operations on one patient for ruptured urethra ; and 10 secondary debridements on casualties previously operated upon by German surgeons.

British casualties were sent from the Arnhem battle area. During the first week of 18th to 25th September Captain T. F. Redman, RAMC, of the 133rd (Parachute) Field Ambulance was the senior British officer. He had been wounded in the DZ and taken prisoner within minutes of landing. He, together with Private H. Jones, and a badly wounded German, were taken on a farm cart to a German RAP at Ede, and in the evening evacuated with an ambulance full of Wehrmacht casualties to the German Military Hospital. Captain Redman's wound was such that he was soon able to move around the wards and to compile a list of British wounded, and render certain medical assistance. He found that his help was being welcomed and he was soon working in co-operation with the German doctors.

Firstly he selected cases for operation and arranged their movement to the theatre. It was agreed with the senior German surgeons [1] that Captain Redman would keep the theatre annexe filled with those cases needing urgent attention. The wounded so collected together were both British and German. It reflected great credit, recorded Captain Redman, that their (the Germans) ethical standards made their selection of the wounded for attention quite impartial, nationality not being considered.

Captain Redman assisted in a number of operations, sharing a table put up in one of the admission halls with a German doctor, taking it in turn with him to perform the operations, and working with a team of German orderlies, who efficiently gave local anaesthetics and evipan injections. Captain Redman was also called upon to give anaesthetics when working with some of the German surgeons, mostly middle-aged men, surgeons in civil life.[2] The speed of their work was considerable, each surgeon worked on two tables, shuttling from one to the other with no time lost between operations.

Seven days passed before the urgent surgical work was

---

[1] Major-Arzt Kaiser and Major-Arzt Peach.
[2] The only aspect of their work, Captain Redman noted, that contrasted with ours was that they always excised skin, however old the wound, and to a greater degree than in British hospitals.

completed—there were during that time some 1,500 German and 300 British wounded in the hospital—and, in consequence, by the fourth day gas gangrene was on the increase, and many amputations became necessary for this reason alone. Serum was available, but in insufficient quantity for general prophylaxis, and sulphonamides too were only available for treatment rather than prophylaxis. There was also a shortage of oxygen and plasma; however, in the rare cases when the German doctors considered blood to be of value it was taken there and then from a donor.

At this hospital the attitude of the German medical staff was one of co-operation, and humanitarian in every way. At the end of the first week Captain Redman's work [1] was that of liaison with Dutch hospitals for admissions and X-rays, and for that purpose he was given a German driver, an ambulance, and complete freedom of movement.

The German plan for the running of the Caserne as a hospital was welcomed by the British, and the policy and action subsequently taken was based on the hope that during the whole period at Apeldoorn a relieving force from Second Army would be in Apeldoorn just as soon as a bridgehead could be established on the north bank of the Neder Rijn. The policy decided upon was to be one of procrastination and, as far as evacuation of patients was concerned, ' one of masterly inactivity '.

The first essential therefore in the British plan was to get a really efficient hospital functioning as soon as possible with the available resources; the next consideration was the hindrance of the German plan by preventing as many wounded as possible from being moved away to the POW camps in Germany. The barracks provided excellent accommodation for the purpose to which they were to be put. There was central heating, excellent washing facilities, good sanitary arrangements, a large central cookhouse designed for cooking for 2,000, and a bath-house equipped with showers.

Three barrack blocks were put at the disposal of the British

---

[1] On the 23rd September Captain Redman was joined by Major P. Smith and Captain J. W. Logan, sent from Arnhem by the Germans.

AFTER ARNHEM

Medical Services. Each block was a three-storey building with entrance hall, office accommodation, lavatories and washing rooms, whilst each barrack room was capable of holding thirty beds, or sixty if they were in double tier.

It was decided that the organisation of the hospital should comprise a HQ [1]; a Registrar's Office [2]; an Administrative Wing,[3] responsible for food, sanitation, staff, supplies and discipline ; and a Medical Wing,[4] the OC of which would be responsible for all treatment and allocation of cases to the wards, for the maintenance of the operating theatres and the transference of cases to and from outside hospitals.

The Airborne Military Hospital was established on the evening of 26th September, and conferences were held to decide on the details of the organisation on the three days that followed, the discussions being attended by Lieut.-Colonel Zingerlin, the Chief German MO, his Staff officer and Dr Trip, the head of the Red Cross Society of Holland in the Gelderland Province. The German Medical Services offered all help possible to equip the hospital and to maintain it with food, medical supplies and fuel.[5]

The general equipment for running the hospital was inadequate, and Colonel Zingerlin agreed to supply blankets, sheets, soap, towels, toothbrushes, bed-pans and urinals. Medical equipment from the Division's own resources was, however, sufficient to run the whole hospital, although certain expendable stores were low. In response to requests for these items to be replenished, Colonel Zingerlin pointed

---

[1] Commanding Officer, Colonel G. M. Warrack ; Second-in-Command, Lieut.-Colonel M. E. Herford ; Liaison Officer, Captain T. Redman of 133rd Parachute Field Ambulance.
[2] Major J. E. Miller, the DADMS, was the Registrar with a staff of all the available clerks.
[3] Commanded by Lieut.-Colonel A. T. Marrable.
[4] Commanded by Lieut.-Colonel M. Alford.
[5] Writing to Colonel A. A. Eagger, Colonel Warrack recorded that in his opinion ' a great deal of help was given to the Airborne Medical Services because the Germans were so impressed with the splendid fighting qualities of the men who had been wounded, and awed by their great gallantry in the recent battle '. ' It was also ', he felt, ' that many of the considerations were in the nature of a second string so that when the collapse, which appeared imminent, took place the victorious British Armies would find that they had treated our wounded very correctly '.

out that they had over 2,000 wounded in the area, and that they too were short of supplies and even if they could 'find' them transportation would be a problem. It was therefore suggested by Colonel Warrack that as all the required supplies were waiting for them on the south bank of the Rhine would it not be possible for arrangements to be made for them to be sent across under a white flag, or if more convenient they could be dropped in the grounds of the barracks by parachute. The Germans agreed to put this suggestion up to the General Staff, which they did, but General Field-Marshal Model would not allow such an arrangement to be made.

The conditions in the British Hospital were not ideal, diets were somewhat 'rough and ready'; there were few comforts, and no nurses. It was agreed, therefore, that the more serious cases would be moved into the two local Dutch civilian hospitals where they would receive better food, more comfortable beds and the attention of trained Dutch nurses. The X-ray facilities at the Dutch hospitals, the Catholicha and the Algemina Zikenhause, were also used, and patients were sent down for X-rays in German ambulances.

Considerable medical assistance was given by the Dutch, who later sent six complete fully equipped surgical teams, including a neuro-surgical team, from The Hague and Amsterdam; they were most anxious to help 'The Tommies' and not the Germans, and rendered every possible assistance. They were not allowed to work in the Airborne hospital, but gave considerable help in the Dutch hospitals at Apeldoorn.

On the day the hospital opened on 25th September over 1,250 wounded were 'admitted'. The speedy organisation of the hospital had been a great achievement, for the situation on the evening of the arrival from the scene of the battle had been somewhat chaotic. Some 1,700 soldiers, the majority wounded, some very seriously, had just been 'dumped' in the bare unoccupied barracks within the preceding thirty-six hours, with no proper accommodation, only one field-kitchen for cooking, and no organisation.

The hospital settled down straightaway to a regular routine and the plans for preventing as many as possible from being taken off to POW camps were put into operation. Speed was essential, for on the very next day following the opening of the hospital the Germans marched off nearly 500 walking wounded, together with two MOs and eight orderlies. They went down to the railway where they were entrained in cattle trucks bound for the Reich. A further 650 wounded were admitted so that the total numbers were not only made up but increased.

The first task of the Registrar and his staff was to compile a complete return of all personnel in the barracks, and he was pressed continuously by the German Commandant for the completion of this information. The preparation of the early returns showed considerable variety and initiative, which was intended as a ' cover plan ' to enable men to escape before the correct numbers were finally established.

As the lightly wounded became fit, they became restless, and many escaped. There was a guardroom at the entrance to the barracks, and guards patrolled in front of, and around, the hospital blocks. The whole camp was surrounded by concertina wire and a ten-foot steel fence, but on the eastern approach there was a barbed-wire fence and no concertina wire, whilst beyond lay open fields. At the outset the guard was provided by the SS, who generally adopted a ' tough ' attitude, but a few days later they were relieved by a Wehrmacht guard, all somewhat elderly men, immediately dubbed ' The Bismarck Youth '.

The arrival of the Wehrmacht and the increasing number of men becoming fit enough to escape led to a steady flow of men through the eastern fence. It was made clear throughout the hospital that any man who intended to escape should report to the MO in charge of the ward or the CO, and that they would be given every assistance. The SS had collected most of the maps and compasses during the first two days, but their searches had not been very thorough and several officers and men had managed to retain theirs, and such were used to advantage.

German concern over the medical situation as a whole, resulting from the battle, was evidenced by the interest taken in the activities of the British Medical Services. Colonel

Warrack and Lieut.-Colonel Herford were invited by Colonel Zingerlin to visit the British wounded in the Dutch hospitals and afterwards to meet General-Arzt Meyer. This they did, visiting the Het Loo Hospital in Queen Wilhelmina's Summer Palace, and the St Joseph's Kriegs-Lazarett. At the British Hospital a round-table conference was held, when the main topic was food, although many other subjects were touched upon. It was felt that the German general looked upon the Airborne Medical Services as a god-send in the light of the heavy commitment of some 5,000 casualties on his hands, which no one could possibly have envisaged; and because the British were prepared to help themselves to the full he was prepared to give all the help he could. ' The whole conference was conducted ', recalls Colonel Warrack, ' on fairly friendly terms ', as it was obvious that the Germans were out to help and ' it was always a case of " doctor to doctor ".'

Considerable help came from the Dutch. The local Red Cross organisation made a house-to-house collection for English books and also provided playing-cards, soap, towels, razor blades, sheets and many other items. A daily supply of whole blood was instituted by Dr Trip, who also brought a neuro-surgical team to the hospital to examine and advise on treatment for those suffering from head injuries.

A number of members of the Dutch underground movement also visited the hospital. They were asked if they could make contact with 21st Army Group to see if fighter-bombers and ' Typhoons ' could shoot up all the railways leading from Apeldoorn into Germany.

By the end of the first week things had settled down to a regular routine. The men from the Field Ambulances rapidly assumed their new duties as hospital orderlies. There was a remarkable absence of serious infection for care had been taken to separate ' clean ' wounds from infected in the different wards. The lists of wounded were finally completed and proper records maintained.

Some fifteen casualties died during the week, mainly resulting from their rough journey from Oosterbeek. They were buried in the nearby Dutch cemetery. The Germans had failed to make proper arrangements for the funeral; there were no coffins, and the bodies were laid on stretchers, covered with blankets and carried on horse-drawn carts.

Colonel Warrack and the Senior Chaplain attended the funeral, as did about 100 Dutch civilians, who were ordered back from the graves by the Germans. The Dutch retaliated after the interments by whistling ' Tipperary ' and giving the ' V ' sign.

During the second week the Germans adopted the procedure of suddenly telling the Commandant, with about two hours' notice, that men were to be moved to other hospitals or away by train. Delaying tactics were employed, and on 2nd October when orders were given for 250 walking wounded to be ready in two hours, their departure was delayed until five-thirty in the afternoon, which gave many the chance to escape in the dark on arrival at the railway station an hour later.

Colonel Herford made it quite clear that he had no intention of permitting wounded to be sent away in ordinary cattle trucks. However, Colonel Zingerlin promised that he would have plenty of straw put into the trucks, that only twenty-one should go into each, that suitable feeding arrangements would be made and that Red Crosses would be painted on the roofs of all carriages. He also assured Colonel Herford that all German wounded were being evacuated in similar manner.

The wounded, selected by the MOs as fit to travel, were paraded and searched, given tea, and allowed to take one blanket.

The staffing of the train presented a problem, for not only did it mean the reduction of the medical staff, but those who went would thereby forego any chance of escape. It was, however, necessary to provide medical staff and one MO from each Brigade (Captain Keesey from 1st Parachute Brigade, Captain Lawson from the 4th Brigade, and Captain Simmons of the Air Landing Brigade), together with Captain Ridler, the Dental Officer of 16th (Parachute) Field Ambulance, were detailed.

Colonel Zingerlin had given permission for Colonel Herford to visit the train to supervise loading, but Colonel Warrack bullied the interpreter into letting him go as well, but it was obvious that he was not wanted, as conditions were far from being what had been promised. There were thirty men to a truck, and no sanitary arrangements at all. The ' rations ' consisted of a loaf of bread and a small piece of sausage per man for twenty-four hours, whilst coffee would only be issued at halts. The waggons were locked, and the locks wired, the Red Crosses on the roofs of the trucks were both small and insignificant. In fact the whole train was very badly organised.

The train moved off, and although Colonel Warrack had been assured that the four MOs on the train would be permitted to move freely to attend to the wounded and to dress wounds, they were in fact locked into their carriages. Under the circumstances they decided that if they could not work they would try and escape. They drew lots to decide who should remain as they felt one should do so, and this fell to Captain Simmons. The other three jumped the train. In the escape Captain Keesey was shot dead by one of the guards, but Captain Lawson and Captain Ridler got clean away in the darkness and successfully escaped.

Both Colonel Warrack and Colonel Herford protested in the strongest terms to the Commandant and Stabsarzt Kramer. They told them forcibly just what they felt about the arrangements, and were so angry that notice was indeed taken of their protests, which resulted not only in an abject apology, but by the fact that on the next occasion that wounded were transported a sumptuous Red Cross train was provided.

It was made quite clear to Colonel Zingerlin that there would be serious trouble if any more wounded were moved in similar manner, and furthermore, that as all the walking wounded had been sent away, there were no more patients fit to move. This the German refused to believe and ordered a team of ' experts ' to examine every man to decide those who were really transportable. Everyone went out of their way to hinder this board in its work with some considerable success. Everyone, except the abdominal and compound fracture cases, was put on the list and all were, in fact, capable of being moved. However, it took the board two whole days to establish this simple fact.

It was on Friday, 6th October, that orders arrived for 500 patients to be moved in three hours' time. Colonel Zingerlin went down to Colonel Warrack very pleased with himself that a proper ambulance train had been provided, as indeed it was. There was a German doctor, a major, on the train staff, with a lieutenant and two nursing sisters. The train was fitted with beds down both sides in three tiers, there was a stove and a WC in each compartment, and in addition it was equipped with operating theatre, staff quarters and a cookhouse. The British medical staff was further reduced in order to fully staff the train. Lieut.-Colonel Alford was sent down to be OC train, together with his own MOs and orderlies.

The train lay in the station all night alongside a German 'flak' train, which went into action early the following morning when an RAF flight of 'Typhoons' swept over the station in an attack on the sidings and marshalling yard. The Germans sweated at their guns without success, to the accompaniment of jeers and ribald shouts from the British wounded. This incident aroused another strong protest from the senior British officers—their theme being 'The brave German gunners had the protection of the Red Cross in direct contravention of the Geneva Convention'. Colonel Zingerlin was furious, he complained bitterly to the local commander and the 'flak' (anti-aircraft) train was removed.

The train was forced to remain in the station for three days as all the suitable engines had been shot up by the RAF and a railway strike called by the Dutch government was in force.

It was shortly after this that the hospital received, at short notice, a visit from 'The Director, Medical Services of the Armies of the Third Reich in the West', one General von Hauhenneiser, who arrived with a large staff. The General, described as 'quite an impressive figure, with his Prussian-style cap, monocle, sword-cuts on his face, and very erect carriage' was obviously impressed with the hospital, particularly with the turn-out and discipline of the orderlies, who, on the approach of the inspecting party, stopped their sweeping, and came to attention, brooms 'at the order'. He paid particular attention to the fractured femurs and jaw cases, showed great interest in the plasma and blood transfusion apparatus, and the more anaemic looking patients obviously concerned him, for he issued instructions that sufficient and adequate food must be made available. Before leaving he told the Commandant that the establishment must, in the first place, be treated as a hospital, in the second as a prison camp, and the needs of the patients had to come first. This was all very encouraging and it was felt that the hospital would remain as and where it was. This, however, was not to be.

During the third week of the hospital's existence, when the original holding of patients was reduced by evacuation to 120, numbers were again increased by the arrival of patients from the Dutch hospitals and from Het Loo, from whence the number of escapes had reached considerable proportions. The St Elizabeth Hospital in Arnhem was closed too, and Major Longland and Captain Lipmann Kessel arrived with their staff and thirty patients. They also reported a number of escapes [1] and the fact that the Dutch underground movement had been in touch with them and were actively assisting all who could break away.

The increasing number of escapes led to a general toughening of the German attitude and a cutting down of privileges, so that the prison camp atmosphere predominated. No longer were the interchange of visits permitted between the Dutch doctors and the Airborne Military Hospital and the padres were the only ones allowed out, but then only three times a week to take communion for the wounded in the Dutch hospitals, and even then they were asked to give their parole.

At the beginning of the third week the number of patients was further reduced and it was then obvious that the hospital

[1] Including the escape of Brigadier (now Lieut.-General) Hackett, who had been seriously wounded on the second Sunday of the battle. He had been operated on by Captain Lipmann Kessel less than twelve hours after he had been hit. Ten days later he got up and walked out of the hospital, eventually reaching 21st Army Group three months later.

was over-staffed, so Colonel Warrack held a meeting of all officers and told them that as far as he was concerned as long as an adequate staff was kept he had no objection to a certain number of officers and RAMC ORs making off if they wished to take the chance, although in the case of the officers of 181st (Air Landing) Field Ambulance they were given specific orders not to attempt to escape as it was decided that the unit as a whole was to continue in being to care for the wounded.

Plans for escaping were to be submitted to him within twenty-four hours and the week-end was to be an ' escape period '. Several officers decided to go and were provided with food and given every assistance.

As soon as they were missed the Germans took immediate precautionary measures. The cookhouse, an easy way out, was put out of bounds, and guards mounted over the cooks at their work ; a counting parade was held each day and sentries constantly patrolled the hospital area.

Great plans went into action to effect the getaways. To cover the escape of two of the surgeons, operations were staged by a number of ORs and great play was made of the ' hallowed atmosphere ' of the theatre—and heads were counted from the door without further investigation of the ' bodies ' lying on the operating tables.

Colonel Herford and Padre McGowan also got away under the cover of a very dark and windy night in pouring rain. When their escape was discovered the next day the Germans issued orders at 8.15 am that with the exception of five MOs, two padres and twenty RAMC ORs all the rest of the medical staff were to be ready to move in half an hour. Delaying tactics again prevailed, and by 11.30 am Colonel Warrack had disappeared. The Germans were infuriated at the continued escapes, and the hospital was compressed into one block, guards were doubled and every movement was controlled.

On 26th October Major S. M. Frazer, who was then in command, was told that the hospital was to be closed, that all British medical staff and patients were to be moved to St Joseph's Kreigs-Lazarett, and ambulances would be arriving in an hour; which indeed they did, and the evacuation took place immediately, despite the fact that there were several severely wounded, including one subaltern who was transported in a bus, receiving all the time a continuous drip from blood from a Dutch girl (who had been kept in the barracks by the Germans for their pleasure) and who willingly acted as a blood donor in an effort to keep this patient alive.[1]

There was an air of stillness as the last vehicle of the convoy wheeled out of the gates of the Caserne, leaving behind the silent Wehrmacht guards—and so that great achievement, the Airborne Military Hospital at Apeldoorn, came to an end.

The whole of the Arnhem operation had been, from the medical viewpoint, far from normal. The medical services had had an extremely difficult task to perform. Every officer and man had been stretched to the uttermost, and they had given of their best. The RMOs and their staffs had distinguished themselves by their devotion to duty under the most difficult conditions, working continually in the very middle of a great battle. The surgical teams had performed feats which have gone down in the history of the RAMC and, in retrospect, one wonders even now how such things as they achieved were possible.

From 26th October 1944 until 13th April 1945 the Germans continued to use the St Joseph's Hospital at Apeldoorn as a prisoner of war hospital. As and when hospital trains were available or the number of cases warranted it, the wounded prisoners were moved into the Reich. After some argument it was laid down by the German Command in Holland that the RAMC staff would be entirely responsible for the medical treatment of allied prisoners of war. This, recorded Major S. M. Frazer,[2] gave the British ' a strong lever in preventing interference from inept young Germans who would regard a prisoner of war as fair practice for their surgery '.

[1] This officer, after transfusion amounting to thirty-two pints of blood and other transfusions of plasma, and despite the loss of a leg, survived.
[2] Second-in-Command of the 181st (Air Landing) Field Ambulance. RAMC.

The hospital arrangements ran comparatively smoothly. Medicaments were in fairly good supply, although there were periodical shortages of dressings and sulphonamides and there was never sufficient plaster of Paris or penicillin after the British supplies were exhausted. The German doctors were always willing to give what help they could, but the non-medical and lower-grade personnel were, as a result of their Nazi outlook and jealousy of the treatment the British were receiving, generally obstructive, particularly over matters of medical and hospital supplies. The German dispenser, however, was a reasonable fellow and, unless ardent Nazis were about, was prepared to let Major Frazer have a fair share of what became available. The hospital was regularly visited by medical generals and consulting surgeons, many of whom were professors from well-known universities; they were invariably courteous and gave much valuable advice. According to the German practice special diets were made available for all serious cases, which included all major amputations and lung wounds and all cases of prolonged pryrexia, otherwise rations were monotonous and somewhat inadequate, being particularly short of proteins.

No Red Cross parcels or mail from home got through to St Joseph's, and all went without cigarettes for two and a half months. The only comforts were brought in, at considerable risk, by the Dutch nurses.

The British wounded were divided by the two doctors' 'firms', but the shortage of RAMC orderlies was acute, one at a time doing night duty. After four months they were exhausted, by sparseness of rations—which were particularly lacking in protein—overwork, and the fact that it had been necessary for them to give of their blood for transfusions—forty pints of blood having been given by the seven members of the staff during this time.

At the outset there were sixty-eight patients in the hospital,[1] but numbers were reduced by the evacuation of wounded when considered fit to move by train to Germany,

---

[1] Amputations, 19; open fractures, 23; head wounds (with hemiplegia), 3; chest wounds (with empyema), 6; abdominal wounds (penetrating), 5; gun-shot wounds (with gross sepsis), 12.

and with them went one of the padres—who had done duty as an orderly, washing and shaving men in the wards—Captain Griffin, and one of the five orderlies, Private Parker. This left only four orderlies and the loss of this staff put an even greater strain on the medical organisation, especially when the patients went up to eighty-three by the admission of captured wounded from the 49th Division [1] and a number of wounded American air-crews.

Some of the first-line surgery that these casualties had received was described as 'shocking', as a result of which, and after strong protests by Majors Frazer and Rigby-Jones, wounded were sent in for surgery and treatment after first aid only.

As the Rhineland battles developed, casualties came in from the First Canadian Army, fighting north of the Reichwald, and Americans from as far south as Roermond.

In January, three patients escaped—Major Sherriff of the King's Own Scottish Borderers, an RAF pilot, and an American—and this brought about a wave of German discipline and the imposition of petty restrictions as a form of mass punishment. It was a great temptation to escape, with the British lines only twenty miles away and the Dutch willing to give every assistance.

As the battles drew nearer, morale reached a very high pitch, but the Germans decided to move the hospital. It was not possible to move the serious cases, but most of the wounded, with Major Rigby-Jones, the Reverend Buchanan, CF, and one orderly, Private Jackson, were sent to Heemstede, near Haarlem.

The fighting drew nearer, and eventually, on the morning of 13th April, a company of Canadian infantry came up through the woods and bushes adjoining the hospital. A burst of cheering broke from the wards as the cheery, triumphant Canadians clattered into the hospital.

That evening Colonel Coke, the ADMS of the 1st Canadian Division, arrived and arranged for rations and medical supplies to be sent up. In the three-day battle that followed all

[1] The 49th (West Riding) Division were holding the left flank of 21st Army Group in the Nijmegen area.

three medical officers of the 1st Canadian Infantry Brigade established their RAPs in the precincts of the hospital, and then as the fighting died down arrangements were made for the evacuation of all the allied wounded into the 21st Army Group lines of communication.

In the seven months that St Joseph's Hospital had functioned as an allied military hospital 208 wounded had been admitted (including thirty-one Americans); 143 had been evacuated; and eighteen had died, whilst 178 operations had been performed by Majors Frazer and Rigby-Jones.

CHAPTER XI

INTO THE BREACH

WITH THE 6TH AIRBORNE DIVISION IN THE ARDENNES

CHRISTMAS was approaching and the whole of the 6th Airborne Division was looking forward to leave, but early in the evening of 20th December all senior officers were urgently summoned to conferences at their unit HQs. It was then that they learned that they would be spending a very different Christmas from that which they had all anticipated.

The seriousness of the threat of Von Rundstedt's Army in their sudden and fierce attack in the Ardennes on 16th December was such that Field-Marshal Montgomery ordered the concentration for the Rhineland battle to stop and switched certain formations from the Geilenkirchen area to west of the Meuse. The 6th Airborne Division was to move almost immediately to help check the German advance.

Every unit was thrown into a great state of activity and hurriedly they embussed and entrained to the ports of embarkation bound for Calais and Ostende. Movement at the outset was hindered by fog, and the advanced elements of the Division travelled by devious routes across the frozen, snow-covered Belgian countryside to arrive in the concentration area between Dinant and Namur on Boxing Day, where its immediate task was the covering of the crossings of the River Meuse. The 195th (Air Landing) Field Ambulance, commanded by Lieut.-Colonel W. M. E. Anderson, moved from Bulford to Purfleet on 22nd December, sailing the next day for Calais, where they arrived on the early morning of Christmas Eve. The Field Ambulance [1] moved

---

[1] The first Airborne unit to go into action was the 195th (Air Landing) Field Ambulance.

from Calais *via* Waeghem and Anseghem to Dinant, where they opened an ADS. The 224th (Parachute) Field Ambulance left Bulford on 24th December, spending Christmas Day in the Purfleet transit camp, embarking at Tilbury the next day. Throughout 26th and 27th December they lay off Tilbury, sailing in convoy for Ostende on the 28th. On arrival the unit, under the command of Lieut.-Colonel A. D. Young, moved from Ostende *via* Tournhout, Roulers, Courtrai, Tournai, Leuze, Ath, Mons, and Charleroi to reach and open up an ADS at Abbaye de Maredsous on 30th December.

By the time the 1st and 2nd Parachute and 6th Air Landing Brigades were in position the German advance had been brought to a standstill, and the British and American formations had taken the initiative in offensive operations. The two Parachute Brigades were sent forward against the tip of the German salient.

Despite the failure of their enterprise, Von Rundstedt's troops were still full of fight, and there was no indication that they were likely to give way.

On the morning of 3rd January the 13th Battalion The Parachute Regiment moved against the village of Bure, launching its attack at half-past one in the afternoon. Severe fighting was immediate, the Germans bringing down heavy fire on the leading company from prepared positions and there were many casualties as the company dashed forward into the village. The company engaged in the flank attack on the rising ground on the right also ran into a fierce and accurate fire from tanks and field artillery and sustained heavy casualties. By the end of the day it had been reduced to one officer and twenty men.

By five o'clock half the village was held by two companies, and throughout the night and the following day they determinedly held on to their positions. Artillery support was given during the day, and that evening they were reinforced by a company of the 2nd Battalion The Oxford and Buckinghamshire Light Infantry.

During the fierce fighting in and around Bure Sergeant Scott of the 225th (Parachute) Field Ambulance went out with an ambulance to collect wounded. Whilst he was so engaged bandaging men, and lifting them into the vehicle, a German Tiger tank clanked up, and slewing on its tracks shuddered to a halt alongside the ambulance. The turret opened, the head and shoulders of the commander appeared and called out in good English to the NCO.: "Take the casualties away this time", he cried, "but do not come forward again as it is not safe!"[1]

The action of the 13th Battalion at Bure was described as ' the most severe of any fought by a unit of the division at that time '—a difficult period followed of hazardous patrolling in the snow-covered country.

During a patrol an NCO and six men of the 22nd Independent Parachute Company made their way into a wood near Marloie, not far from the border of Luxembourg. The leading man touched off a mine and fell, the corporal went forward to rescue him and he too trod on a mine. He called out for a message to be sent for medical help and a mine detector. In response five medical orderlies arrived on the scene, but before they could reach the two wounded men two of them were blown up by mines. Just at this time the MO of the 13th Battalion, Captain D. J. Tibbs, arrived. He immediately ordered all the men away from the minefield. No one was to move into the area until the arrival of the mine detector. The MO then went straight towards the wounded men. He stopped by the first and bandaged him, stopping the bleeding, then moved on, dealing with each man in succession until he reached the last man. By then he was in his shirt-sleeves, having wrapped his jerkin and battle-dress blouse around the worst of the wounded. The snow was crisp and hard and the temperature well below freezing point.

Then a party arrived with the mine detector and a path was swept through the minefield. Volunteer stretcher-bearers followed and the wounded were carried out, and when the NCO with one of the mine detectors reached Captain Tibbs he found the officer supporting a wounded man in a sitting position. Sweeping the ground around, the buzz in the earphone located a mine immediately behind the wounded man, in the very spot his shoulders would have rested had

[1] ' The Red Beret ' by Hilary St George Saunders.

the officer laid him down. Two more mines were detected within twelve inches of Captain Tibbs's feet.[1]

In the last week in January the Division was moved back from the Ardennes into Holland and took up positions along the line of the River Maas between Roermond and Venlo. Here the Division was engaged in patrol activities of an unusual and extremely hazardous character, involving the crossing of the river, then in full flood, in small craft, which the strong currents often swept well off their course; this frequently resulted in the patrols landing in minefields along the east bank and right in enemy positions.

In the early hours of 10th February two men of the 22nd Independent Parachute Company were blown up in an uncharted minefield some three hundred yards west of the River Maas opposite Tegelen. Captain J. D. Fisher of 195th (Air Landing) Field Ambulance hurried down with stretcher-bearers to a point on the road about twenty yards from the wounded men. The enemy, attracted by the explosion, were putting up flares and firing onto the area. One man was howling with pain, and the other shouted out that each had had a leg blown off. Captain Fisher decided that immediate medical aid had to be given, so, instead of awaiting the arrival of a mine-detector, crawled into the minefield, pushing a stretcher before him as a rough detector and with a marking tape in his mouth. He pulled the first man onto the stretcher then on to the next man, prodding the mud with his fingers searching for mines. Reaching the man he dragged him back into the safety lane he had marked, along which the stretcher-bearers followed to bring out the wounded.[2]

It was in the third week in February that the whole Division was withdrawn from 21st Army Group. It concentrated at Ghent, and thence moved to Ostende to embark for Tilbury, and back to Salisbury Plain to prepare for its forthcoming Airborne Operation in the Crossing of the Rhine.

---

[1] ' The Red Beret ' by Hilary St George Saunders.
[2] For this gallantry Captain Fisher was awarded the Military Cross.

CHAPTER XII

OVER THE RHINE

THE 6TH AIRBORNE DIVISION'S AIRBORNE LANDING

FOR the crossing of the Rhine, designated 'Operation Varsity', the 6th Airborne Division, commanded by Major-General E. Bols, DSO, came under command of the 18th United States Airborne Corps.[1]

The plan for the operation took into consideration the previous experience of the airborne landings in Normandy and at Arnhem, and in consequence it was decided that all troops, both parachutists and glider-borne, would be transported in one air-lift, also that the landing would be right on the objective, thereby saving warning time to the enemy in an approach march, and, lastly, that the operation would take place in daylight. This decision, it was realised, was a considerable risk in loss of life, but to outweigh this factor a daylight landing would enable every man to see where he was, where he could find his unit and equipment, and also see the enemy and his objectives. Lastly, the airborne attack was not to take place until ground operations had been successfully launched. The Rhine crossing was first to be achieved by Commandos and troops of the Second Army, the 15th (Scottish) Division being the assault formation. Their objective was to seize and hold Wesel and not until this was achieved would the Airborne force arrive over their DZs.

The DZs for the 6th Airborne Division were in the wooded area of the Diersfordterwald, the high ground to the east of the villages of Bergen and Hamminkeln, and a number of bridges to the east over the River Issel.

The 3rd Parachute Brigade, with 224th (Parachute) Field

---

[1] Commanded by Lieut.-General M. B. Ridgway, with Lieut.-General R. N. Gale as his Second-in-Command.

Ambulance, were to drop at the south-eastern area of the Diersfordterwald, and secure the Schneppenberg feature; the 5th Parachute Brigade, with 225th (Parachute) Field Ambulance, to the north of the forest; and the 6th (Air Landing) Brigade, with 195th (Air Landing) Field Ambulance, between the line of the railway running north-east to south-west diagonally across the forest, and the line of the River Issel, around the village of Hamminkeln.

The Parachute Brigades were to drop first and would be closely followed by the gliders of the Air Landing Brigade.

Unlike all previous airborne operations there was no secret about their destination. Before ' D ' Day in Normandy, the landing area was kept secret to the last moment; again, this was so for the Arnhem landing; but, this time, everyone knew that their forthcoming task was the crossing of the Rhine, it was only the final details which had to be disclosed at the briefings at the transit camps where the Division assembled in the four days prior to take-off.

The fact that, for the first time, an Airborne landing was to take place in broad daylight on a heavily defended area was a matter of considerable concern to the planning staff in estimating possible casualties. The CO of 224th (Parachute) Field Ambulance was warned to expect 600—nearly one-third of the 3rd Brigade's strength. This estimate, it is recorded, set a difficult if not insoluble medical problem.

It was decided that a section of the Field Ambulance, comprising an MO and sixteen ORs, would be attached to each battalion of the Brigade. This meant that once the battalions had moved off from the DZ towards their objectives and the HQ and surgical team had gone to establish the MDS there would be less than twenty men left behind to collect and evacuate the wounded and injured scattered all over the Brigade DZ.

Despite the situation envisaged there was a great feeling of suppressed excitement and eagerness throughout the Division. Typical of the addresses to the men, as an opening to the final briefings, was that made by Brigadier S. J. L. Hill, Commanding the 3rd Parachute Brigade.

" Gentlemen ", he said, " the artillery and air support is

fantastic ! And if you're worried about the kind of reception you'll get just put yourself in the place of the enemy. Beaten and demoralised, pounded by our artillery and bombers, what would you think, gentlemen, if you saw a horde of ferocious bloodthirsty paratroopers, bristling with weapons, cascading down upon you from the skies ? And you needn't think just because you hear a few stray bullets flying about that some miserable Hun is shooting at you. That is merely a form of egotism. But if, by any chance,' you should happen to meet one of these Huns in person, you will treat him, gentlemen, with extreme disfavour."

Reveille on the morning of 24th March 1945 for the units of the 6th Airborne Division was at 2.45 am. Breakfast of bacon and eggs was served half an hour later in the ' blacked-out ' messes and dining halls. There was a shuffling, crumping of boots on gravel and some shouting of orders as the units fell in on parade, the men bumping each other with their full packs as they formed up in the darkness to embuss, soon after four o'clock, for the airfields. Here they donned their ' Mae Wests ' and parachutes, queued up for a mug of tea and an issue of anti-sickness pills.

The HQ and three sections of the 224th (Parachute) Field Ambulance had waited for the day in the transit camp at Hill Hall, near Epping—the rest of the unit being at Mushroom Farm. The unit took off, with the 3rd Parachute Brigade, from the airfields at Chipping Ongar and Weatherfield shortly after seven o'clock in the morning of 24th March, after a reveille at a quarter to three. The air-lift of the Field Ambulance for the operation divided the unit into seven ' sticks ' each of eighteen all ranks, whilst the ' jeeps ', trailers, motor cycles and the RASC drivers were airborne in three gliders. The unit moved in three waves.

In the first wave was the COs ' stick ', and a ' stick ' comprising No 2 Section, which was to drop with the Brigade HQ and the 8th Battalion The Parachute Regiment. No 1 Section dropped in two ' sticks ' in the second wave with the 1st Canadian Parachute Battalion. The Second-in-Command's and No 3 Section's ' sticks ' went in the third wave, dropping with the 9th Battalion The Parachute Regiment.

The flight was uneventful, except for the breaking of the tow-rope of No 1 Glider over France. The first wave dropped at three minutes to ten, followed by the second and third waves at four-minute intervals, whilst the gliders with the transport landed forty minutes later. The DZ area on the southern fringe of the Diersfordterwald was occupied by the enemy, a neck of woodland running out from the Brigade HQ and Field Ambulance RV being particularly strongly held. There were immediate casualties on landing from enemy small-arms and mortar fire.

A number of the unit came down among the high trees and three [1] were killed as they hung helpless suspended from the branches by their parachute harness. Others, however, made miraculous escapes. Sergeant-Instructor Slater of the Army Physical Training Corps cut himself down from the trees by slashing his lift webbs and fell twenty feet, but was unharmed. The QM, Captain E. D. Anderson, was brought to earth by the shattering of the tree, in which he was suspended, by a mortar bomb, but on landing, when he went to the aid of a wounded man, was shot through the shoulder, but eventually managed to get to the RV.

The other RAMC personnel disentangled themselves from their parachutes—the section officer of No 2 Section found two bullets embedded in the basic pouch carried on his chest —and made off to the RV under heavy fire.

As they neared the position, Captain C. A. Chaundy of the Army Dental Corps was shot through the neck and killed instantly. The others reached their RV safely and immediately set up a CCP in the wood. The enemy were strongly entrenched around the wood, and in addition to a number of machine-guns there were two well-camouflaged field-guns. Twenty minutes from the time of the landing most of the unit had been accounted for. Soon the DZ was littered with parachutes, discarded quick-release gear, kit-bags and other jettisoned equipment, the men having doubled off to their respective RVs.

The first task, that of clearing the DZ of casualties, was undertaken under heavy mortar fire, the section attached

---

[1] The Reverend J. F. Kenny, RAChD, Corporal L. F. Nicholson, RAMC, and Driver Shelton, RASC.

L

to the battalions moving the wounded and injured to the battalion RVs from whence the casualties were evacuated by No 4 Section to the Field Ambulance ADS. The wounded lying out in the open were under constant fire and there was a continual call for stretcher-bearers. It was during this work that Staff-Sergeant Walsby was badly wounded and died a few hours later at the MDS.

At midday the Brigade Commander ordered 224th (Parachute) Field Ambulance to move to the 1st Canadian Parachute Battalion area, and following a reconnaissance by the CO the unit moved into the church at Bergenfurth, which had been shelled by British artillery from across the Rhine. The nave was littered with fallen plaster and smashed pews. A party of prisoners were put to work in clearing the church and by half-past two in the afternoon one surgical team was in operation.

The priest's house adjoining the church had been quickly converted into an operating theatre, the church being used as the reception and minor treatment department. The innovation of carrying ready-sterilised instruments by the surgeons and their assistants proved its worth, as did also the carrying of a bottle of plasma in the basic pouch of every member of the unit's HQ. These supplies proved adequate until the forward units of the Second Army brought up fresh supplies. In cases of severe shock, however, plasma alone was not enough, and as whole blood was not available in containers it was taken from donors on the spot, but such source of supply was, of course, limited.

There was a continual flow of casualties, British, Canadian, German, both soldiers and civilians, some very gravely and hideously wounded—one man was found to have a solid piece of metal, weighing nearly ten pounds, embedded in his pelvic region, whilst a middle-aged German civilian, found gazing at his exposed intestines, died quietly following an injection of morphia.

The death of Captain Chaundy had left the surgical team without an anaesthetist, and in consequence all the MOs were called upon to assist during operations, but there were not enough doctors to go round, and it was not long before the assistant anaesthetists were giving pentothal by intravenous injections and anaesthesing other patients with mixtures of ether and chloroform.

The casualties were so numerous that the supply of stretchers gave out. As soon as the gliders began to land—crashing down on the DZ—Private P. M. Lenton, knowing that each glider carried medical supplies, proposed going out to get more stretchers. " You'll never get there and back alive ", said his Section NCO, pointing out across the open ground, but Private Lenton and Private T. Downey insisted that they could try. Off they went and not only brought back a supply of much-needed stretchers, but carried in some of the wounded men lying out on the DZ.[1]

There was a continual flow of casualties ; the Canadian parachutists had met with considerable opposition, and during their drop were subjected to heavy enemy fire from light anti-aircraft guns and small-arms fire. They sustained a number of casualties, including the CO, who was killed on landing.

Foremost among those tending the wounded was Corporal F. G. Topham, one of the Canadian medical orderlies. About eleven o'clock, soon after the landing, cries for help came from a wounded man lying out in the open on the DZ. Two medical orderlies from 224th (Parachute) Field Ambulance went out to render aid, but both were killed as they knelt beside the wounded man. Then, to quote from the citation which led to the award of the Victoria Cross, 'without hesitation, and on his own initiative, Corporal Topham went forward through intense fire to replace the orderlies who had been killed before his eyes. As he worked on the wounded man he was himself shot through the nose. In spite of severe bleeding and intense pain he never faltered in his task. Having completed immediate first-aid, he carried the wounded man steadily and slowly back through continuous fire to the shelter of a wood.' For two hours Corporal Topham refused all offers of medical help for his own wound and continued to work in bringing in wounded. Later in the day he came

[1] For this act of gallantry Private Lenton was awarded the Military Medal and Private Downey mentioned in Despatches.

up with a carrier which had received a direct hit, the vehicle was blazing and its mortar ammunition was exploding. Despite an order that no one was to approach the carrier, Corporal Topham [1] went forward alone, dragged out three men, and carried them back one at a time in the open and under heavy fire. ' His magnificent and selfless courage ', concluded the citation, ' inspired all those who witnessed it.'

The 225th (Parachute) Field Ambulance, commanded by Lieut.-Colonel N. J. P. Hewlings, concentrated on their DZ and established themselves in a large farm on the outskirts of the Diersfordterwald, making use of the outhouse, and the two surgeons, Majors A. Macpherson and P. Essex-Lopresti, were soon at work.

The Diersfordterwald was strongly held by the Germans, and in consequence casualties from the 225th Field Ambulance ADS were being evacuated to the east, further into Germany, into the area occupied by the 5th Parachute Brigade. The Germans, still in some strength, lay between the 3rd and 5th Brigades all day, but during the night withdrew from their positions, one company actually marching through the farm occupied by the 225th Field Ambulance. However, they did not pause, or halt to look round the buildings, and the Field Ambulance was too outnumbered and not properly equipped to deal with the situation, so they lay low and watched the laden infantry march by.

By the end of the day the 224th (Parachute) Field Ambulance had lost two officers and five NCOs and men killed. Captain E. D. M. Anderson, the QM, and seven ORs were wounded and seven more missing.[2] A total of 212 casualties[3] had been treated by the unit and nine surgical operations were performed.

At Earls Colne Airfield the Horsa gliders and Halifax aircraft awaited the 195th (Air Landing) Field Ambulance and the unit emplaned at seven o'clock. The towing aircraft

---

[1] Royal Canadian Army Medical Corps.
[2] Of these 3 were taken prisoner but later recaptured.
[3] 181 British, 41 Canadian, and 70 German prisoners of war.

engines warmed up, the glider ropes taughtened and, one by one, the gliders became airborne. They circled the airfield as the airborne force assembled. At times gliders and tug aircraft could be seen at all points of the compass as far as visibility permitted.

At a given time the airborne force headed towards the coast, and were soon over the sea. The Channel crossing was soon over, and life-belts were discarded. Weather conditions were such that many of the gliders had very ' bumpy ' flights. One glider's tow-rope parted from its ' tug ', and the glider fell behind and downwards from the main stream of aircraft.[1] However, most of the planes and gliders kept their stations and formations during the flight.

By ten-thirty the gliders carrying 195th (Air Landing) Field Ambulance were between the lines of River Mass and the Rhine, a vast smoke-screen obscured most of the country below, fighter aircraft were among the gliders in considerable strength, and a number of Dakotas could be seen returning from the DZ—side doors still open. In front the puffs of bursting AA fire could be seen, soon the flashes and the crumps and cracks of explosions could be heard, and both aircraft and gliders began to ' weave '.

Soon the gliders turned into a steep glide and were cast off from their ' tugs '. Men peered through the smoke and mist as they tried to identify landmarks from the maps, particularly the church spire and windmill at Hamminkeln. The DZ was soon distinguishable, parachutes were lying about over the fields, and men could be seen moving about all over the area.

Down came the gliders, crashing through hedges, wire fences, and trees, ' juddering ' to a halt in a sickening grinding crash. The noise of battle welled up around the men as the doors were ripped open and they scrambled out on to German soil, and lay down under the wings and tails of the gliders until they received the order to start unloading. The low landing speed of the gliders had made them very vulner-

---

[1] Glider No. 177 carrying Captain S. I. Green, and a ' stick ' of 195th (Air Landing) Field Ambulance. The glider landed near Deurne in Holland, and the RAMC personnel rejoined the Division the following day.

able to light AA fire and small-arms fire and because of their somewhat flimsy and inflammable construction almost every hit had most damaging effects. At the outset the casualties in the 6th Air Landing Brigade were assessed at 40 per cent of personnel and 50 per cent of equipment. Many of the gliders crashed on landing. Of those due to land on the DZ of the 3rd and 5th Parachute Brigades less than half arrived safely. The glider carrying the medical equipment to the 9th Battalion turned upside down in the trees, Sergeant Miller being killed in the violent impact on landing.

No 3 Section of 195th (Air Landing) Field Ambulance landed in their glider at a quarter to eleven. They were soon unloaded and ready to move. Captain J. S. Binning, RAMC, put his section in a defensive position. His fighting personnel, the two glider pilots, arrived with a bren, the ACC cook, the Sapper and RASC driver, being distributed in a close perimeter around the glider, and the RAMC personnel, although armed, were held in reserve under the glider's wings and tail. Not far away some gunners were unloading from their glider. Captain Binning made his way over to them, and in discussion with the Gunner subaltern established their position—a little to the north-west of Hamminkeln and north of the wood in which the Divisional HQ was to concentrate.

The section set off across country, picking up on the way an American paratrooper with a broken leg. They soon came under heavy mortar fire, went to ground, but sustained no casualties and pressed on. Reaching a farmhouse they found a troop of the Light Regiment, RA, under mortar and small-arms fire, preparing for action. Captain Binning checked his position with the OC, who said quite calmly, in a manner reminiscent of giving directions to a stranger in a London street, " Oh, this is Bunters "—one of the code names for selected locations.

Moving on, the section covered over a mile of country without mishap, and by midday had reached Divisional HQ, where on seeking out a senior officer Captain Binning inadvertently reported personally to the GOC, who welcomed him and directed him to Brigade HQ. The section was ordered to move into a corner of a wood and dig in, the OC going over to the CCP at Divisional HQ, where a chaotic situation obtained due mainly to the presence of an excitable German MO and a number of voluble German orderlies who were not organising anything, and were rushing around giving brandy to every wounded man. "Tetanus! Tetanus!" shouted the German doctor, pointing at random to the wounded. Captain Binning took control of the CCP and tried to direct the Germans into some form of organised work, but in the end was forced to give up the attempt and had the Germans removed to a POW cage. Thereafter, with the RSM of the Field Ambulance and four medical orderlies, the CCP settled down to a routine to compete with the constant flow of wounded, and it was not long before every room in the house in which the CCP had been established was full of lying cases.

The main problem arose from lack of transport to bring in casualties, and to evacuate them to the Field Ambulance. It was not until after nine o'clock that evening that the required transport was organised by the DADMS in the form of a captured German lorry, which took five stretcher cases and three sitting wounded. By this means the CCP was relieved of congestion and after ten o'clock no further cases were admitted.

The section at the CCP had started medical treatment at midday with one medical pack for minor treatment and six Thomas splint sets. During the day a considerable amount of medical equipment had been used, including the application of three Thomas splints, but by the evening the situation had improved by salvaging of both British and American medical panniers from gliders, the acquisition of German medical supplies, and the arrival of Gunner Moffatt, the medical orderly of the Light Regiment, RA, with a pannier of medical equipment for an RAP.

During the forty-five hours that the 224th Field Ambulance MDS spent at Bergefurth, Major H. D. Johnson and Major N. A. Miller, assisted by their surgical teams and with Captains D. E. Freeman, G. R. W. Gray and S. P. C. O'Regan as the anaesthetists, had each performed fourteen surgical operations. The wounded selected for operations were in far too critical a condition to have survived evacuation across the Rhine.

Of the twenty-eight cases operated on, fifteen were suffering from multiple wounds, the majority of which were bullet wounds, the remainder, about a third, resulted from shells and mortar bombs.[1] Resuscitation commenced immediately with plasma until whole blood became available on 25th March, although this was in short supply.

Stocks of pentothal, ether and chloroform carried by the personnel of the surgical teams was adequate, and every case was given an intra-muscular injection of penicillin. For wound toilet, pulverised sulphanilamide was replaced by penicillin and sulphathiazole powder, whilst for amputations and laparotomies hot saline was always ready in addition to a continual supply of sterile instruments and jaconet towels, all boiled in camp kettles, and a plain steriliser heated over two primus stoves. Plaster of Paris bandages were used for all fractures and also for some severe flesh wounds when it was considered that this immobilisation would facilitate the patient's journey back to the base hospital.

During the afternoon of 25th March there was cheering outside the 224th (Parachute) Field Ambulance MDS; everyone paused in their work to look out as the first vehicles of the 6th Battalion The King's Own Scottish Borderers, the spearhead of the 15th (Scottish) Division, went by, pressing on towards the retreating Germans.

In their wake came a jeep in which rode the ADMS of the Division, Colonel MacEwan, who brought the news that the beachhead was secure, the line of evacuation was now clear and casualties could now be sent back to the safety of the General Hospitals west of the Rhine.

The whole airborne operation had been a success and the German resistance completely broken, although the casualties had been heavy, numbering nearly 3,000 killed, wounded

---

[1] An analysis of the injuries showed: Penetrating wounds of abdomen, 6; Fracture femur, 5; Penetrating wounds of chest, 2; Amputations, 4; Fracture tibia, 3; Other injuries, 8. No burns or head injuries were treated in the theatre.

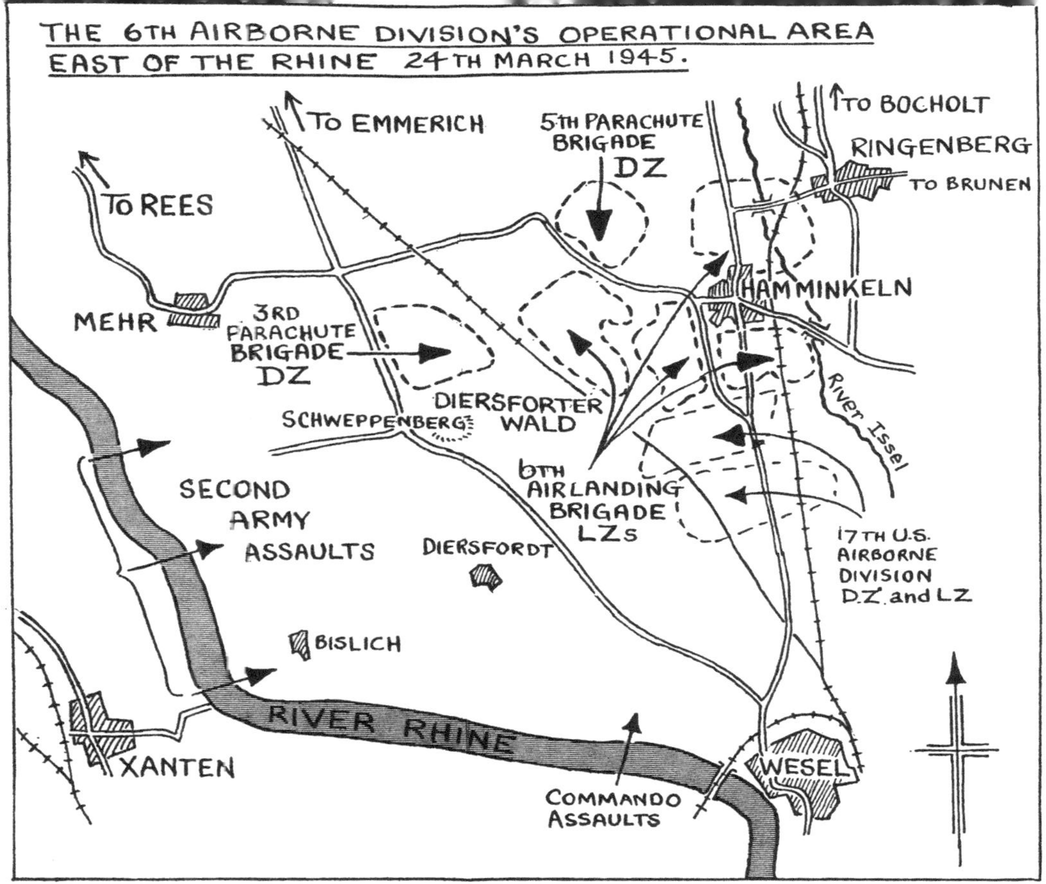
THE 6TH AIRBORNE DIVISION'S OPERATIONAL AREA
EAST OF THE RHINE 24TH MARCH 1945.
TO EMMERICH
TO REES
5TH PARACHUTE BRIGADE DZ
TO BOCHOLT
RINGENBERG
TO BRUNEN
HAMMINKELN
MEHR
3RD PARACHUTE BRIGADE DZ
DIERSFORTER WALD
SCHWEPPENBERG
River Issel
6TH AIRLANDING BRIGADE LZs
SECOND ARMY ASSAULTS
17TH U.S. AIRBORNE DIVISION D.Z. and LZ
DIERSFORDT
BISLICH
RIVER RHINE
XANTEN
WESEL
COMMANDO ASSAULTS

and missing, the glider casualties having been particularly severe, outnumbering the parachutists in the ratio of three to one. 1,600 aircraft and over 1,300 gliders had put some 14,000 troops on the ground. About fifty-five aircraft and just under 4 per cent of the gliders had been destroyed.

Despite the reduction in the strength of the 6th Airborne Division by one-third, the formation reorganised and prepared that night to take its place in the forward pursuit move on the heels of the retreating Germans.

CHAPTER XIII

FROM THE RHINE TO THE BALTIC

THE ADVANCE THROUGH GERMANY

THE forward route of the Division took them from Hamminkeln on 25th March to Wismar, which they reached on 2nd May, their advance taking them across the River Ems, and the Weser, passing just south of Osnabruck, through Minden, Celle, thence north-west through Ulzen across Luneburg Heath, over the River Elbe and on to the shores of the Baltic, some 330 miles in five weeks.

The Division's advance gathered momentum, moving forward some thirty to forty miles a day. In such an advance the Field Ambulances were deployed on the orders of the ADMS in order that one should always be open at the right place at the right time to clear the casualties from the forward battalion; the second was in reserve ready to move; and the third ready to clear its casualties, pack up and be ready to take the reserve ambulance rôle. In all airborne operations the Field Ambulances were brigaded, they trained and operated at all times with their own brigades, and thereby became an integral part. This was all very well in an airborne rôle, but now the Division was fighting as an infantry formation and it took a lot of diplomacy on the part of the divisional medical staff officers to prevent proposed changes in the medical plan in order that the brigades could have their 'own' Field Ambulance in support at all times, but generally speaking the divisional medical organisation worked smoothly. The main CCS was still on the west bank of the Rhine and as the advance continued and the evacuation route lengthened, RAMC detachments had to be left as staging posts along the lines of communication.

By ten o'clock in the morning of 25th March the link-up between the assault forces of the Second Army and the airborne forces was fully established, and preparations were made for the immediate advance into Germany.

The 224th Field Ambulance remained in their position near Bergen until 26th March. On the 25th the unit treated a further ninety-nine cases, and the surgical team carried out fifteen operations, and during the day Major Murray was slightly wounded by the accidental explosion of a ' gammon ' bomb. At four o'clock in the afternoon of the 26th the unit closed its ADS and moved to a brigade concentration area at Isselrot, where sections were attached to battalions for a forward move.

The next day the unit reached Elmers and on the 28th moved to Schloss Raesfeld where it was the only Field Ambulance open in the Divisional area, and received twenty-six casualties and a further ninety-three the next day [1] and eighteen surgical operations were performed. On the 30th the 225th Field Ambulance ' leap frogged ' the ADS of 224th Field Ambulance which moved the next day to Greven, where it remained for four days, admitting 199 casualties.[2]

The 4th of April was spent on the move, with an overnight halt at Nieder Lengerich. On 5th April the unit reached Lubbecke, where it remained for two days, during which it took over the German Military Hospital at Minden, but soon after Minden came into the area of the 9th US Army, so that the hospital had to be evacuated, and whereupon two sections set up an ADS at Friederdue. The 8th of April saw the Field Ambulance at Wunstorf, and two days later it moved to Negenborn, where it remained until the 14th. Then followed three days on the move, halting near Celle on the 14th, Eschede the next day and Stadensen on the 16th, where the unit opened an ADS until 20th April.

In the twenty-eight days since they parachuted down on the east of the Rhine the 224th Field Ambulance had admitted 1,139 casualties, and the 225th received 1,083.[3]

---

[1] Made up of 85 British ; 2 Canadian ; 1 Australian ; 2 Americans ; 25 German prisoners of war ; and 4 civilians.

[2] Of which 165 were British.

[3] British casualties were made up of 549 wounded (454 from the 6th Airborne Division), 168 sick, 67 accidental casualties, and 24 cases of exhaustion. 35 Americans ; 177 German prisoners of war ; and 61 German civilian and displaced persons were also treated. The analysis of 95 surgical operations performed were as follows : fractures of femurs, 17 ; other fractures, 25 ; abdominal wounds, 10 ; traumatic amputations, 5 ; flesh wounds, 37 ; burns, 1.

On 26th March the 195th (Air Landing) Brigade started their forward move from the Hamminkeln area, crossing the eastern part of the DZ, littered with shattered gliders, lying across the railway track, crushed against trees and buildings, the landings in this area having been made in the face of considerable opposition from AA guns. On they went on the track of the enemy, here and there lay sprawled-out groups of German dead, among shattered buildings marking the lines of attack of the rocket-firing Typhoons. The Devons and Royal Ulster Rifles advanced along parallel roads and there were a number of casualties in the constant brushes with enemy rear-guards. An RAP and a CCP were set up by the RMOs, Captain Kaye with the Devons and Captain D. I. Rees with the RUR, in a farm near Postmanshof, to deal with both British and German wounded.

On 28th March the advance continued, the roads being packed with vehicles, and the RAMC sections with the infantry battalions marched as well, shrouded in a dull grey haze of dust, over the broken roads, and through shelled villages where every house standing displayed white flags, made from sheets suspended from long sticks and poles, and with the civilians standing in apathetic groups staring at the continuous flow of marching men, vehicles and guns. Now and again they passed groups of twenty to thirty unarmed and unguarded groups of Germans marching back towards the Rhine.

The little town of Rhade was reached that night, and in the morning the advance was continued to Limbeck, where the columns turned off the road to march across country, leaving the roads clear for the forward movement of Second Army's artillery and transport.

As the advance continued the Field Ambulance was continually passed by groups of unarmed and unescorted Germans plodding wearily to the rear, among them were a considerable number of members of the Todt organisation.

The going was hard, it was overcast and raining and it was sheer 'footslogging' over heavy ploughland and through thick woods, where every track and road was deep in mud. At last, in the darkness of the night of 29th/30th March, the

Field Ambulance plodded into Coesfeld. Two sections were allotted billets in undamaged houses amid the rubble of the badly shattered town, resulting from heavy air attack on the 21st, and No 1 Section in a farmhouse on the outskirts. The next day was spent in Coesfeld, where a few casualties were treated, and on the 31st the advance was resumed, but slowly, with several long halts, when the infantry 'debussed' to move forward to dislodge enemy rear-guards. Eventually Greven was reached, the ADS was established in a secluded and palatial German Schloss, and here Captain Binning, who did not arrive until 2 am in the morning, recorded in his diary 'found Captain Rees, still fully dressed and equipped, resting in a luxurious armchair with an empty bottle of champagne at his side'.

The ADS functioned at the Schloss throughout the following day, admitting a number of casualties, but was on the move again by the evening and continued throughout the night up to the Dortmund-Ems Canal, which was crossed at first light on 2nd April under fire from enemy artillery using air-burst shells. Later in the morning the Germans put up some strenuous resistance at Lengerich, and the ADS was hurriedly opened as a CCP and within five minutes was receiving casualties. As the infantry pressed forward, a recce was made in Lengerich leading to the setting up of an ADS in the basement of the local civil hospital to deal with a steady stream of wounded which included an increasing number of Germans.

After an early reveille on the morning of 4th April the Field Ambulance moved at 8.30 am. It moved fast, the whole Brigade was speeding forward in all its vehicles. They swept along through rolling hilly country, past fields of bright-green corn and light-brown ploughland and along roads fringed with apple and cherry trees on which early blossoms were showing. The convoy raced on to Wissenden where the Brigade formed up in battle groups, infantry clambering onto tanks to go forward in front of marching troops. An MDS was opened in Wissenden and soon after casualties began to arrive.

During the engagement earlier in the day Captain Naysmith, the Dental Officer, had been taken prisoner whilst putting up direction signs to the MDS, but by afternoon had been 'liberated' by the RUR. He had done his best to persuade a German company commander to surrender but without avail, and his stubbornness resulted in few prisoners being taken that day by the RUR, who laid waste to a large sweep of countryside, leaving many German dead, and a trail of smoke and fire from farms and buildings in their wake. News travelled fast, and the burgomasters of the next few villages on the forward route came out and surrendered to the first British tank to approach.

It was in this area that the Field Ambulance first encountered crowds of liberated prisoners of war, French, Russians, Poles, and even Italians, one of whom leapt up and down by the side of the jeeps and ambulances excitedly waving his arms and shouting " Redda Crossa! Redda Crossa!". 'The Russians', recorded Captain Binning, 'literally went crazy with joy, crowded out to shake hands, shouting, weeping, cheering, and waving their caps—all this joy and excitement was all the more noticeable in the heart of Germany, where hitherto our reception in most villages was sullen to say the least. The plight of the Russians was truly dreadful: they were lean; more than half starved—a half biscuit was instantly seized and crammed into a hungry mouth. The French, by comparison, were well dressed and looked, at least, as though they had eaten *some* food recently.

After leaving this area a faint air of welcome could be detected in some of the little villages. Women and children would smile or wave their hands, but on the whole the men remained unmoved, regarding the soldiers with stolid, cold, staring eyes. . . .'

The advance continued towards the River Weser, through Minden and north-west to Petershagen, where the 195th (Air Landing) Field Ambulance set up an ADS in a large barrack-like house to which they had been directed by an English-speaking lady doctor. The accommodation was ideal but the sojourn was short and on went the Field Ambulance towards Ladhe, then over the Weser and on to Bad Remburg.

By 10th April the Division had reached the Steinhuder-

meer. From then onwards the days ran into each other with
constant movement, brushes with the enemy, air attacks,
especially at night, constant changes of location, long drives
through blinding dust, through sleepy, shuttered villages or
others shattered and burnt out in the course of determined
little battles as company met company in desperate fighting,
the Germans goaded by despair into desperate resistance,
the British by determination to reach their goal by smashing
the opposition before them. Moving north-westwards, leaving Celle and Hanover on the right flank, the Division entered
Ulzen, where many of the buildings were still smouldering in
the shell-shattered town, and then on again over Luneburg
Heath, into Luneburg and on towards the River Elbe.

It was felt that the River Elbe would be a severe obstacle,
and that the Germans would stage a last-ditch resistance.
One Parachute Brigade was earmarked for an airborne attack
on the east bank, but on nearing the river line advance
patrols reported signs of disorganisation and but weak resistance. A hasty attack was launched and was completely
successful and, early in the morning of 2nd May, the Division
crossed the Elbe over a pontoon bridge. By the afternoon
the leading troops of the 3rd Parachute Brigade made contact near Mecklenburg with Russian patrols advancing from
the east, the 6th Airborne Division being the first formation
to link up with them, and later in the afternoon the advanced
troops of the Division entered Wismar on the Baltic coast,
some sixty miles from the Elbe. They had taken some 3,000
prisoners and the leading company riding on tanks had never
dismounted for action.

The undamaged town of Wismar was still and silent, the
inhabitants having barricaded their doors and windows and
shut themselves in. Following the leading unit into the town,
Major J. C. Watts,[1] the DADMS, established a medical HQ
in a large house in the southern sector of the town, whilst
two of the Field Ambulances followed up to occupy a large
Luftwaffe hospital which lay about a mile to the west.

[1] Now Colonel J. C. Watts, OBE, MC, MB, FRCS, Professor of Military
Surgery, Royal Army Medical College, author of ' Surgeon at War ' (Allen
& Unwin) (1955), from which the description of the incident on page 176 has
been taken.

Major Watts had just installed himself at the Medical HQ when an officer of one of the Parachute battalions reported a large number of German wounded in the eastern area of the town. Hurrying in that direction, he came into the main square, where an astounding sight met his eyes. Moving into the square was a straggling and pitiful column of wounded with blood-stained bandages around heads, arms and legs, some with limbs in plaster—the column, he discovered, was spread out over nearly two miles of the main road leading in from the east, and at the end of the long slow-moving line of men came the more seriously wounded, lifting and dragging themselves along, helping each other in their great stress. Among them were a number of German nurses, who were helping men in plaster and even some whose limbs had been amputated, others lay on small carts and were being dragged along over the bumpy stones.

By questioning the nurses Major Watts learned that they were all in a hospital train travelling west which had run out of fuel and had been brought to a standstill a few miles east of Wismar. Whilst halted a Cossack patrol had arrived on the scene, had sacked the train, taken any valuables, shot any of the wounded who had resisted, and on leaving had swept the train with a machine-gun and set it on fire. All the wounded, with the medical and nursing staff, had hurriedly abandoned the blazing train and had set off westwards in search of relief and safety.

Major Watts loaded four of the worst cases on to his jeep, which was fitted for stretcher carriage, gave instructions to the German nurses to halt the column so that the wounded could rest until he could arrange for their collection, and drove off with his load of wounded to the Luftwaffe hospital, where one of the Field Ambulances made arrangements to take in the wounded. Returning to the scene of the pitiful march Major Watts still found the column on the move, for nothing could stop them in their westward move—fear of Russian pursuit was intense—so he continued to ferry wounded back to the hospital, jeep load after jeep load, until all reached the hospital in this manner, or through their own slow, painful efforts.

Early the next day the Brigade was faced with an additional problem. A trickle of refugees, which soon grew into a steady stream, came into the town from the east. They had left all their possessions and their homes to get away from the advancing Russians. A reception camp was hurriedly set up by 195th (Air Landing) Field Ambulance, who took on the care of the increasing number of refugees. Among them were a number of civilian doctors who were put to work to cope with the inevitable dysentery, which soon broke out.

The rest of the Division followed on the heels of the 3rd Brigade, passing through villages filled with liberated British and American prisoners of war—shouting, cheering, waving, singing ' Tipperary ', calling out " Give 'em socks ", " Get after the bastards ! ". They were thin and worn but their spirits were terrific—there was handshaking and more cheers, and on went the Division, on to the Baltic shore, passing whole battalions of disarmed, shuffling Germans, moving westwards, and groups of Russian and Polish prisoners who grinned and waved to the passing columns, which did not halt until they were in sight of the sea at Wismar.

From 3rd to 7th May the Field Ambulances of the Division remained in their locations [1] in and around Wismar, tending the wounded and sick British and American released prisoners of war, and countless German soldiers and civilians, as well as the hundreds of refugees and displaced persons who came into the area.

Great was the excitement when news came through on the morning of the 7th that all the German Armies in Europe had surrendered in the early hours. The next day, the official ' VE ' Day was celebrated with parades, concerts and a great general relaxation, although the general conditions and the necessary adjuncts to such a celebration were missing.

On 11th May the Field Ambulances turned out in strength for the Victory Parade in Wismar where the Divisional Com-

---

[1] 224th (Parachute) Field Ambulance was ordered to send a surgeon to the notorious concentration camp at Belsen. This officer was Major H. Daintree-Johnson.

mander took the salute as the Royal Scots Greys drove past in their tanks and the 3rd Parachute Brigade marched past to the pipes and drums of The Greys.

The next day Brigadier Austin Eagger, the DDMS of the 1st Airborne Corps, accompanied by Colonel M. McEwan, the ADMS, visited the Field Ambulances ; a proud day for them to see the airborne medical units with which they had been associated since their formation ; to see them during the first days of peace after the final defeat of Germany, and to recall all that they had achieved in the past five years. . . .

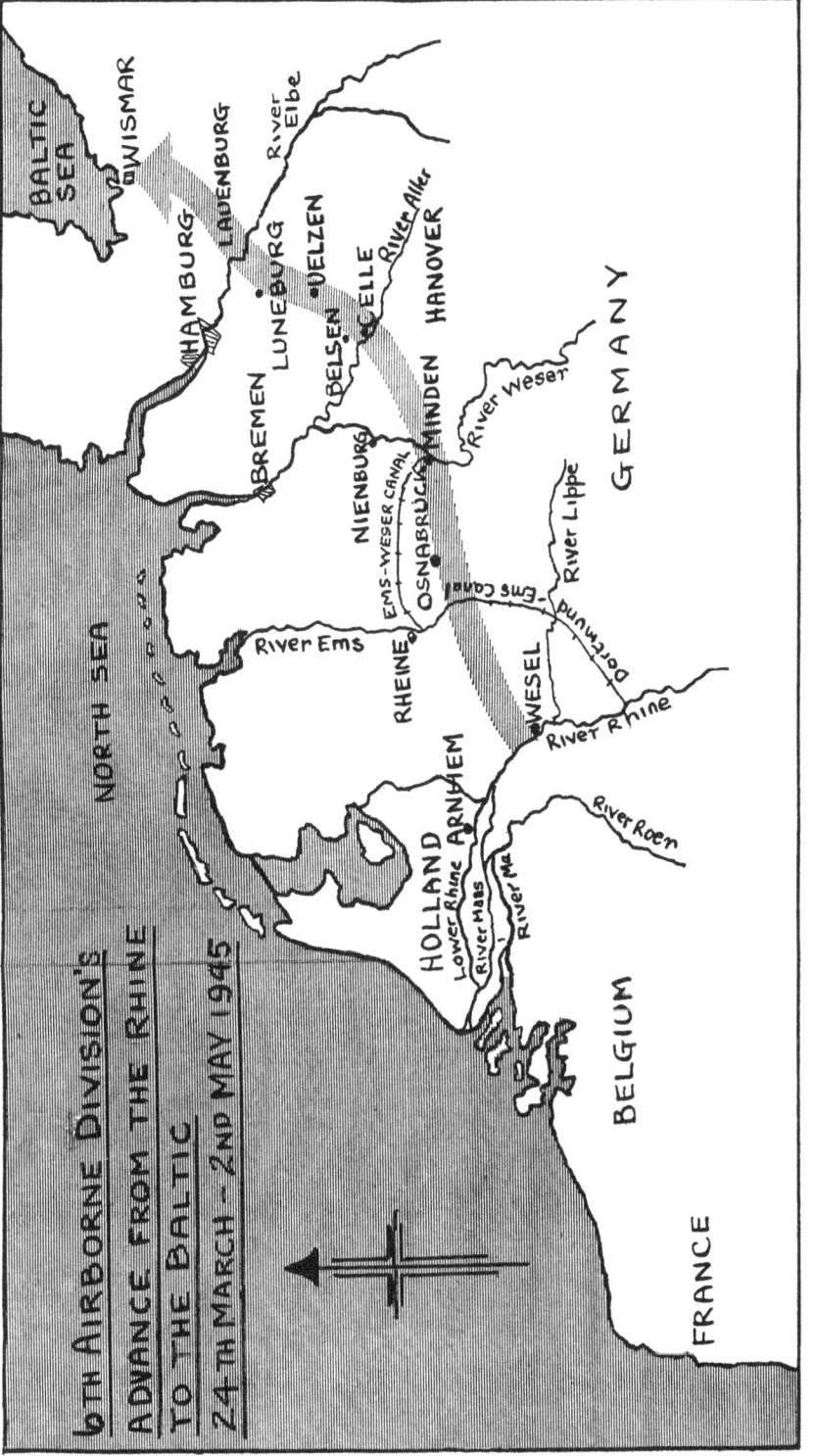

CHAPTER XIV

THE LIBERATION OF NORWAY

PLANNING for the liberation of Norway had commenced as far back as October 1943 at HQ Scottish Command, and consideration was given to every possible contingency, but it was not until the final defeat of the Wehrmacht in Germany itself that these plans were put into operation.

At the time of the final collapse of the German armies and the unconditional surrender at Luneburg Heath on 8th May 1945 there were some 400,000 German troops in Norway, and the immediate task of the Allied Liberation Forces destined for Norway was the control, disarmament and evacuation of the large German garrisons. In step with this objective was the work of succouring and repatriating Allied prisoners of war and 'displaced persons', and finally the Allied force was to be available to render any assistance required by the Norwegian authorities.

The Allied force of a strength of 39,000 all ranks which was to operate under the direction of SHAEF [1] was composed of Norwegian,[2] American,[3] and British troops, the latter under the command of HQ Allied Land Forces, Norway. The British element of the force comprised the re-formed 1st Airborne Division, HQ 50th (Northumbrian) Division, the 1st SAS Brigade, the 303rd and 304th Infantry Brigades, and No 88 Group, RAF.

On 7th May the German Forces in Norway surrendered unconditionally and German officers flew to Scotland to give full details of the German dispositions and defences.

Two days later a Sunderland aircraft landed in Oslo harbour and four Allied officers went ashore to ensure that the Allied

---
[1] Supreme Headquarters Allied Expeditionary Force.
[2] The Norwegian Mountain Brigade, trained in the United Kingdom, and units of the Royal Norwegian Navy and Air Force.
[3] A US Task Force of one regiment composed of three battalions.

force's orders were carried out.[1] On the same day the 1st Airborne Division took off from airfields in the United Kingdom to land at Oslo and Stavanger.

The RAMC units of the 1st Airborne Division were the re-formed 16th (Parachute) Field Ambulance, commanded by Lieut.-Colonel N. J. P. Hewlings ; 133rd (Parachute) Field Ambulance, commanded by Lieut.-Colonel W. C. Alford, OBE ; and the 181st (Air Landing) Field Ambulance, which had been re-formed on 1st March 1945,[2] under the command of Lieut.-Colonel I. C. Gilliland,[3] with Major G. Rigby-Jones as Second-in-Command.

The 16th (Parachute) Field Ambulance flew out to Oslo and the 133rd[4] took off from Barkston Heath to land at Sola Airfield at Stavanger on 10th May. The 133rd (Parachute) Field Ambulance took over the St Joseph's Roman Catholic Hospital at Kristiansand and other smaller hospitals at Evji-Nlosen, Moi and Bergen, and one section was detached for service with the 1st SAS Brigade at Kristiansand, where they were primarily engaged in the care of Russian prisoners of war, of which there were some 1,500 around Kristiansand and another 3,000 around Bergen, many of whom were suffering from diphtheria and scarlet fever.

The Air Landing Field Ambulance took off from Tarrant Ruston and Earls Colne Airfields on 11th May, and landed at eight-thirty in the evening at Gardia Airport near Oslo : moved to the city by train, and two days later was established at Norstrand on the Oslo Fjord : here it was quartered in the school which had previously been used by the Germans as an emergency hospital, and opened up a General

[1] The control of the German forces (which outnumbered the Allied force by ten to one) was enforced by making full use of the German organisation and existing chain of command.

[2] Made up of the seaborne element of the unit which went to North-Western Europe to join up with the glider-borne Air Landing Field Ambulance at Arnhem, with a few survivors of the original 181st Field Ambulance from Arnhem, together with 5 officers and 165 ORs from the 23rd Field Ambulance.

[3] Succeeded by Lieut.-Colonel A. T. Marrable in July.

[4] Less one section which flew to Copenhagen with the HQ of the 1st Parachute Brigade on 8th May. This section was in Copenhagen with the 1st Parachute Brigade, which formed part of the SHAEF mission to Denmark, until 10th July.

Hospital. By the end of the month 107 patients had been admitted and twenty-nine operations had been performed.

The medical units of the Airborne Division were committed to the work in connection with the supervision of a large number of sick Russians in the German prisoner of war camps and with the evacuation of the German army. Every man was subjected to a careful medical inspection to ensure that he was completely free from any infections before he was permitted to leave the country. By the end of July sufficient shipping had been assembled to allow the start of the transportation of the Germans back to their country.

At the end of June the 1st Airborne Division started its withdrawal from Norway to return to the United Kingdom, where it was to refit for its new rôle as part of the force to be designated the Imperial Strategic Reserve. The 133rd (Parachute) Field Ambulance returned to England on 29th June, flying from Stavanger to Culverthorpe and then moving on to Winthorpe. On 11th October the unit returned to Bulford.

On 15th November orders were received for the unit to be placed in ' suspended animation '. The personnel were posted away in batches, and the unit finally closed down on 1st December.

The 16th (Parachute) Field Ambulance also flew back to England and was disbanded in October, when the 1st Airborne Division ceased to exist.

In caring for the Russians, one section of the 181st (Air Landing) Field Ambulance was embarked on a Swedish hospital ship to care for some 250 Russians, the majority of whom were in the advanced stages of tuberculosis, for the voyage to Murmansk. On arrival at Murmansk it was made clear to the SMO by the Russians that it was their responsibility for unloading the sick from the ship, and a party of troops with fixed bayonets went aboard to supervise the disembarkation. In their haste to get ashore, one man died of a fatal haemoptysis whilst attempting to hurry up a companion-way. The section had shore-leave in Murmansk, thereby becoming the first unit of the British Army to land in North Russia since 1919.

The 181st (Air Landing) Field Ambulance sailed from Oslo in the MV *Stratheden* on 3rd September.

181st (Air Landing) Field Ambulance on its return to England was quartered at Busigny Barracks, at Perham Down, near Tidworth. Here orders were received for the unit's disbandment and it was disbanded on the 14th November 1945 when the number of Airborne Divisions was reduced from two to one.

CHAPTER XV

IN INDIA AND BURMA

WITH THE AIRBORNE FORMATIONS OF THE INDIAN ARMY

IT was at Delhi Cantonment in October 1941 that the 50th Indian Parachute Brigade was formed.[1] It was composed of the 151st (British),[2] the 152nd (Indian),[3] and 153rd (Gurkha)[4] Parachute Battalions, together with a British-Indian Brigade Signal Section, and a section of Sappers raised from the Kirkee Sappers and Miners.

The 151st (British) Parachute Battalion was raised from a nucleus of volunteers drawn from all units of the British Army in India, and the 152nd (Indian) Battalion from all sections of the Indian Army.

There were considerable difficulties in the formation of the Brigade for there were, at that time, no precedents in India.

An Air Landing School was established at Willingdon Airport at New Delhi in September 1941, and although this was an RAF unit all the parachute instructors were, at the outset, drawn from the army.

[1] Commanded by Brigadier W. Gough, MC (formerly 2nd Gurkhas).

[2] The 151st (British) Parachute Battalion, commanded by Lieut.-Colonel M. Lindsay, DSO (RMO, Captain John Buck, RAMC), was transferred to the Middle East in 1942, where it was renumbered 156th—see page 32.

[3] The 152nd (Indian) Battalion (RMO, Captain F. G. Neild, RAMC) was the most interesting experiment, as it contained all races, creeds and castes. This had not previously been attempted and the experiment can hardly be counted as successful, for when the (Indian) Airborne Division was eventually formed, the Battalion split into two—Hindu and Mussalman—by simple fission rather than by parthenogenesis. *Vide* 'Indian Airborne Reminiscences'—Captain F. G. Neild, RAMC. 'Journal of the Royal Army Medical Corps', Vol XCI, No 6, December 1948.

[4] The 153rd (Gurkha) Battalion (RMO, Captain A. G. Rangaraj, IAMC) 'had the smoothest passage forming, as it consisted of one class who spoke one language and was officered by British officers of the Gurkha Brigade'. It was commanded at the time by Lieut.-Colonel F. T. Loftus-Tottenham, DSO, who subsequently became GOC of the 81st (West African) Division.

The only equipment available for parachute training was a dozen 'statichutes', a trapeze, and aircraft with the fuselage having a good clearance of about three feet. The aircraft available for training comprised a flight of Vickers Valencias. Courses at the Air Landing School for thirty men at a time lasted three weeks, one week's physical training and two weeks parachute training, five jumps being necessary to qualify for the parachute 'wings'.

In March 1942 all training ceased due to the flight of Valencias being withdrawn to assist in the withdrawal from Burma and Assam. During the period 7th March to 10th May 1942 British forces were forced into the fighting withdrawal from Burma in the face of the Japanese drive to India which was at last halted on the 800-mile front from the north of Akyab, in the south-west Arakan area on the Bay of Bengal, *via* Imphal to Ledo, the terminus of the Calcutta-Assam railway.

Shortly after the withdrawal from Burma, in June 1942, the first operational parachute drop in Burma was made by a mixed detachment of British and Gurkha parachute troops, under the command of Major J. O. M. Roberts; they dropped in the Myitkyina area, with the object of endeavouring to find out the future intentions of the Japanese in that sector. The force later withdrew, by a march northwards several hundred miles, to Fort Hertz, from where they were flown back to India.

The Japanese advance to the eastern borders of India had far-reaching repercussions throughout the country. In July the 152nd (Indian) Parachute Battalion was called upon to drop in the Sind desert to help in rounding up the Hurs, a lawless tribe of Muslims, and in the following month, following the arrest of Ghandi and other leaders of the Congress Party, the whole Brigade was engaged on internal security duties and deployed in and around Old and New Delhi.

The operations in Burma had increased the importance of Delhi as an air-base, and in consequence the Air Landing School was moved to Chaklala in the North Punjab, redesignated No 3 Parachute Training School and became an entirely RAF unit.

For administrative and training purposes the 50th (Indian) Parachute Brigade was also moved to Campbellpur, and it was here that the 154th (Gurkha) Parachute Battalion [1] was raised from the remnants of the 3/7th Gurkha Rifles to take the place of the 151st (British) Battalion, which had been sent to the Middle East in October 1942.[2]

At Campbellpur parachute training was stepped-up following the arrival of some Hudson aircraft and a squadron of Wellingtons. On the formation of South East Asia Command a complete Wing of Dakota aircraft became available.

At the end of October 1943 General Browning, then GOC Airborne Troops, visited the 1st Airborne Division in Italy and had ordered the ADMS, Colonel A. Austin Eagger, to fly out to India to advise on the organisation of the medical services of the 50th (Indian) Parachute Brigade.

After discussions with Brigadier Hope-Thomson, MC, the Commander of the Indian Parachute Brigade, and the Staff at GHQ India at New Delhi, Colonel Eagger recommended that a similar organisation to the British Airborne Medical Services should be adopted, with one exception, that Parachute Mobile Surgical Units should be formed and that these should only be attached to the Parachute Field Ambulance prior to operations. This organisation was sanctioned, and, his work in India completed, Colonel Eagger flew back to rejoin the 1st Airborne Division in England at the end of December.[3]

Meanwhile the 50th (Indian) Parachute Brigade was reorganised and its supporting arms were increased. Among them was the first Indian Parachute Field Ambulance, numbered 80th,[4] which included a surgical team. At the same time the Indian Airborne Forces Depot was formed to take the place of the Parachute Training Centre.

Training of the Brigade continued throughout 1943 and

[1] RMO, Captain Banerjee, IAMC.
[2] See page 32.
[3] Shortly after, in January 1944, Colonel Eagger was promoted Brigadier and appointed DDMS of the Airborne Corps.
[4] Commanded by Lieut.-Colonel R. B. Davis, IMS, with Major P. G. McGrath, RAMC, Captain W. Thompson, RAMC, and Lieut.(QM) F. A. Hine, RAMC.

their air training culminated in three weeks' jungle warfare courses at Rai Wala, near Dehra Dun. It was there that the 153rd (Gurkha) Parachute Battalion carried out the first battalion jump in India—after an approach flight of four hundred miles from Chaklala. This was followed by an Exercise which was a rehearsal for Operation 'Eagle', a combined assault on the Arakan coast planned for early in 1944. Phase I of the Exercise was held in the North West Frontier Province, the landing zone being that point between the convergence of the Kabul River and the River Indus above the fort at Attock.

Although training had reached the stage when airborne operations could be launched, Phase II of the Exercise was not held as all aircraft were suddenly withdrawn, the Brigade was converted to a 'mule-pack' basis of organisation and moved to the Kohima area for advanced jungle training.

The Brigade entrained at Campbellpur on 24th February leaving behind the 154th (Gurkha) Parachute Battalion to complete its air training. Four days by rail right across India brought the formation to Calcutta and thence on to the riverhead at Sirajganj Ghat where the Brigade embarked in river paddle steamers to move slowly up the broad Brahmaputra River to their destination at Pandi. The move on to Kohima was carried out in three-ton lorries and for the final stage of the journey the Brigade marched ten miles to their camp at Chakabama.

Here the 50th (Indian) Parachute Brigade came under command of the 23rd Indian Division, which formed part of the IV Indian Corps. The 1st Battalion The Assam Regiment joined the Brigade to take the place of the 154th (Gurkha) Parachute Battalion; and the 152nd (Indian) Parachute Battalion moved into positions in the area designated 'Sheldon's Corner' to the south-east of Ukhrul—an area which was a mass of jungle-covered mountains intersected by deep ravines.

On 19th March orders were received for the 50th Parachute Brigade to move. The Brigade, less the 152nd Parachute Battalion and the 1st Battalion Assam Regiment, marched a distance of ten miles up and up, some 3,500 feet to Kohima,

IN INDIA AND BURMA 187

where they embussed for an eighty-mile drive down the Manipur road to Imphal.

Unbeknown to the Brigade the Japanese had suddenly advanced from the south-east and had descended upon the 152nd Parachute Battalion in their positions eight miles from Ukhrul.

In consequence the situation had become somewhat confused. The transit camp, where the Brigade should have stayed overnight, had moved, so the men dug in and waited.

Orders soon came for one company to move to Ukhrul to join the 152nd (Indian) Parachute Battalion and then as many men of the 153rd (Gurkha) Parachute Battalion as could be crammed into twenty fifteen-cwt. trucks were ordered to join them.

The next day the HQ of the 50th Parachute Brigade, the 153rd (Gurkha) Battalion and the 80th (Indian) Parachute Field Ambulance, commanded by Lieut.-Colonel R. B. Davis, IMS, concentrated in a defensive position on the Sangshak Plateau. Here they were joined by the remnants of the 152nd (Indian) Parachute Battalion and the rear-party of the 49th Indian Brigade.[1]

The total medical personnel of the force comprised seven MOs,[2] including the RMOs with the battalions and sixty mixed British and Indian ORs. The organisation consisted of a skeleton Field Ambulance HQ and two sections with a surgical team of a surgeon, anaesthetist and six ORs.

The equipment was limited to essential materials carried in 'man-pack' with the aid of 'Everest Carriers'; and in 'mule-packs' were additional supplies of blood plasma, glucose-saline, cellona plaster and one collapsible airborne-pattern operating table.[3]

Hardly had these troops arrived when the Japanese

[1] 4th/5th Mahratta Light Infantry and a battery from each of the 9th Mountain Regiment Indian Artillery and the 158th Field Regiment, RA.
[2] Lieut.-Colonel R. B. Davis, IMS; Major Hislop, RAMC (surgeon); Major P. G. McGrath, RAMC; Captain H. Pozner, RAMC (anaesthetist); Captain K. Swales, RAMC; Captain F. G. Neild, RAMC; and Captain A. G. Rangaraj, IAMC.
[3] 'Medical History of an Action' by Captain H. Pozner, RAMC. 'Journal of the RAMC', Vol LXXXIII, No 4, October 1944.

launched a fierce attack and every man was immediately committed to violent action. The hurriedly formed perimeter was so small that the 153rd (Gurkha) Parachute Battalion's RAP ' shared a flat piece of ground, about the size of a badminton court, with a section of mortars '.[1]

During the next three days there was heavy fighting in the whole area. Finally on 23rd March the whole force [2] was, on the orders of HQ 23rd Indian Division, concentrated in a defensive ' box ' on a jungle ridge at Sangshak, which was soon surrounded and besieged by the Japanese intent on destroying the garrison. Time and time again attacks were launched against the ' box ' only to be driven off by the sheer determination of the defenders, who just would not give ground. Their position was, however, worsening; the Japanese were firmly established on the high ground and the ' box ' was continually shelled.

The ADS of the 80th (Indian) Parachute Field Ambulance had to be moved and in consequence ' several hundred wounded were wandering about seeking shelter, many of them horribly torn and ghastly to look upon '.

The wounded in the ADS lay in dips in the ground with but the minimum shelter. The surgeon worked in an eight-foot-square pit, five feet deep, protected only by a thin covering of bamboo, planks, tarpaulins and corrugated iron. The ' walls ' were lined with dark-coloured parachutes in order that lights could be used at night. The surgeon ' did what little could be done ', wrote Captain Harry Pozner,[3] anaesthetist to the surgical team, ' to save lives and patch up the wounded so that they could be transferred if—it was a very big " if "—it were possible to get them back to Imphal '.

[1] *Vide* Captain F. G. Neild's (RMO, 152nd (Indian) Parachute Battalion) ' Indian Airborne Reminiscences '. ' Journal of the RAMC', Vol XCI, No 6.

[2] HQ 50th (Indian) Parachute Brigade with the 152nd and 153rd Parachute Battalions and 80th (Indian) Parachute Field Ambulance; the 4th/5th Battalion The Mahratta Light Infantry; the Kali Bahadur Regiment; 15th Battery, 20th Mountain Regiment, RA; one troop of 581st Field Battery, RA; and 74th Indian Field Company.

[3] Now Colonel H. Pozner, MC.

'That night', continues Captain Pozner's story,[1] 'it rained with all the sadistic violence of a tropical storm. Water seeped in everywhere, fox-holes and bunkers became morasses—the wounded slid into the mud, and the floor of the operating dugout became a treacherous maw into which precious surgical instruments and dressings were washed and finally disappeared. In the rain-lashed dark the wounded shivered in sodden blankets, and a few silently died. Every available piece of dry clothing was heaped upon them, and all who could be spared from the defences, from the Brigadier to the sweeper, worked unceasingly under the supervision of the SMO to provide a modicum of comfort for the sick.'[2]

The 'box' was reorganised to meet the continued Japanese attacks. By 26th March Sangshak was 'a shambles. The few buildings in the box were gutted, the trees were many of them blackened stumps ; the wounded groaned and cried out for water, the dead lay unburied and the stench from these corpses fouled the air.'

The situation was now desperate and a message to the effect that it was doubtful if the Brigade could resist further sustained attack was sent to Divisional HQ. Back came an order from the GOC ' Fight your way out. . . .'

In obeying this order the Brigade's main concern was for its wounded. The SMO—Lieut.-Colonel R. B. Davis— volunteered to stay behind with them, but the Brigadier ruled out

[1] 'The First Stand' by Harry Pozner (now Colonel H. Pozner, MC, RAMC) published in 'Victory—The Weekly for India Command', Vol XIV, No 8, 6th August 1945.

[2] Approximately 60 per cent of the total wounds treated at the ADS were in the upper limbs, chest and throat, these had been mainly caused by small calibre bullets, grenade and shell splinters and mortar bomb fragments. Twenty major surgical operations were performed either to arrest excessive haemorrhage, to explore wounds which endangered life, or to immobilise compound fractures of the limbs with severe destruction of tissues.

In the operations the anaesthetic used was intravenous pentothal sodium for rapid induction following by chloroform. A total of eighteen pints of blood plasma and six pints of glucose saline was used, the criteria for their use being severe haemorrhage and the probable prognosis of the patient. Intravenous fluids were given in slit trenches in the open under heavy fire with the bottles of fluid suspended from bamboo poles stuck in the ground.

(*Vide* 'Medical History of an Action' by Captain H. Pozner, RAMC. 'The Journal of the RAMC', Vol LXXXIII, No. 4, October 1944.)

this suggestion. The 'box' was to move in its formation and the wounded to move with them, each wounded man accompanied by a comrade. Ten stretcher cases and 120 walking wounded moved with the force.

Then followed six days of battling through forty miles of dense jungle, up mountains and down into valleys. On the high ground there was no shade to ward off the fierceness of the sun; many of the men were in the last stages of exhaustion and near breaking-point but on they went and, at last, came upon the outposts of the 5th Indian Division and passed through the wire into the comparative safety of the defensive perimeter of Imphal.

Such was the 50th Indian (Parachute) Brigade's first action. The battle of Sangshak had halted the Japanese advance and had diverted the numerically superior enemy force. Vital time had thereby been gained by the defenders of Imphal to strengthen their positions and deploy the 5th Indian Division, which had been flown in from the Arakan.

For their services during the battle of Sangshak the CO of the 80th (Indian) Parachute Field Ambulance, Lieut.-Colonel R. B. Davis, was awarded the DSO, Captain H. Pozner the MC, and the Military Medal to Corporal Hughes,[1] RAMC, and an Indian Havildar, IAMC.

The 50th (Indian) Parachute Brigade was then reorganised in a defensive 'box' in the 4th Indian Corps area. The Parachute Battalions—particularly the 152nd—were sorely in need of reinforcements, but these were not immediately forthcoming and, in any case, it must be borne in mind that they were the only parachute-trained troops available to GHQ, India, so the Brigade HQ took command of three unattached battalions to form an infantry brigade, whilst the 152nd (Indian) Parachute Battalion was 'kept on ice', the 153rd (Gurkha) Battalion was placed under command of the 17th Indian Division.[2]

One section of the 80th (Indian) Parachute Field Ambu-

[1] This was a posthumous award as this gallant NCO disappeared and was reported as missing, believed killed, on the march out of Sangshak.
[2] The 153rd (Gurkha) Battalion served, in turn, under command 17th, 20th and 23rd Indian Divisions around Imphal, until the Japanese advance had been firmly held and beaten back.

lance, commanded by Captain W. Thompson,[1] attached to the 1st Battalion The Assam Regiment, was withdrawn with the Battalion to Kohima—where it went through the siege— whilst the surgical team was moved to Bishenpur.

Another section of the Field Ambulance was later parachuted into the jungle on to the lines of communication of the 3rd Indian Division (' The Chindits '—General Wingate's Special Force) where Captain K. Swales, RAMC, and Captain E. Tarleton, IAMC, established a medical staging post.

In August 1944 the 50th (Indian) Parachute Brigade returned to Rawal Pindi.

Early in 1944 the 44th Indian Airborne Division, as it was designated, was formed,[2] under the command of Major-General E. E. Down, CBE, by the conversion of the 44th Indian Armoured Division. It was intended that the Divisional Units should come from the Armoured Division, and that the Division would comprise the 50th (Indian) Parachute Brigade; a British Parachute Brigade from Europe; and an Air Landing Brigade raised from The Chindits.

In May 1944 Lieut.-Colonel P. R. Wheatley, DSO, was flown out to India to take up the appointment of ADMS to the new Division.

Whilst the Division was being formed the 50th Parachute Brigade remained available for operations under Headquarters ALFSEA[3] in support of the Fourteenth Army. The airfields around Secunderabad were, however, unsuitable for Dakotas, and eventually the Brigade was sent back to Chaklala for its continued training for its intended airborne operation near Shwebo, on the Fourteenth Army's advance to Mandalay, timed for the beginning of February 1945. Training continued, with this object in mind, until December, when the rate of advance of the Fourteenth Army had so increased that they had in fact already overrun the planned DZs, and it was decided that no further airborne operations were possible before the monsoon season.

At this time, the 2nd Independent Parachute Brigade

[1] Captain Thompson, wounded at Kohima, was awarded the Military Cross. He was killed later in an accident at Rawal Pindi.
[2] At Secunderabad.
[3] Allied Land Forces South East Asia.

Group which, it had been planned, would join the 44th Indian Airborne Division from Italy, had been fully committed to service in Greece. In consequence it was decided to split the 50th (Indian) Parachute Brigade to form the two Parachute Brigades needed for the new Division. In similar manner the 152nd (Indian) Parachute Battalion was also split to form two battalions. Two new British Parachute Battalions, the 15th and 16th, were raised from volunteers from among what was left of Wingate's Special Force—' The Chindits '—then at Jhansi. The new Air Landing Brigade was formed from the 2nd Battalion The Black Watch, then at Bangalore, the 4th/6th Rajputana Rifles and the 6th/16th Punjab Regiment.

The medical services of the new Airborne Division comprised the 7th (British) Parachute Field Ambulance, commanded by Lieut.-Colonel D. G. C. Whyte, DSO ; the 60th (Indian) Parachute Field Ambulance, commanded by Lieut.-Colonel J. Duerdon, IAMC ; and the 80th (Indian) Parachute Field Ambulance, commanded by Lieut.-Colonel J. Young, DSO, IMS, and a Field Hygiene Section (OC, Major Saki).

These were new types of Field Ambulances, each composed of an HQ and five sections, two of which were British. To each Field Ambulance were attached two Indian mobile surgical units.

In June 1944 the Division moved to Bilapur, near Nagpur in the Central Provinces, to commence air training, operating from a group of airfields constructed during the threat of Japanese invasion.

Whilst the Division was reorganising and training at Bilapur it was suddenly called upon to mount an airborne operation to neutralise the Japanese guns at Elephant Point, commanding the mouth of the Rangoon River. The task was such, however, that it was possible for it to be carried out effectively by one composite parachute battalion made up from all the battalions of the original 50th (Indian) Parachute Brigade, and a parachute field ambulance section with a surgical team [1] accompanied the battalion.

[1] Major Dunlop (surgeon) ; Captain Thornton (anaesthetist).

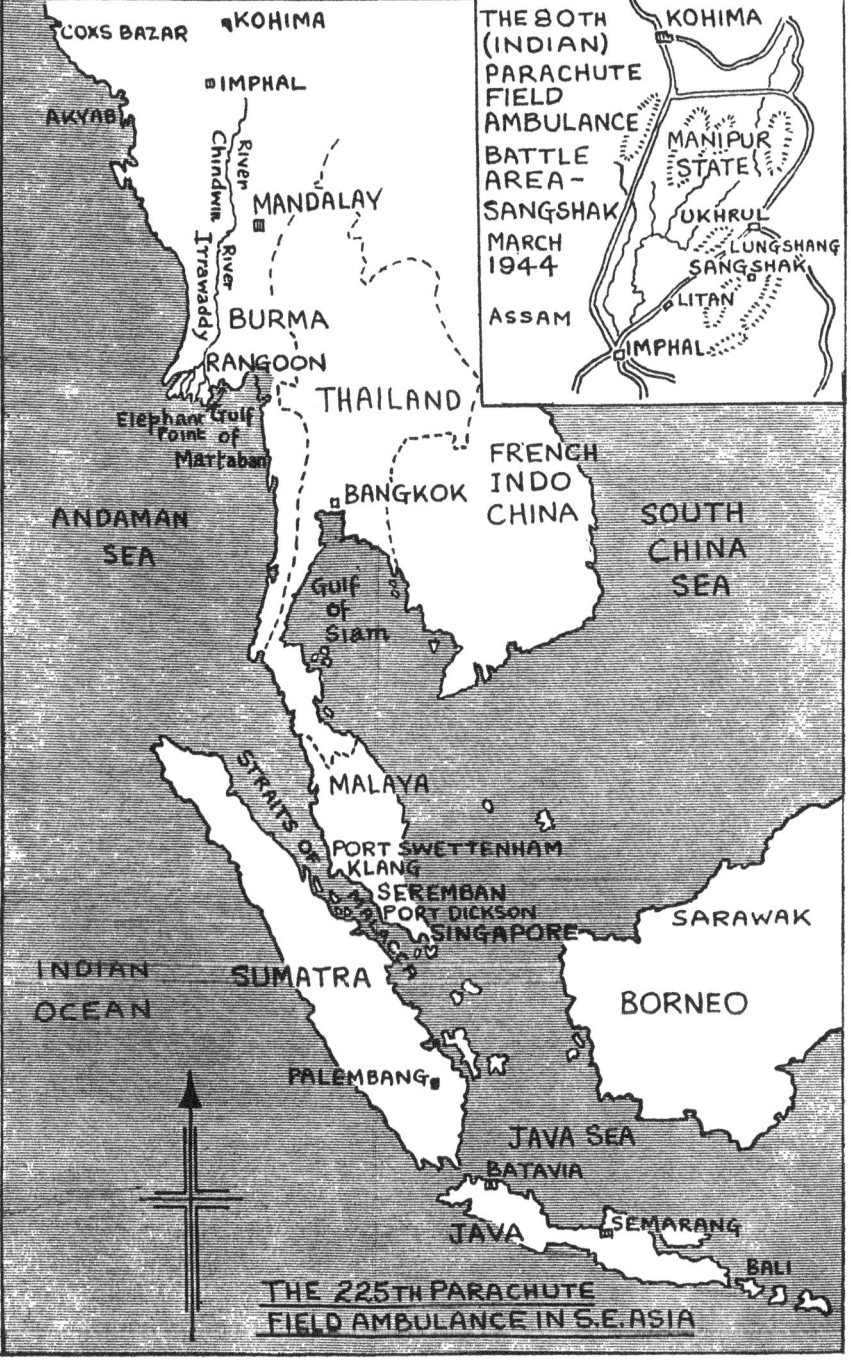

The operation was successfully concluded and shortly after, whilst the battalion was actually participating in the Victory March through Rangoon, news of 'VE Day' and the conclusion of the war in Europe was announced.

All attention was then focused on operations for the final defeat of the Japanese. In these plans an Airborne Corps, composed of the 44th Indian Airborne Division and the 6th Airborne Division from Germany, were earmarked for special operations.

The capitulation of the Japanese on 8th September had come suddenly and unexpectedly, and with the exception of the 5th Parachute Brigade which arrived in India at the end of July[1] the move of the 6th Airborne Division to India was cancelled.

The changed situation in the Far East brought about a very different type of employment for the 44th Indian Airborne Division, for they were called upon to provide the medical teams which were parachuted into Malaya, Thailand, French Indo-China and the Dutch East Indies, and to go to the urgent assistance of Allied prisoners of war scattered in their camps throughout these countries.

Prominent in these teams were personnel of the three Parachute Field Ambulances of the Indian Airborne Division. The MOs and orderlies for these teams flew from Bilapur to Ceylon to report to HQ, South East Asia Command, and awaited in camp in Trincomalee, until taking off on their errands of mercy in dropping to succour the prisoners of war in Japanese hands.

The rôle to which these teams were committed was difficult and not without danger.

One party flew in to Palembong in Sumatra, and here Captain Mackler was killed by local terrorists in an ambush.

Captain J. Wraith of the 7th (Indian) Parachute Field Ambulance was dropped at Port Swettenham in Malaya where there was a large camp of White Russians and Eurasians. He found malnutrition widespread: the men were surviving on a diet of sweet potatoes, whilst the medical situation among the local population was serious. Severe

[1] See Chapter XVI.

skin sepsis, beri-beri, malaria and intestinal infections were rife among the Malays. Captain Wraith moved on to Kulang, near Singapore, to the Sikh and Gurkha prison camps—the latter being in a deplorable condition—and thence to Singapore, where he supervised the distribution of medical stores to all allied centres throughout SEAC.

Another party, with Captain P. James (RMO, 2nd Black Watch) and a medical orderly of the 7th (Indian) Parachute Field Ambulance, was dropped, on the 22nd September, from 400 feet into a clearing thirty miles north of Bangkok, moving on to the aid of the men in the camp in the grounds of Bangkok University, and finally on to Kanchanwoburi, the northern point of the infamous 'death railway', where they established a small hospital which was soon expanded to a general hospital of 1,200 beds.

Such work as this continued into the early months of 1946.

Towards the end of 1945 the formation, redesignated the 2nd Indian Airborne Division, was moved from Bilapur to the Karachi-Quetta area, where it was engaged in internal security duties.

During 1946, with the approach of Indian independence, the British units were withdrawn from the Division to become the 6th British Independent Parachute Brigade, and gradually the Indian and Gurkha battalions and units were disbanded, except for the original 50th (Indian) Parachute Brigade, with the 60th (Indian) Parachute Field Ambulance, which in 1947 became part of the new Indian Army.[1]

[1] The Brigade was subsequently employed in Kashmir, and the 60th Indian (Parachute) Field Ambulance Indian Medical Corps, under the command of Lieut.-Colonel A. G. Rangaraj, MVC, later served with distinction in Korea, landing on 20th November 1950 and joining the 27th Commonwealth Brigade at Uijongbu on 14th December.

The Indian Parachute Field Ambulance served with the 1st Commonwealth Division until August 1953, when it was transferred to the Indian Custodian Force on its arrival in Korea.

CHAPTER XVI

MALAYA AND JAVA

THE 225TH (PARACHUTE) FIELD AMBULANCE IN THE FAR EAST

THE 6th Airborne Division rested at Wismar on the Baltic for two weeks after 'VE' Day, and then came the orders for the formation to return immediately to England. The Division moved back across the Elbe to Luneburg, where they passed through the transit camp at the former Luftwaffe Barracks, before emplaning from an airfield near Ulzen, from which they flew *via* Brussels back to England to land at Netheravon and Greenham Common near Newbury and thence, once again, back to Bulford.

In the Far East the war against Japan was still being hard fought ; the Japanese were being pressed and driven back at all points. The forward movement down through Burma, up from New Guinea and across the chain of Pacific islands was gathering momentum and yet there was no sign of the slackening of Japanese resistance, or any indication of capitulation.

As the war in Europe drew to a close, so plans were being drawn up at the HQ of the Supreme Allied Commander, South-East Asia, which would lead to the final crushing of the Japanese. In these plans the employment of an Airborne Division was to be one of considerable importance.

It was the 6th Airborne Division which was selected for this task, and as soon as this was announced immediate preparations commenced to fit the formation for the work ahead. Early in July 1945 the Tactical HQ of the Division, together with the HQ of the 5th Parachute Brigade, were flown out to India, and the staffs were immediately engaged in planning what was to have been the Division's third major airborne operation. By 9th July Lieut.-Colonel A. D. Young,

DSO, the CO of the 224th (Parachute) Field Ambulance, who flew to India with the Advanced Planning Party of the Division, had submitted his first report to the ADMS covering the reception of the 5th Parachute Brigade Group, operational planning for the Group, and the equipment and organisation obtaining in India.

The 5th Brigade was originally destined for an independent rôle in an airborne operation in Burma and this necessitated its arrival in India in advance of the rest of the Division. The Brigade, together with the advance party of the 225th (Parachute) Field Ambulance, commanded by Lieut.-Colonel J. C. Watts, MC, was flown out from England to India ; the Brigade's flight covering eight days, from 20th to 27th July. Landing at Bombay, the formation remained in India until the beginning of September. The HQ of the Field Ambulance arrived by air at Karachi on 27th July, flying on to Bombay. The rest of the unit, which travelled to India by sea, landed at Bombay, and was moved to a large transit camp at Kalyan, a railway junction midway between Bombay and Poona.

At the time of its move to India the Brigade was intended for employment in an airborne rôle, in operation ' Zipper ', the overall plan for this operation being the formation of a bridgehead in the heart of the Malay peninsula between Singapore and the Japanese armies in Northern Malaya, with the objects of turning south and crossing the Straits of Johore to Singapore, and northward to engage the main Japanese force. Seaborne landings were planned at Port Dickson and Port Swettenham, whilst the Parachute Brigade would carry out an airborne attack to recapture Singapore.

However, on 6th August 1945 the first atomic bomb was dropped on Japan at Hiroshima, the second at Nagasaki on 9th August. This action was the final blow and brought about, on 15th August, the capitulation of the Japanese. In consequence there was a complete change in all plans in light of the new situation obtaining throughout the whole of South-East Asia.

The 5th Parachute Brigade sailed from Bombay on 9th September for Malaya, carrying out a seaborne landing at Morib Beaches on the 17th. The landing craft grounded on a sandbank some 500 yards off the beach, and the men had to wade ashore in water above their chests. Only part of the force got ashore, the 7th and 12th Battalions The Parachute Regiment spending a night sheltering among the rubber trees in pouring rain.

Next morning the troops re-embarked on the transports, and the force sailed for Singapore, where they landed on the 21st and received a tumultous welcome from the seething crowds of Malays, Chinese and Indians. The Brigade immediately settled down to the work of garrisoning Singapore Island.

Near the Field Ambulance HQ at Alexander Barracks, into which they moved on the 23rd, was a small group of bungalows which had served as a Japanese internment camp for the German Naval Mission to Malaya and the crews of two German submarines. These Germans came under medical control of the 225th (Parachute) Field Ambulance, and in the interests of their health they were provided with work, the first task being the levelling of ground and the laying out of a football pitch which was opened with a match between the Field Ambulance and the German sailors. The Field Ambulance was also responsible for the medical control of the Japanese POW camp at Busau and McArthur Camp, which housed Koreans and Formosans.

Early in December the Brigade Group was moved to Serembam to take the place of the 23rd Indian Division, which had been hurriedly withdrawn from Malaya to move to Java.

At that time Java and Sumatra were in a state of turmoil. Instead of maintaining law and order until the arrival of a British force, the Japanese commander in the Dutch East Indies had ordered his troops to hand over their arms to the rebel forces of the Indonesian puppet 'provisional government' which was then engaged in an all-out effort to prevent the return of Dutch control.

Christmas was spent by 225th (Parachute) Field Ambulance at Batavia. A typical military programme covered the first post-war Christmas. Carols on Christmas Eve. ' A nice hot cup o' tea ' organised and served at 7.30 am on Christmas Day by the officers and senior NCOs. Breakfast at nine. Then a Church Service, followed by a Comic Football Match—officers and sergeants versus ORs—teams in fancy dress, and played with a rugby ball ; and then, the traditional dinner at two o'clock—soup, turkey and stuffing, pork and apple sauce, roast potatoes and sprouts, Christmas pudding, custard with rum, mince pies ; coffee, beer, minerals, cigarettes, cigars, and dessert. A buffet tea at five o'clock —for those who could take it—and at eight o'clock a show by the unit concert party.

At the end of December the 5th Independent Parachute Brigade Group, under the command of Brigadier Poett, was put under orders for service in the Dutch East Indies, and sailed for Java from Singapore, landing at Batavia, where the formation came under command of the 23rd Indian Division. The British force in Java was then engaged in the difficult task of maintaining law and order among the Javanese, organising the public services and a normal way of life amid the chaos, and controlling the Japanese forces. The Field Ambulance embarked at Singapore in HMS *Rocksand* on 17th December and landed at Batavia on the 20th. Here they established their HQ, and opened up a hundred-bedded hospital in the Van Heutz Plein.

Immediately on arrival the 5th Parachute Brigade was involved in Operation ' Pounce '—the clearing of Batavia— and on 30th December went forward to clear a number of kampongs (native villages) on the outskirts of Batavia. Early in January the formation moved to Semarang to relieve the 49th Infantry Brigade. The Field Ambulance embarked at Batavia in HMS *Orouna* on 9th January, arriving in Semarang Roads on the morning of the 11th, disembarking the next day.

Here the Brigade found themselves in occupation of a large town with a population of some 210,000—the town in ruins, scarred with fire and from the street fighting ; there were no public services, the shops were closed, and there was little food available.

'The medical problem', wrote Lieut.-Colonel J. C. Watts,[1]

[1] Now Colonel J. C. Watts, OBE, MC, MB, FRCS, Professor of Surgery, Royal Army Medical College.

' was serious, as in addition to the Indonesians there were about 30,000 Chinese, 3,000 Dutch and about the same number of Koreans. None of these communities would cooperate with the others and there was a vast shortage of drugs.'[1]

Around Semarang the Indonesian rebel forces were concentrating. Their aim, they announced, was to throw out the British and the slaughter of all the Dutch and Chinese.

The parachute battalions deployed in a defensive perimeter around the town and a rearmed Japanese battalion was brought in to man a sector.[2]

The Sapper squadron set to work in resurrecting the public services, the RASC detachment took over the handling and distribution of food, and the artillerymen took over the town police duties. The Field Ambulance was established in the Dutch Military Hospital, which lay across a canal from the main road, where it set up a MDS, where Major A. Macpherson, the surgeon, was kept fully occupied in the theatre. ' Unit morale was immensely high ', recorded Lieut.-Colonel Watts, ' for we had a picked bunch of both officers and men.'[3] Colonel Watts himself was engaged on duties he described as a ' sort of Medical Officer of Health to Semarang ' organising and administering the hospital and sanitary services and the work of the general practitioners.

[1] ' Surgeon at War ' by Lieut.-Colonel J. C. Watts, MC, FRCS, RAMC. (Allen & Unwin.) (1955.)

[2] The Commander of the Japanese Garrison Battalion at Semarang had been appalled, when informed by the British team from the 44th Indian Airborne Division which had parachuted into Semarang, that the orders of the local Japanese General to hand over his arms to the Indonesians were contrary to his Emperor's commands as shown to him in the Imperial rescript of the surrender terms. On his own initiative he ordered his unarmed men into action. They recaptured an Indonesian machine-gun post with the loss of seventy men, and thus armed from this small beginning finally rearmed his battalion with all the weapons handed over a few days before to the rebels. (' Surgeon at War.')

[3] ' Outstanding among the latter were some ten conscientious objectors, who, finding the non-combatant corps full of skrimshankers and malingerers, had taken the only step they could to get into a forward unit. This was to volunteer for parachuting, which had caused them to be transferred to the RAMC and posted to airborne units. Most of them were highly educated and very intelligent, the Quakers especially being most industrious and zealous.' (' Surgeon at War ' by Lieut.-Colonel J. C. Watts.)

Gradually organisation triumphed over the shambles of Semarang, life under British rule returned to normal, and to a certain extent prospered. The Brigade kept the rebels well in check, and life in the community was quite peaceful, although the Battalions remained constantly on the alert.

At the end of May 1946 the first Dutch troops arrived to relieve the British and shortly after the Brigade returned to Malaya. The 225th (Parachute) Field Ambulance left Semarang in the MV *Empire Pride*, bound for Singapore, on 2nd May. They landed on the 5th, and moved to Sagil, where they remained for eight days before moving to Muar.

Two months were spent in Malaya, and then orders came for the 5th Independent Parachute Brigade to move to Palestine to rejoin the 6th Airborne Division. On 19th July the 225th (Parachute) Field Ambulance embarked at Singapore. Madras was reached on the 23rd, where the unit landed and went for a route-march. This was repeated at Colombo on the 28th. Port Said was reached on 7th August. Here the unit disembarked and the following day entrained for Palestine; they reached Camp 22 at Nathanya on 9th August.

Ten days later orders were received for the unit to be disbanded. It was broken up and the personnel posted as reinforcements to the other three Field Ambulances of the 6th Airborne Division.

CHAPTER XVII

INTERNAL SECURITY

PALESTINE, 1945-48

FOLLOWING the capitulation of Japan in August 1945 the military situation in the Far East changed completely, and, as far as the 6th Airborne Division was concerned, it was no longer required, not even in an occupational rôle.

The future of the airborne forces was reconsidered and re-planned. With the 6th Airborne Division originally committed to service in the Far East, the 1st Airborne Division, on its return from Norway, had been allocated a rôle in the Imperial Strategic Reserve based in the Middle East, but the fall of Japan resulted in the decision to reduce the Airborne Divisions to one. Although the younger formation, it was decided that it would be the 1st Division which would be disbanded, and the 6th retained on account of the relative strengths of the two formations and the composition of the 'age and service' groups of the personnel. The 6th Airborne Division, which from the beginning of July had been preparing for service in SEAC, therefore became part of the Strategic Reserve, and it was warned for service in the Middle East. The 5th Parachute Brigade having been despatched to India, the Division was brought up to strength by the inclusion of the 2nd Parachute Brigade, which had just returned from Greece.

On 24th September the Tactical HQ of the Division flew out to Palestine, for that country was to be the destination of the formation. It was chosen, in the first place, on account of the training facilities and available airfields, and although the need for an increased number of troops in Palestine was, in the light of the political situation, foreseen, the Division's rôle was clearly laid down as part of the Strategic Reserve. On arrival of the formation it was planned that it should concentrate on airborne training, and it was not originally intended that it should be employed on internal security duties.

The Division [1] moved to Palestine between 15th September and 6th November, the RAMC units of the Division being the 127th [2] and 224th [3] (Parachute), and 195th [4] (Air Landing) Field Ambulances, and the 74th Field Hygiene Section. The 3rd Parachute Brigade landed at Haifa on 3rd October. It was followed seven days later by the 6th Air Landing Brigade [5] and on 22nd October by the 2nd Parachute Brigade.[6] The Division moved to a concentration area some six miles south of Gaza, the main Divisional HQ being situated at the Nuseirat Ridge Camp, and here the formation settled down to acclimatise the men to a new way of life in a sandy, barren country, but a country simmering with a growing political tension, for both the Arabs and Jews were alert to the immediate post-war political problems of Palestine.

As soon as the war was over the Jews immediately reopened the question of the clauses of the British Government's White Paper of May 1939, which had limited Jewish immigration into the country to a given maximum over a period of five years, after which no further immigrants would be permitted without the consent of the Arabs. In 1944 the British Government decided to extend the time limit of five years in consequence of delays resulting from the war, but no increase in the total number of immigrants was allowed, and by the end of 1945 the total number of permitted immigrants—75,000—had nearly been reached.

Tension began to rise when the Jewish community realised

[1] Under the command of Major-General E. L. Bols, CB, DSO, the ADMS being Colonel M. MacEwan, DSO, OBE, DFC, TD, who handed over to Colonel M. J. Kohane, MC, in 1946.
[2] Commanded by Lieut.-Colonel F. Murray, RAMC.
[3] Commanded by Lieut.-Colonel A. D. Young, DSO, RAMC.
[4] Commanded by Lieut.-Colonel S. Smith, RAMC.
[5] The 195th (Air Landing) Field Ambulance had sailed from Liverpool in HMT *Duchess of Bedford* on 2nd October, and on arrival at Haifa had moved to Mughazi Camp.
[6] The 127th (Parachute) Field Ambulance moved from Greenham Lodge at Newbury to Liverpool on 26th October, and embarked on the SS *Ascania* with the 1st Battalion Argyll and Sutherland Highlanders and detachments of the 6th Airborne Division. They arrived at Haifa on 7th November.

the position and it was openly said among them that the British were continuing the Nazi policy of anti-semitism. To the Jews the all important matter was the throwing open of Palestine as a home for displaced Jews from all over Europe, and that for the immigration quota to be adhered to was regarded as inhuman. The Palestine Jews began to say that if the immigrants could not be legally admitted then they must be brought in by any other means. The British Government was of course bound by the terms of the White Paper of May 1939 [1] and could not agree to increasing the number of Jewish immigrants unless the Arabs agreed, and such agreement was not forthcoming.

The political situation in Palestine at the time of the arrival of the 6th Airborne Division was such that it was soon apparent that the matter of internal security was of growing importance and, although the 1st British Infantry Division with a number of independent units and ancillary troops were already in the country, it was obvious that the airborne formation would also be called upon for internal security duties, and such had to be understood and learned by the Division.

The position too called for re-deployment of the British forces in Palestine. At the end of October the 6th Airborne Divisional HQ moved to Bir Salim ; the 3rd Parachute Brigade (with 224th (Parachute) Field Ambulance) to Lydda District (which included Jaffa and Tel-Aviv) ; the 6th Air Landing Brigade (with 195th (Air Landing) Field Ambulance) to the Samaria District ; and the 2nd Parachute Brigade (with 127th (Parachute) Field Ambulance) on arrival from England went to Nuseirat Ridge Camp in the Gaza District.

The Division was soon involved in the situation for there was widespread railway sabotage in the Divisional area on the night of 31st October and the following day a nightly road curfew was imposed.

[1] Palestine had, from 1923, been administered by Great Britain under a mandate given by the League of Nations, one of the terms of which permitted the formation of a Jewish organisation to advise the Palestine Government on the interests of the Jewish community and on matters affecting ' the Jewish National Home '.

On 14th November large-scale riots developed in Tel-Aviv and the 3rd Parachute Brigade was moved in to restore order, Tel-Aviv being placed under martial law for six days. This operation set the pattern of the Division's internal security work and henceforth ' Cordon and Search ' was the order for maintenance of law and order, and the rounding-up of terrorists, suspects, and illegal immigrants.

In March 1946 the 1st Parachute Brigade sailed from England to join the Division. It landed in the Middle East at Port Said, moving on to Palestine on 8th April. On arrival the Brigade took the place of the 6th Air Landing Brigade in the Division, which, on the 13th April, broke its association with the formation with which it had served since it was raised, and became the 31st Independent Infantry Brigade. The Air Landing Brigade's Field Ambulance, the 195th (Air Landing) Field Ambulance, commanded by Lieut.-Colonel S. Smith, RAMC, retained its airborne rôle, was re-designated, re-trained [1] and became the 195th (Parachute) Field Ambulance with the 1st Parachute Brigade.

The situation in Palestine was gradually worsening. On 22nd July 1946 a party of Jews disguised as an Arab working party entered the King David Hotel in Jerusalem—the offices of the Government Secretariat and the HQ of British troops in Palestine and Transjordan. The Jews unloaded from a lorry a number of milk churns—filled with explosives —carried them into a basement wing—lit the fuzes and ran. The explosion which followed was described as ' devastating ' —the whole wing of the building collapsed. Many of the occupants were killed outright, others were trapped and injured.[2]

The outcome of this outrage was the launching a week later of Operation ' Shark ', the object of which was a

[1] Training in Palestine was limited, because of the operational situation, and plans for airborne exercises were restricted, although, in May 1946, ' Exercise Gordon ' took the 3rd Parachute Battalion (with a company of the 8th Battalion, together with detachment of other arms including RAMC personnel) to Khartoum.

[2] Rescue work and clearance of rubble was carried out by the 9th Airborne Field Squadron, RE, and ninety-one bodies were recovered.

INTERNAL SECURITY

thorough search of every house and every person in the whole of Tel-Aviv to find members of the terrorist ' Stern Gang ' and the ILZ (the Irgun Zuai Leumi—the Jewish national military organisation).

Operation ' Shark ', the cordoning and searching of Tel-Aviv by sectors commenced at 5 am on 29th July 1946 and lasted until 3rd August. The search was carried out by the 6th Airborne Division, with additional troops under command, totalling in all some 15,000 all ranks.

The city, with a population of some 170,000, contained three large hospitals and four smaller ones, together with numerous nursing homes and clinics. There were also about 1,500 medical practitioners, but security consideration precluded any prior planning with the civic medical and health departments. The rigid curfew to be imposed forbade the movement of all doctors or the civic medical services and, in consequence, the maintenance of these services would devolve on the Army.

The British Medical Services comprised the three Field Ambulances of the 6th Airborne Division; a Field Ambulance of the 1st Infantry Division; the RMOs with all units employed, and one MO with each Brigade (Sector) HQ. In addition there was No 12 British General Hospital, another *ad hoc* Military Hospital, and a Casualty Reception Station at Latrun Detention Camp.

The tasks of the Medical Services were wide and numerous. Firstly the care and evacuation of sick and wounded from the British force ; then the provision of MOs for ' Searching Teams ', who would examine bedridden in houses ; ' Screening Teams ', for the examination of alleged sick,[1] and bogus plaster cases—there were several cases of feigned broken limbs set in plaster in attempts to avoid facing the ' screening teams '—and suspect ' women '—men disguised in female attire—the maintenance of the cordon by ensuring no movement through the line by alleged or real sick people ; the evacuation of wanted wounded ; taking over the re-

---

[1] On several occasions medical officers in searching hospitals suspected bogus patients and, after examination, exposed them as such.

sponsibility of day-to-day running and maintenance of the civilian hospitals ; the provision of general practitioner services ; special drugs for out-patients, milk for babies and other cases ; ice for preservation of civil stocks of vaccines and sera ; maintenance of essential services, including sewage and refuse disposal ; and finally the disposal of dead together with attendant legal and ritual formalities. It was in all indeed a formidable task.

The RAMC organisation efficiently carried out its many tasks. All lightly wounded, together with ordinary unwounded detainees, were evacuated to Latrun Detention Camp; seriously wounded were taken to 'C' Military Hospital under escort ; alleged sick from outside the cordon were diverted to Petah Tigua if Jews, whilst the Arabs were sent to Jaffa; whilst those within were taken to the Sector Screening Post, seen by the Brigade MO, screened and either sent to hospital, returned to their homes or detained in the Sector cage.

The ADMS South Palestine District had compiled nominal rolls by hospitals of civilian doctors who in the past had been screened by the police and recommended for passes. These lists were handed over to the Sector SMOs, who collected these doctors from their homes, together with the minimum essential staff of nurses, kitchen orderlies and boiler-room operators in order to maintain the civil hospital services. Food for the hospital staff and patients was provided by the RASC. Good reserves of drugs were held by all hospitals, but blood plasma had to be provided from military reserves. One of the main problems was that of laundry services, particularly for the operating theatres and accouchement wards, and this was only partially solved by the end of the operation.

The majority of admissions were into the Hadassa Municipal Hospital, where a military medical control centre, composed of a Lieut.-Colonel and two RAMC officers with thirty ORs, was established. All cases were passed through the control centre on to the Jewish civilian doctors, who decided on admission or return to homes.

Sick calls within the Sectors were passed to the street patrols, who passed the cases on through platoon and company HQs to the RMO at battalion HQs. Here the case was dealt with, or, if hospital admission was necessary, transferred to the military medical control centre in an ambulance car.

A complication arose because there were no general practitioners as such in Tel-Aviv and the specialists had their cases in different hospitals throughout the area. In consequence it became necessary to allocate the various specialists to hospitals irrespective of whether the hospitals contained a majority of their patients. Professor Marcus, formerly a Professor of Surgery in Vienna, was provided with military transport and an escort to move about and act as consultant to all civilian hospitals as required.

Other unforeseen incidents had to be faced. No plans had been made for the provision of such services as the continuation of anti-rabic treatment, and on the second day it was reported that there were fifteen such cases undergoing treatment. Just prior to the start of the operation a case was admitted to the Assuta Hospital for a Caesarean operation the next day, and the specialist concerned had to be found and brought to the hospital under escort.

Throughout the Operation 'Shark'[1] the work of the Airborne Field Ambulances was considerably varied, as was their rôle at all times, ranging from dealing with casualties from actions with the terrorists to midwifery.

Operations of 'cordon and search' continued following the destruction by the Jews of railway communications, mining of roads, ambushes, and acts of sabotage of varying magnitude.

The first RAMC casualty occurred on 22nd September when Corporal T. McInnes of 224th (Parachute) Field Ambulance was killed; and on 31st October, during a search for arms and members of the IZL by the 1st Battalion The Parachute Regiment at Petah Tigua, a vehicle of 195th (Parachute) Field Ambulance was mined, killing two of the RAMC

[1] Over 100,000 Jews were screened during the operation, five dumps of arms and large quantities of ammunition and explosives were uncovered.

occupants, Lance-Corporal C. W. Voce and Private J. B. Eyre, and wounding two others.[1]

On the arrival in Palestine in August 1946 of the 5th Parachute Brigade Group from Malaya, the 225th (Parachute) Field Ambulance commanded by Lieut.-Colonel J. C. Watts was broken up to provide reinforcements for the other three Field Ambulances of the Division, Colonel Watts being posted to the command of the 195th (Parachute) Field Ambulance in place of Lieut.-Colonel S. Smith.

In January 1947 the 2nd Parachute Brigade Group, and with it the 127th (Parachute) Field Ambulance, commanded by Major D. C. J. B. Nixon, RAMC, returned to England, and the remainder of the Division re-deployed—the 1st Parachute Brigade, with 195th (Parachute) Field Ambulance, commanded by Lieut.-Colonel J. C. Watts, MC, moving to the Galilee area; and the 3rd Brigade, with 224th (Parachute) Field Ambulance,[2] commanded by Lieut.-Colonel A. T. Marrable, DSO, going to Haifa.

At Haifa the 3rd Brigade was concerned with the protection of the port and the nearby oil installations, and with the ever-increasing problem of the transhipment of illegal immigrants who arrived with increasing frequency from different European ports.

On these occasions the Medical Services were involved, the task of the Field Ambulances being the establishment at the landing quays of an RAP, complete with stretcher-bearer parties and ambulances, ready to treat and evacuate as necessary sick or injured from among the illegal immigrants and troops engaged in the operation. Wounded, resulting from tussles with the more desperate immigrants, were evacuated to the British Military Hospital, whilst sick immigrants were moved to the Government Hospital.

[1] Between 1945 and 1948 the 6th Airborne Division sustained forty casualties, killed and died of wounds, of which the RAMC sustained these three, although in October 1947 Lieutenant A. McK. Elliott, RAMC, the RMO of the 3rd Parachute Battalion, and Private B. G. Hall of 195th (Parachute) Field Ambulance, died on active service.

[2] In 1947 the 224th (Parachute) Field Ambulance was renumbered, taking the original Parachute Field Ambulance Number '16'.

Four MOs were usually sufficient to deal with each shipload, two going on board with the boarding-party to deal with any urgent medical cases and two remaining at the RAP. Simple although the arrangements seemed, it was inevitable that trouble arose. The very nature of the immigrants and the conditions under which they had been living and had travelled was such that many needed treatment and gangways became congested whilst small crowds accumulated around the RAP, which was composed of an MI Room and a DDT tent organised by a staff-sergeant of a Field Hygiene Section.

The work was not easy. On 31st March 1947 over 1,500 illegal immigrants were transhipped from the *San Filipo* amid considerable obstruction by the Jews. On 14th April strong resistance was put up against the Royal Naval boarding party when the *Guardian* arrived with over 2,500 immigrants. During this transhipment three were killed and five wounded. Eight days later another ship brought in nearly 800 immigrants, and so the work went on throughout 1947.

Nineteen hundred and forty-eight saw a changing situation in which British troops found themselves between two fires as a result of increasing clashes between Arabs and Jews in border raids and between the divided communities in the frontier areas, when the British were called upon to restore order. Their task, however, was drawing to a close, and as far as the 6th Airborne Division was concerned the days of the formation were numbered. In the plan for the gradual withdrawal of all British troops from Palestine up to the end of the British Mandate in May the Division had been scheduled to leave in April. It was expected that, after a short spell at home, the formation would rejoin the 2nd Parachute Brigade in Germany, but this was not to be for on 18th February it was announced that the Division would be disbanded later in the year. In consequence part of the Divisional HQ, one Parachute Battalion and an Airborne Squadron, Royal Engineers, remained until the last. Units of the Division began to leave Palestine in March, and on 7th April the last airborne medical unit, the 16th (Parachute) Field Ambulance,[1] commanded by Lieut.-Colonel A. T. Marrable, DSO, embarked from Haifa on the *Georgic* bound for home.

The British Mandate ended on 15th May. Three days later the Tactical HQ of the Division [2] embarked with the 1st Parachute Battalion, and by 30th June the last British troops left Palestine.

---

[1] The last ADMS of the Division was Colonel P. J. Richards, DSO, OBE, who took over from Colonel M. J. Kohane, MC, at the end of 1947.

[2] The 16th (Parachute) Field Ambulance was subsequently reorganised as a Field Ambulance, and the following year was again on service—in Malaya.

CHAPTER XVIII

SINCE THEN . . .

THE AIRBORNE MEDICAL SERVICES, 1947-61

EARLY in 1947 the 2nd Parachute Brigade Group, which included the 127th (Parachute) Field Ambulance, was withdrawn from the 6th Airborne Division in Palestine, and sailed from Haifa on 27th January.

On arrival in England the Brigade Group was stationed in Wellington Lines and Stanhope Lines at Aldershot, occupying in the former the original 1856-59 infantry barracks, and in the latter the red brick 1890 barracks. The 127th (Parachute) Field Ambulance had originated in the pre-war TA unit, the 127th (East Lancashire) Field Ambulance, RAMC(TA) and, in consequence, when the TA was re-formed on 1st April 1947, the Parachute Field Ambulance had to give up the number '127' and it was given a Regular Army number, '23rd'.

The Brigade Group remained in Aldershot until February 1948, when it crossed from Harwich to the Hook of Holland to entrain for Hanover, where it was accommodated in the spacious former Wehrmacht barracks between the autobahn and the north of the city and took its place in the Order of Battle of the British Army of the Rhine.

In the summer of 1948 it was decided that the 6th Airborne Division would be disbanded, and the Regular Airborne Forces reduced to a single Brigade Group. The 2nd Parachute Brigade, in Germany, was selected to become this permanent airborne element of the Regular Army. The formation was re-numbered and re-designated the 16th Independent Parachute Brigade Group.

In November 1949 the Brigade returned from Germany to Aldershot, and on 19th July the following year, on the occasion of the presentation of the first Colours to the 1st, 2nd and 3rd Battalions of the Parachute Regiment by HM King George VI on the Queen's Parade, at Aldershot, the 23rd (Parachute) Field Ambulance, commanded by Lieut.-Colonel W. R. Lamb, MC, played their part in the ceremony, in keeping the ground.

Although the Regular Army element of the Airborne Medical Services had been reduced to one Parachute Field Ambulance, three such units had come into being in the TA.

On the re-formation of the TA in April 1947 it was reorganised to meet the needs of the day. Old units were reconstituted in new rôles and many new units were raised. One feature of the post-war TA was the introduction of a new formation—the 16th Airborne Division (TA) the medical services of which comprised the 4th, 5th, and 6th (Parachute) Field Ambulances (TA).

The 4th (Parachute) Field Ambulance, commanded by Lieut.-Colonel G. Rigby Jones, MC, was raised at the Duke of York's HQ at Chelsea, and was formed from the pre-war 141st (County of London) Field Ambulance, RAMC(TA).

The 5th (Parachute) Field Ambulance, raised in Sheffield under the command of Lieut.-Colonel C. W. P. Bradfield, was an entirely new unit, but the 6th (Parachute) Field Ambulance, formed in Liverpool and commanded by Lieut.-Colonel A. T. Burn, descended from the pre-war 164th (West Lancs.) Field Ambulance (TA).

In addition there were two Parachute Field Surgical Teams (TA), Nos 61 and 62, and Light Field Ambulance Sections with four of the Battalions The Parachute Regiment (TA).

In 1950, on the reorganisation of the TA, the numbers of the parachute field ambulances of the 16th Airborne Division were changed to 44th, 45th, and 46th (Parachute) Field Ambulances.

Annual training of these TA units took them back to the war-time training area at Bulford; to the Stanford Battle Area; and to Strensall, Rhyl and Colchester; post-war Territorials were trained as parachutists and airborne exercises were held. In 1954 part of the 46th Parachute Field Ambulance took part in the Regular Army's exercise ' Battle Royal ' in Germany.

In the Coronation Procession in 1953, the honour of representing the whole of the Airborne Medical Services fell to the lot of a Territorial officer, Major R. McL. Archibald, RAMC (TA), the Second-in-Command of the 46th (Parachute) Field Ambulance.

In 1956, following another reorganisation of the TA, the 16th Airborne Division (TA) was disbanded,[1] as were also a number of the TA units which comprised the formation, and among these were the 45th and 46th (Parachute) Field Ambulances. The remaining unit, the 44th (Parachute) Field Ambulance, was commanded by Lieut.-Colonel D. R. Urquhart, who was subsequently succeeded by Lieut.-Colonel R. J. Howat.

In April 1951 the 16th Parachute Brigade Group went to North Wales for training in the Llanbedr area, but after two weeks was rushed back to Aldershot and held in readiness for service overseas in consequence of the situation in the Middle East arising from the Abadan crisis, for the loss of the oil refinery and the withdrawal of the British staff following nationalisation of the Persian oil industry had immediate effects on the whole situation in the Middle East.

On their return to Aldershot seventy-two hours' leave was granted to the Brigade, then back to barracks ready to move.

On 5th June the Brigade marched down through the town to Aldershot station to entrain, with the bands playing the traditional ' Auld Lang Syne ' on the departure platform, for Portsmouth, where the battalions embarked on the aircraft carrier HMS *Warrior*. The 23rd (Parachute) Field Ambulance embarked at Southampton on HMS *Triumph* to sail for Cyprus.

Landing at Famagusta, the Field Ambulance moved into quarters at the British Military Hospital at Nicosia, alongside the 2nd Field Ambulance.

The whole Brigade immediately commenced hardening and acclimatisation training and was so engaged up to the

---

[1] During its existence three officers held the appointment of ADMS—Colonel M. E. M. Herford, DSO, MBE, MC (1947-50) ; Colonel G. Rigby-Jones, MC (1950-55) ; and Colonel T. F. Redman, TD (1955-56).

autumn of 1951 when it was suddenly called out to emplane for Egypt to reinforce the garrison in the Canal Zone following the denouncement by Egypt of the long-standing Anglo-Egyptian Treaty. The Parachute Field Ambulance left Nicosia by air on 18th October to land at Suez, where it was quartered at the British Military Hospital. It was here that the unit was brought up to strength by a draft of forty non-airborne reinforcements from the RAMC Depot—who after but a short time all volunteered for parachute duties.

The Brigade was stationed in the Canal Zone and took part in internal security operations with both the 1st and 3rd Infantry Divisions, the Field Ambulance being stationed in a camp of their own at Fanara. In October 1952 the unit moved to Ferry Point at Ismailia with two sections at the ' outstations ' of Suez-el-Ballah and Tel-el-Kebir.

During their stay in Egypt the unit carried out parachute training and took part in a number of exercises in Jordan with the Arab Legion, in the Sinai desert, and an airborne landing in Cyprus.

The Brigade remained in Egypt until August 1954, at the start of which the general withdrawal of British troops commenced, the 23rd (Parachute) Field Ambulance with the 2nd Battalion The Parachute Regiment being the last units of the formation to leave, sailing in the troopship *Empire Ken* for Southampton, where they landed on 27th August. The Field Ambulance returned, with the Brigade, to their old quarters in Aldershot.

In October 1954 Lieut.-Colonel A. D. Young, DSO, who had commanded the Field Ambulance for three years in the Middle East, handed over the unit to Lieut.-Colonel J. L. Kilgour, who commanded it on the occasion of the visit to the 16th Parachute Brigade Group by HRH The Duke of Edinburgh, who inspected the formation in Rushmoor Arena, Aldershot, on 15th April 1955.

The rest of the year passed quietly, routine duties interspersed with field and parachute training, but the Brigade was, at all times, ready to fulfil a ' fire-brigade ' rôle. In consequence leave was taken in a ' block ' period instead of a percentage being on leave at all times. The leave period concluded on 9th January 1956, and two days later one section of the Parachute Field Ambulance was flying out to Cyprus with the 1st and 2nd Battalions of The Parachute Regiment. The remainder of the unit remained at Aldershot at forty-eight hours' notice to follow—straight into an operation area.

At this time the situation in Cyprus was worsening, brought about by the post-war revival of the issue of Enosis, or the union of Cyprus with Greece. Early in 1955 an organisation called EOKA, formed by a few hundred terrorists, had brought an element of violence into the unrest which until then had been confined to political demonstrations. EOKA had started to open fire on the British Security Forces, and to plant explosives and bombs at vital points of communication.

The situation deteriorated in consequence of support for EOKA from Greece and the fact that the Turkish Cypriots were violently opposed to the aim of Enosis. The British Government was then faced with the dual problem of suppressing EOKA and finding the best means of granting independence to Cyprus. To carry out the former the British Force in Cyprus had to be reinforced.

In June the 2nd Battalion The Parachute Regiment moved to Cyprus accompanied by another RAMC Section, and on 5th August the remainder of the unit followed on the aircraft carrier HMS *Theseus*, reaching Famagusta on the 11th.

On arrival in Cyprus the Field Ambulance concentrated in the Terra Santa School, whilst they built their own camp on the outskirts of Nicosia, where they set up a small tented Medical Reception Station and settled down to training whilst waiting, ready to be called into action.

The advent in July of the ' Suez Crisis ' had slowed down the tempo of the operations against the EOKA terrorists, for more units in Cyprus earmarked for possible service in Egypt were devoting their time to training. In consequence there was a feeling of irritation among these troops, for although it was fully appreciated that the time spent on training was necessary it was frustrating to see, and be aware of the increasing number of incidents, ambushes and actions by EOKA in places which had been well under control.

The situation in Cyprus, aggravated by the increased activities of EOKA, led in September to the change of employment of the 16th Parachute Brigade Group. From training they switched to a period of intensive anti-EOKA operations, the first of which, 'Operation Sparrowhawk' carried out in the Kyrenia Mountains, achieved considerable success, and in the latter part of October 'Operation Foxhunter' was launched in the Paphos Forest.

Between August and the end of October the 23rd (Parachute) Field Ambulance took part in these large-scale anti-terrorist operations during which the unit tried out their new operational sub-units, which were used to bring a hospital and a general practitioner service into the cordoned-off areas —which on occasions were up to a hundred square miles in size.

The success of these anti-EOKA measures was gratifying, added to which the weather had been perfect, with warm sunny days and cool nights, and the mountain slopes brightened by autumn crocus and mountain cyclamen, whilst the cultivated land on the outskirts of villages was covered by terraced groves of oranges and olives.

Whilst still engaged in operation 'Foxhunter' orders were received for the Brigade Group to return to its camps around Famagusta and Nicosia ready to participate in operation 'Musketeer'—the landing in Egypt, where the situation had reached the stage at which the British and French Governments had agreed on joint action.[1]

The situation in Egypt had arisen from that country's general attitude towards Middle Eastern affairs, and its own economic position resulting from the Aswan Dam project and expenditure on arms from Iron Curtain countries.

In July 1956 the Egyptian Government had suddenly seized the Suez Canal and expropriated the Suez Canal Company, taking over all its financial resources. The British

---

[1] In consequence of impending operations close liaison was established between the Parachute Brigade Group and the 10th Parachute Division of the French Army, and this resulted in practical liaison and training with their French medical colleagues by the 23rd (Parachute) Field Ambulance.

Government decided that the Egyptians could not be allowed to take over the control in this manner in complete defiance of the existing international agreements, which had been recognised ever since 1888. In this view they were supported by the French Government.

The crisis gradually mounted during a period of international discussion between July and October, and at the end of the month another factor brought the Middle East crisis to a peak. Israel mobilised, and on the 29th moved against Egypt.

The British and French Governments decided to call on both nations to cease hostilities and withdraw their forces to a distance from either side of the Canal. If either or both did not comply then an Anglo-French force would intervene and would occupy Port Said and Suez thereby ensuring free passage through the Canal if it was threatened by operations between the Egyptians and Israelis. This meant putting into operation the plan prepared by the Anglo-French military staff following the events of July.

The Israelis pressed on with their operations in the Sinai Desert and the Egyptian Forces were withdrawing—withdrawing towards the Canal. The Anglo-French operations were launched.

The operation involved an airborne and a sea assault on the area of Port Said, to be followed by an advance to the south along the Suez Canal and the Treaty roads.

The airborne landing was to be carried out by a battalion group (the 3rd Battalion The Parachute Regiment)—the object.ve, Gamil Aerodrome—whilst a French Parachute Regiment accompanied by a ' stick ' from the Guards Parachute Company would drop over the interior basin to the south of Port Said. The remainder of the 16th Parachute Brigade Group, with Royal Marine Commandos and other French troops, were to land by sea.

The Air Assault Party, RAMC, comprised : the RMO and Regimental Medical Section of the 3rd Battalion The Parachute Regiment ; a Collecting Section of one MO and thirteen ORs ; and a Surgical Team of one surgeon, one anaesthetist and four OTTs.

The seaborne element of the assualt force carried in one ship the ADS of forty all ranks, with all equipment loaded into ten ' Jeeps ' each with a trailer, whilst a second personnel ship carried one MO and fourteen ORs equipped on a man-pack basis ; and a reinforcement group for the ADS of fifteen ORs.

One section of the 23rd Parachute Ambulance, commanded by Captain M. Fearnley, with a Surgical Team dropped with the 3rd Parachute Battalion Group on Gamil airport in the early morning of 5th November.

Despite the considerable opposition and heavy fire, the only RAMC casualty sustained during the ' drop ' was the RMO of the Battalion, Lieutenant A. Cavenagh, who was hit during the descent. He was struck in the eye by a shell fragment. In the same burst the nylon rope holding his equipment, suspended below him, was cut through by a splinter. However, he landed safely and, despite being blinded in one eye, continued to carry out his duties as the RMO until, after the main fighting had died down, he was ordered to leave the scene of action, in a casualty evacuation aircraft.

As soon as possible after the drop a casualty collecting post and an operating theatre were set up by the airport's control tower and here the unit surgeon, Captain N. Kirby, with Captain J. M. Elliott the anaesthetist and Captain M. Fearnley were soon busily engaged. The senior NCO at the CCP was a Reservist, recalled for the emergency—Sergeant L. Goodall—who was later Mentioned in Despatches for his conduct on that day.

During the brisk engagement in and around the cemetery adjoining the airfield, and in the fighting for the control of the barracks and schools beyond, a number of wounded were brought in by jeep, under heavy fire, by Captain J. M. Elliott, a National Service officer, the anaesthetist with the Surgical Team. It is recorded that ' He personally picked up wounded men in the heat of the action in a forward area at great personal risk. His conduct was in the highest traditions of the Corps and a source of inspiration to all who saw it '. For this action Captain Elliott was subsequently awarded the Military Cross.

Whilst the fighting was in progress around Gamil airport, the remainder of the Field Ambulance with the rest of the Parachute Brigade Group which had embarked from Cyprus in LCTs had lain offshore during the night and were landed on the morning of 6th November near the de Lesseps Statue, in the wake of the assault force of the Royal Marine Commandos.

As soon as they were ashore the ADS group of the Field Ambulance linked up with the 15th Field Ambulance in the Casino Palace Hotel. Early the next morning they moved out to the southern outskirts of Port Said to set up a battle ADS in preparation for the development of further operations to the south. Another section went forward with the 2nd Battalion The Parachute Regiment as it thrust forward to just beyond El Cap where its advance was brought to a halt by the order to ' Cease Fire '.

The positions held were rapidly consolidated whilst the force awaited further developments. Meanwhile the ADS was engaged in tending and treating Egyptian casualties and rendering considerable help to the Egyptian hospitals in the town in the provision of food and medical supplies.

On 9th November the unit entertained four representatives of the International Red Cross, who had arrived from Cairo, and the DDMS made arrangements with them for the passage of a hospital train. The train was loaded on the 11th by the medical orderlies of the 23rd (Parachute) Field Ambulance and taken into the Egyptian lines by the Second-in-Command, Major P. F. Knight.

Shortly after, the Parachute Brigade Group was withdrawn from Suez and returned to Cyprus to prepare, and stand by for, further operations if they were required. Following the cease-fire the British and French Governments were pressed by the United Nations to withdraw their forces from Egypt, and this was done when a United Nations Force was assembled in sufficient strength to take over control of the Canal Zone, the withdrawal of the Anglo-French Force being completed by 22nd December and the UN contingents took over.

By the end of the year the whole Brigade Group returned home, back once again to Aldershot, where it is still stationed, the 23rd (Parachute) Field Ambulance, commanded by Lieut.-Colonel R. H. Freeman [1] being at Parsons Barracks, at the eastern end of Wellington Lines.

Normal training continues, for the 16th Parachute Brigade Group is always ' at the ready ' . . . ready for service anywhere and at any time to move and fight if necessary in the traditions of the Airborne Forces, and, in the case of the 23rd (Parachute) Field Ambulance—the traditions of the Royal Army Medical Corps. In this they are supported by the one remaining Airborne Medical Unit of the TA, the 44th (Parachute) Field Ambulance, RAMC(TA), commanded by Lieut.-Colonel D. MacMillan,[2] which has its HQ in London at Jamaica Road, Bermondsey, and with detachments in Birmingham and Nottingham.

For an appreciation of the work and the services of the Airborne Medical Services one cannot do better than to quote from an article by Lieut.-Colonel H. B. Coxen, DSO, MC, then commanding the 2nd Battalion The Parachute Regiment, writing in the ' Army Medical Services Magazine ' in January 1954 :—

> ' During the War we were blessed ', wrote Lieut.-Colonel Coxen, ' with an establishment which included an RMO, a sergeant, four corporals and thirteen privates of the RAMC with each parachute battalion. There is no doubt but that their value was inestimable ; it is of great importance to morale that the parachute soldier should have available to him expert medical attention should he be wounded in battle in an airborne operation. The presence of these RAMC personnel, together with the surgical teams of the Parachute Field Ambulance, provided that expert attention. In fact experience proved that though denied proper hospitalisation the

---

[1] Lieut.-Colonel J. L. Kilgour, who had commanded the unit in the Middle East, handed over the command in November 1957 to Lieut.-Colonel A. M. Ferrie, who commanded the Field Ambulance until January 1961.

[2] Who succeeded Lieut.-Colonel J. S. Binning.

immediate availability of expert treatment for head and stomach wounds saved many lives that might have been lost had treatment been delayed in normal evacuation. The parachute soldiers were quick to realise this and their confidence in their own comrades of the RAMC contributed largely to the high performance in battle of airborne units. . . . The battle knowledge gained by the RAMC personnel enabled them to anticipate where casualties might occur, and the RMO could deploy his staff where they were most needed . . . and always to the fore, operating often in regimental aid posts, the surgical teams of the Field Ambulance set a standard that can seldom have been equalled in the history of their Corps.

' Many other advantages of such attachments can be equally appreciated. . . . It will be a great day in the Regular Battalions of the Parachute Regiment when we can see our own RAMC attached once again, fully integrated in our training and operations.'

. . . . Such is the story of the Airborne Medical Services over a period of just twenty years. Twenty years of service of which all who have worn the Red Beret, the Pegasus Badge, the Red Cross Brassard, and the badges of the Royal Army Medical Corps, or the Royal Army Dental Corps, can look back upon with a sense of achievement and a justifiable feeling of pride—a pride which is shared by all ranks of the Army Medical Services and all those whose privilege it has been to serve or be associated with them. How apt indeed can be applied the words from the ' Hymn for the fallen of the Royal Army Medical Corps ' by Brigadier R. B. Price :—

> ' Unarmed they bore an equal burden
> Shared each adventure undismayed
> Not less they earned the victor's guerdon
> Not least were these in the crusade.'

APPENDIX A

COMPOSITION OF A PARACHUTE FIELD AMBULANCE ROYAL ARMY MEDICAL CORPS

Headquarters of Field Ambulance

Officer Commanding (Lieut.-Colonel)	1
Second-in-Command (Major)	1
Specialists, or graded surgeons (can be Majors, Captains or Lieutenants)	2
Specialist, or graded anaesthetist (can be Major, Captain or Lieutenant)	1
Quartermaster (Captain or Lieutenant)	1
Regimental Sergeant-Major	1
Quartermaster-Sergeant	1
Sergeant Clerk	1
Dispenser (Sergeant)	1
Nursing Orderly (Sergeant)	1
Sanitary Assistant (Sergeant)	1
Clerks (including one Corporal)	2
Masseur	1
Nursing Orderlies	6
Nursing Orderlies for duty as—	
Barber	1
Batmen	3
Pack Storeman	1
Sanitary Dutyman (Lance-Corporal)	1
Stewards Storemen (including one Corporal)	2
Stretcher-bearers (including one trained as a shoemaker)	5
Water Dutyman	1
Operating Room Assistants (including three Lance-Corporals)	6

Four Sections, each composed of—

Officer Commanding (Major, Captain or Lieutenant)	1
Staff-Sergeant (a Nursing Orderly for duty as Regimental NCO)	1

APPENDIX A

Clerk 1
Nursing Orderlies (Lance-Corporals) 3
General Dutyman 1
Stretcher-bearers (including one Corporal and a Lance-Corporal) 13

Personnel of other Arms of the Service attached—

Royal Engineers (Carpenter and Joiner) 1

Royal Army Service Corps—

    Captain 1
    Company Sergeant-Major 1
    Sergeant 1

    Drivers for duty as—

        Clerk 1
        Vehicle Drivers 34
        Motor Cyclists 4
        Driver/Mechanics 4
        Electrician 1
        Vehicle Mechanics 5

Royal Army Dental Corps—

    Captain or Lieutenant 1
    Clerk/Orderly (Corporal) 1

Army Physical Training Corps (Instructor) . . . 1
Army Catering Corps (Cooks) 5

BIBLIOGRAPHY

1. 'By Air to Battle'—The Official Account of the British 1st and 6th Airborne Divisions. (HMSO.) (1945.) Prepared by The Ministry of Information.
2. 'The Red Beret'—The Story of the Parachute Regiment at War, 1940-45. By Hilary St George Saunders. (Michael Joseph.) (1950.)
3. 'With the Red Devils at Arnhem.' By Marek Swiecicki. (Maxlove Publishing Co. Ltd.) (1945.)
4. 'Arnhem Lift'—Diary of a Glider Pilot. (Pilot Press.) (1945.)
5. 'Arnhem.' By Major-General R. E. Urquhart, CB, DSO. (Cassell & Co. Ltd.) (1958.)
6. 'Inter-Allied Conferences on War Medicine, 1942-45.' (Staples Press, Ltd., London.) (1947.)
    (i) 'Airborne Medical Services in Operations in Holland.' By Brigadier A. Austin-Eagger, CBE, DDMS, 1st (British) Airborne Corps.
    (ii) 'The RAMC at Arnhem.' By Colonel G. M. Warrack, DSO, OBE, ADMS, 1st Airborne Division.
    (iii) 'Medical Organisation and Experiences in an Airborne Operation, Sicily.' By Major C. J. Longland, RAMC, Surgical Specialist, Parachute Field Ambulance.
7. 'With the 6th Airborne Division in Normandy.' By Lieut.-General R. N. Gale, CB, DSO, OBE, MC. (Sampson Low, Marston & Co. Ltd.) (1948.)
8. 'Over The Rhine'—A Parachute Field Ambulance in Germany. (Written and produced by Members of 224th Parachute Field Ambulance—privately printed by the Field Ambulance.) (The Canopy Press (1946), at Sarafand, Palestine.) (Edition limited to 300 copies.)
9. 'Red Devils'—A Parachute Field Ambulance in Normandy. Written by Members of 224th Parachute Field Ambulance, 1945.

10. 'Surgeon at War.' By Lieut.-Colonel J. C. Watts, MC, FRCS, RAMC. (Allen & Unwin, Ltd., London.) (1955.)
11. 'Prelude to Glory.' By Group-Captain M. Newnham, OBE, DFC. (Sampson Low, Marston & Co. Ltd.)
12. 'Cordon and Search'—With 6th Airborne Division in Palestine. By Major R. D. Wilson, MBE, MC. (Gale & Polden Ltd.) (1949.)
13. 'The Journal of The Royal Army Medical Corps.'

   (i) October 1944, No 4, Vol LXXXIII—
   'Medical History in Action.' By Captain Harry Pozner, RAMC.

   (ii) November 1947, No 5, LXXXIX—
   'The Parachute Field Ambulance.' By Lieut.-Colonel A. D. Young, DSO, RAMC.

   (iii) December 1948, No 6, Vol XCI—
   'Indian Airborne Reminiscences.' By Captain F. G. Neild, RAMC.

14. 'Army Medical Services Magazine.' (January 1948.)
15. 'The Lancet', 18th March 1944—
    'The Parachute Field Ambulance.' By C. J. Longland, MB(Lond), FRCS, Major RAMC; and Lipmann Kessel, Captain RAMC.

ABBREVIATIONS

AA	Anti-Aircraft.
AA & QMG	Assistant Adjutant and Quarter Master General.
ACC	Army Catering Corps.
ADC	Aide-de-Camp.
ADC	Army Dental Corps.
ADMS	Assistant Director of Medical Services.
ADS	Advance Dressing Station.
A/L	Air Landing (Brigade).
CAEC	Casualty Air Evacuation Centre.
CCP	Casualty Clearing Point.
CCS	Casualty Clearing Station.
CF	Chaplain to the Forces.
CO	Commanding Officer.
CP	Car Post.
CRA	Commander Royal Artillery.
CRASC	Commander Royal Army Service Corps.
CRE	Commander Royal Engineers.
DADH	Deputy Assistant Director of Hygiene.
DADMS	Deputy Assistant Director of Medical Services.
DMS	Director of Medical Services.
DS	Dressing Station.
DSO	Distinguished Service Order.
DZ	Dropping Zone.
EAM	Ethnikon Apeleutherotikon Metopan (Greek National Liberation Front).
ELAS	Ellinikos Laikos Apeleutherotikos Stratos (Greek People's Liberation Army).
EOKA	Ethniki Organosis Kyprion Agoniston (National Organization of Cypriot Combatants).
FAP	First Aid Post.
FDS	Field Dressing Station.
FSU	Field Surgical Unit.
GOC	General Officer Commanding.
HQ	Headquarters.
IAMC	Indian Army Medical Corps.
IZL	Irgun Zuai Leumi.
LCI	Landing Craft Infantry.
LCT	Landing Craft Tank.
LZ	Landing Zone.
MAC	Motor Ambulance Column.
MC	Military Cross.
MDS	Medical Dressing Station.
MI	Medical Inspection.
MM	Military Medal.
MO	Medical Officer.
MTB	Motor Torpedo Boat.

ABBREVIATIONS

NCO	Non-Commissioned Officer.
OC	Officer Commanding.
OR(s)	Other Rank(s).
OTT	Operating Theatre Technician.
POW	Prisoner of War.
QM	Quartermaster.
RA	Royal Artillery.
RAF	Royal Air Force.
RAChD	Royal Army Chaplain's Department.
RAMC	Royal Army Medical Corps.
RASC	Royal Army Service Corps.
RAP	Regimental Aid Post.
RE	Royal Engineers.
RMO	Regimental Medical Officer.
RUR	Royal Ulster Rifles.
RV	Rendezvous.
SAS	Special Air Service.
SCF	Senior Chaplain to the Forces.
SEAC	South East Asia Command.
SHAEF	Supreme Headquarters Allied Expeditionary Force.
SMO	Senior Medical Officer.
SP (Gun)	Self Propelled (Gun).
SS	Schutzstaffel (Nazi Blackshirts).
SS	Special Service.
TA	Territorial Army.
TCV(s)	Troop Carrying Vehicle(s).
UN	United Nations.
US	United States.
USAF	United States Air Force.
USS	United States Ship.

www.ingramcontent.com/pod-product-compliance
Lightning Source LLC
Chambersburg PA
CBHW031947080426
42735CB00007B/301